THE
CHURCH
EDUCATION
HANDBOOK

T H E
CHURCH
EDUCATION
HANDBOOK
KENNETH O. GANGEL

The contents of this book originally appeared as a series of articles in *The Sunday School Times and Gospel Herald*, and is adapted with permission of Union Gospel Press, Cleveland, Ohio.

Unless otherwise noted, Scripture is quoted from the *Holy Bible: New International Version* (NIV), © 1978 by the New York International Bible Society; used by permission of Zondervan Bible Publishers. Other Bible quotations are from the *King James Version* (KJV); *The Living Bible* (TLB), © 1971 by Tyndale House Publishers, Wheaton, IL; *The Amplified Bible Old Testament*, © 1962, 1964 by Zondervan Publishing House. Bible quotations used by permission.

Recommended Dewey Decimal Classification: 268.1
Suggested Subject Heading: RELIGIOUS TRAINING AND INSTRUCTION: ADMINISTRATION

Library of Congress Catalog Card Number: 85-50318
ISBN: 0-89693-602-3

VICTOR BOOKS
A division of SP Publications, Inc.
        Wheaton, Illinois 60187

CONTENTS

PART THREE: IMPROVING CLASSROOM TEACHING

PART FOUR: STRENGTHENING CHURCH-HOME RELATIONS

PART ONE

ORGANIZING
AND ADMINISTERING
CHURCH EDUCATION

How to Be an Encouraging Christian Leader

The renowned Jewish philosopher Martin Buber once wrote, "The fact that people can no longer carry on authentic dialog with one another is the most acute symptom of the pathology of our time." Whether or not the philosopher's diagnosis is exactly accurate does not in any way detract from the fact that encouraging other people is one of the greatest needs of the Christian church today.

Like most other things in the ministry of Christian education—or for that matter any part of the total ministry of the church—encouragement begins with the leadership. How can you be an encouraging leader? Perhaps the best answer to that question is embodied in biographical form in the New Testament record of Barnabas, one of the dynamic leaders in the early church.

Originally named Joseph (Acts 4:36), Barnabas emerged in the New Testament as a lay leader whose important ministry was characterized by his ability to draw attention away from himself. Instead Barnabas majored in uplifting and encouraging other people in God's family.

ENCOURAGING LEADERSHIP IN PERSONAL LIFE

We learn from Acts 4:36-37 that Barnabas was a Levite landowner from Cyprus. This son of encouragement was also "a good man, full of the Holy Spirit and faith" (11:24).

Possibly Barnabas was a bachelor, though we cannot positively discover whether this is true from the New Testament. Paul asked the rhetorical question, "Don't we have the right to take a believing wife along with us, as do the other apostles and the Lord's brothers and Cephas? Or is it only I and Barnabas who must work for a living?" (1 Cor. 9:5-6)

We have no record of a wife for Barnabas, but the argument from silence is not conclusive. There does seem to be a hint in the Corinthian passage that Paul compared Barnabas with himself as one who was serving the Lord as a single.

With all the emphasis on the family in our day, we sometimes tend to make singles feel as though they must be out of the will of God. Such is not the case. Several notable New Testament leaders were single people, and Barnabas may have been among them.

I am impressed that Barnabas did not feel the need to start some new sect or group of his own. As a popular leader, he easily could have formed a divisive group that would have been destructive to the fragile workings of the early church. But Barnabas was not a divisive man. On the contrary, he exemplified a cooperative spirit when he gave the proceeds from the sale of his land to the church (Acts 4:37).

An encouraging leader understands the difference between *stewardship* and *ownership*. Barnabas was a steward of his land and acknowledged God as its Owner. Barnabas had the resources; the church had the need. It didn't take him long to determine what God wanted him to do.

ENCOURAGING LEADERSHIP IN PUBLIC MINISTRY

An encouraging leader is a man or woman of faith, the kind of faith that was obvious in the public ministry of Barnabas.

Barnabas demonstrated his *faith in the church.* Luke indicates that Barnabas trusted the leaders of the church at Jerusalem with his money (Acts 4:34-37). It is important to keep in mind that his donation preceded the judgment of Ananias and Sapphira for lying to the Holy Spirit (5:1-10). Indeed, since Luke recorded the passages back to back in Acts 4–5, we see an almost deliberate contrast between the open, trusting attitude of Barnabas and the selfishness and devious mistrust of Ananias and Sapphira.

Do you want to be an encouraging leader in your congregation, a help to other leaders, and an example to other members of the workteam? Then be a person who has faith in the church. It is easy to criticize the church because churches, like people, are imperfect. The reason is obvious—churches are made up of people. I don't doubt that the Jerusalem church was imperfect in its embryonic state as it suffered persecution and tried to formulate a definitive New Testament theology.

But think what the presence of Barnabas meant to that group! Without question he presented both his financial resources and himself for service to Christ in the church. No wonder his fellow Christians called him "Son of Encouragement."

Barnabas also showed *faith in people.* This is clearly demonstrated by his attitude toward Saul: "When he came to Jerusalem, he tried to join the disciples, but they were all afraid of him, not believing that he really was a disciple. But Barnabas took him and brought him to the apostles. He told them how Saul on his journey had seen the Lord and that the Lord had spoken to him, and how in Damascus he had preached fearlessly in the name of Jesus. So Saul stayed with them and moved about freely in Jerusalem, speaking boldly in the name of the Lord" (9:26-28).

We should not be surprised that the other leaders in the Jerusalem church were suspicious of the great persecutor. The real point of the passage is that their trust in Barnabas was greater than their distrust of Saul. It is a clear display of an attitude apparently prevalent in the church: "Any friend of Barnabas is a friend of ours." Barnabas was known as a man who trusted people; therefore, he was trusted. Integrity was a strategic component of Christian leadership then—and it is now.

We can imagine that Barnabas had been most interested in the dramatic conversion of Saul and had probably watched his development since his conversion, notably his preaching at Damascus. On the basis of all the evidence Barnabas had, and probably having carefully prayed about the situation, he boldly moved forward with the leading of the Lord to introduce the former scourge of Christians to the church of Jerusalem. His recommendation erased all questions and Saul was accepted as one of the brethren.

Barnabas also demonstrated his faith in people by his attitude toward his own nephew, John Mark. We read in Acts 15:36-40: "Sometime later Paul said to Barnabas, Let us go back and visit the brothers in all the towns where we preached the word of the Lord and see how they are doing. Barnabas wanted to take John, also called Mark, with them, but Paul did not think it wise to take him, because he had deserted them in Pamphylia and had not continued with them in the work. They had such a sharp disagreement that they parted company. Barnabas took Mark and sailed for Cyprus, but Paul chose Silas and left, commended by the brothers to the grace of the Lord."

This is one of those realistic passages that establishes the Bible's credibility. It would have been easy for Luke as a historian to gloss over this dispute between two great church leaders, but he recorded it as it happened.

Certainly, there could be some family feeling in the case of Barnabas toward John Mark, and one hesitates to say whether he or Paul represented the correct position in the dispute. No doubt Mark had been undependable on the first missionary journey. Paul, the perfectionist, was not going to put up with that kind of incompetence again. But Barnabas, the Son of Encouragement, was willing to give the young man another chance.

The fact that Barnabas passed out of history at this point is not disturbing. Mark reenters not only as a valued companion of the Apostle Paul but also as the writer of one of the synoptic Gospels. It is genuinely fascinating to hear Paul's words from a Roman prison cell: "Only Luke is with me. Get Mark and bring him with you, because he is helpful to me in my ministry" (2 Tim. 4:11).

What made Mark profitable for Paul's ministry? Certainly not the apostle's rejection of the young man because of his early mistakes. Quite possibly Barnabas, the Son of Encouragement, patiently tutored Mark and helped him become a faithful servant of God. Later Mark would be one of the Bible's writers.

Another positive factor of the early church leader Barnabas is the fact that he had *faith in himself.* When things were beginning to develop at Antioch, the church at Jerusalem sent Barnabas to help the believers there. When he arrived and saw that the grace of God was clearly evident in that city, "He was glad and encouraged them all to remain true to the Lord with all their hearts" (Acts 11:23).

As the work developed, Barnabas did an unusual thing. He went to Tarsus to seek Saul, "and when he found him, he brought him to Antioch. So for a whole year Barnabas and Saul met with the church and taught great numbers of people. The disciples were first called Christians at Antioch" (11:26).

That's an amazing twist to the contemporary understanding of leadership! Here was a man who was willing to be vulnerable. Barnabas had complete faith in himself and his own abilities, but he also recognized the limitations of those abilities. What the new believers at Antioch needed was a man who could institute in-depth teaching of the Bible, a man capable of applying Old Testament Scripture to New Testament Christianity. Though Barnabas was a Levite, he hardly had the schooling of the brilliant young Pharisee from Tarsus; and he knew that Saul was the man for the job. Barnabas was not insecure, he was not threatened, and he was not defensive about his position at Antioch.

Here was his big chance. Barnabas could have had "a church of his own," perhaps even larger than the one at Jerusalem. But Barnabas did not think like the rulers of the Gentiles (cf. Mark 10:42) when it came to his understanding of leadership. He had a New Testament servant's mentality. His calm faith in himself, in God's call, and in God's provision for leadership enabled him to send for Saul so that the church at Antioch could profit from Saul's unique teaching abilities.

Finally, it is important to recognize that Barnabas had *faith in the mission of the church* as it related to world evangelization. Antioch was destined in God's plan to become the first missionary church. When it came time for the members of the church to send forth their first missionaries, they waited before the Lord until the Holy Spirit said, "Set apart for me Barnabas and Saul for the work to which I have called them" (Acts 13:2).

From landowner to donor to helper to leader to pioneer missionary—what a career for the Son of Encouragement! And what an example for us! Perhaps the key to dynamic growth and spiritual unity in your church's Christian education program is a new commitment to encouragement. And that kind of attitude may have to begin with you.

How to Be a Creative Administrator

Many people in the educational program of a local church have administrative positions and don't know it. They think of the pastor or perhaps the chairman of the official board as administrators, but they fail to see that many other people who work with the daily and weekly programs of instruction are primarily responsible for the administration of those programs.

I am thinking about officers such as the chairman of the Christian education committee, Sunday School superintendent, departmental superintendent, librarian, director of the Vacation Bible School, and many others. One of the simplest definitions of *administration* is "getting things done through people." In short, anybody who has responsibility to supervise the activities of other workers is an administrator.

Creative administration is just the opposite of custodial management. The custodial manager wants to "hold things together" and "keep things going," but he is not particularly interested in innovation, progress, and creativity. The creative administrator, on the other hand, seeks new solutions and does not base his decision-making on tradition, precedent, and standard controls.

He steadfastly resists the seven last words of the church: "We've never done it that way before!"

CREATIVE ADMINISTRATION MEANS
WORKING WITH PEOPLE

Quite obviously, if administration is getting things done through people, leaders must be oriented toward that kind of ministry. Yes, "ministry" is the proper word. It is biblical for the church to place relations with people above the accomplishing of numerical goals because it represents one of the major goals of the New Testament, a theme repeated in numerous passages.

To be specific, a church leader who wants to be a successful educational administrator must concern himself with what management scientists call "human relations." Satisfactory relationships must be established and sustained; frustration, confusion, and misunderstanding must be reduced; and the potential of "people power" must be maximized so that persons achieve their own goals and meet their own needs while serving Christ through the church.

Manipulation and exploitation are both dangerous and patently unbiblical. Certainly, it is possible for a manager who understands something of the psychology of behavior modification to get people to do things they don't want to do and which are really contrary to their interests in order that the organization will be served. But that is not creative administration; it is political manipulation like that of the kings of the Gentiles (Luke 22:25).

A church administrator who wants to work with people effectively must understand their wants and needs before he can concentrate on meeting them. The needs and wants of people have been classified and codified in many different ways, but basically they boil down to a desire for development, opportunity for fullest use of gifts and abilities, appreciation and credit for work done well, recognition of achievement, attention as an individual, interest and challenge in the work task, firm but kind supervision, and a fair understanding of what can be expected from the organization in return for their efforts.

One of the best classifications of human need in relation to motivation is that provided by Abraham Maslow in *Motivation and Personality* (Harper and Row). The following chart represents Maslow's "hierarchy of human needs," which gives us interesting guidelines regarding our work with people in administration.

When a need has been satisfied, it is no longer considered a need, so the leader must direct his attention to unsatisfied needs in his effort to motivate people. The point is that we spend too much time thinking about the physiological needs and not enough time thinking about the top of the triangle—self-actualization. In another of my books I raise some questions about this whole concept of working with people in the church:

> What is there about Christian ministry that is self-actualizing? Is it possible that the discouraged pastor or a Sunday School teacher ready to quit finds himself in that position because no one has taught him to think of his service as self-actualizing? Has the Christian service dropout developed a distorted, slave-to-the-church concept of his task? Is it possible that the task itself has very little self-actualizing potential? *(Building Leaders for Church Education,* Moody)

CREATIVE ADMINISTRATION REQUIRES THE GIFT OF ADMINISTRATION

God is restoring to His church in the late 20th century a new emphasis on spiritual gifts. People in congregations around the world are seeking to understand their own spiritual gifts, to develop them, and to use them in serving Christ. We have had this instruction before, because it has always been in the New Testament. But it seems to be characteristic of the Lord to emphasize or reemphasize during certain eras of the church's history various aspects of biblical truth. That was true of the doctrines of justification by faith and the authority of Scripture during the time of the Reformation and also the emphasis on foreign missions which came out of the Moravian movement. The Wesleys and Whitefield restored an emphasis on evangelism, and so it goes.

Now we have a focus in the church on the leadership of the laity through an understanding of spiritual gifts. And one of those gifts is the gift of administration. The central passage on the gift of administration is 1 Corinthians 12:28, where the *King James Version's* word "governments" might better be rendered "administration" in our day, as it is in the *New International Version.* The word actually means "helmsman," the responsible decision-maker on a ship, usually the head man.

How can you tell if you have the gift of administration? One answer would be an understanding of *how others assess your work.* If you have been appointed or elected Sunday School superintendent, it may well be because your fellow Christians have sensed the gift of administration in your life.

Another signal is the *joy or interest you have in managerial activity.* Many people detest administration, considering it pedantic, unnecessary, and even sometimes unspiritual. But a person who truly has the gift of administration will find himself drawn toward directing the tasks of other people, and he will find a genuine spiritual enjoyment in exercising his spiritual gift.

Of course, there is also the matter of the *Holy Spirit's witness in your life.* As He gives us inner assurance that we are God's children, so He can give us an understanding of our spiritual gifts and a motivation to develop and use them in His power.

CREATIVE ADMINISTRATION
BEGINS WITH PLANNING

In actuality, planning is one of several tasks under the general umbrella of administration. But it is so crucial, and comes so close to the front end of the administrative trail, that I want to include it right in the foundational section of our chapters on effective administration. One of the reasons people do not plan effectively is because they see planning time as an expense rather than an investment.

In reality, time spent in effective planning will be more than saved in the execution or implementation stage. A businessman who carefully plans his day, a housewife who organizes the necessary activities of housework, shopping, and so forth, and a Sunday School superintendent who maps out a teaching seminar for his workers well in advance, have all learned to invest planning time in order to maximize available working time.

Planning is also important because it forces us to think ahead. An administrator, unlike a worker who is constantly being supervised by others, must spend a good portion of his or her time thinking about the future. One can think about the future without planning, but one cannot plan without thinking about the future. A forward-looking, goal-oriented person is the most effective planner because he refuses to be trapped into the position of constantly putting out fires in the present. Sone have called this syndrome "the tyranny of the urgent."

Planning also requires careful attention to immediate choices because they profoundly affect goals and other options down the line. We plan on the basis of evaluation; that is, the more we know about what we have done in the past, the better we can plan for the future.

Let's go back to that Sunday School superintendent and his annual teachers' seminar. The more he knows about last year's seminar (how many came, what the costs were, how good the advertising was, what kind of critical remarks were made, what parts of the program people appreciated most, and so forth), the better he will be able to plan for this year's seminar. That is one reason why a creative administrator always insists on a full-scale evaluation of a major project immediately after it has finished.

Let's not forget the idea mentioned several times throughout these paragraphs—GOALS. The creative administrator plans by setting specific goals for his organization.

So how can you become a creative administrator? Certainly the beginning is to identify and develop your spiritual gift of administration, if the Holy Spirit has given you that gift. Then you want to read some of the literature now available from a genuinely evangelical viewpoint which deals with church administration in its various phases. The library of a good seminary or Bible college would be of help if you have one nearby, or your Christian bookstore can certainly direct you to helpful titles. I have written several books in this area, and almost all of them contain bibliographies of many other titles.

The following chapters should help introduce you to some basic concepts. Because there is some administration in all teaching, and some teaching in all administration, this entire book should be helpful.

How to Delegate Effectively

Because an administrator takes responsibility for the successful functioning of his organization, or at least for some part of it, he invariably has a job that never ends. Consequently, in addition to carefully setting priorities, he must learn to effectively give tasks and responsibilities to others, thereby maximizing his own output. Remember that administration is getting things done through people. The more tasks the administrator can delegate effectively, the more time he has to engage in long-range planning and facilitation of goal achievement for his organization.

An effective delegating administrator not only enlarges his own area of action and multiplies his own efficiency but also gives others opportunities to prove themselves and, at the same time, encourages their initiative in personal growth. He gets more done in less time with a minimum of personal frustration and exhaustion.

In an article that appeared in the December, 1971 issue of *Supervision,* Martin Polk suggested ten questions, the answers to which may indicate whether you are deficient in delegation.

1. Is your work piling up too fast?

2. Do you spend several evenings each week "catching up" with work?
3. Are you usually pressed for letter-answering time?
4. Do you find yourself with too little time to see people on business matters?
5. Do you lack time to relax?
6. Are you frequently late in meeting deadlines?
7. Are you habitually swamped by details?
8. Do you feel stale?
9. Are you worried about your work load?
10. Have you been irritable lately?

No doubt some of these questions must be answered affirmatively by all of us at least some of the time. But if too many of them are drawing an immediate and responsive yes, you may want to check your delegation efficiency.

WHY SHOULD A LEADER DELEGATE?

In addition to all the logical reasons just mentioned, there is also the most important reason of all—it's biblical! One of the classic management stories in the Bible is the record of Jethro in Exodus 18. Moses may have been trained as a politician and a prophet, but he had little skill in administration. At least he did not understand the fundamentals of delegation. Read carefully through the chapter. Jethro recommended a complete overhauling of the organization, based on the central principle of delegation. Moses was simply taking charge of too much himself and not allowing his subordinates to share the load. The key is probably verse 18: "You and these people who come to you will only wear yourselves out. The work is too heavy for you; you cannot handle it alone."

WHAT SHOULD A LEADER DELEGATE?

It is tempting to answer the above question by saying, "Everything he cannot do himself." But actually, that is the wrong answer because it tempts us to overload ourselves and to share the tasks of the organization in a miserly fashion. Certainly no one can do your job as well as you can now, but perhaps one of your subordinates can do it well enough to get by, with the expectation that someday he'll be able to do it as well as you or maybe even better.

Incidentally, that's why some leaders don't delegate. There is an innate fear, sometimes not even understood by the leader himself, that the one who receives a delegated task may end up doing it better than his superior. If you harbor such an attitude, remember the words of Jesus: "He will do even greater things than these" (John 14:12).

If you have never had any experience in delegating, the first step is probably to prepare an exhaustive list of the duties you perform on a regular basis. Then identify in that list those tasks which *only* you can do, separating them from the tasks which might conceivably be done by somebody else.

Don't forget the negative side of the second question, "What should a leader delegate?" It is not possible to delegate everything, so something must be left on the check sheet when your exercise is finished.

To Whom Should a Leader Delegate?

Every leader needs to build around himself a core of people who could take his job if a transfer of the mantle becomes necessary. Moses trained Joshua; Eli trained Samuel; Elijah trained Elisha; and Paul trained Timothy, along with a host of others. It takes a certain amount of security, of course, to feel that way about your subordinates, but then security is healthy for you, and the ministry. Ideally you should have around you only subordinates to whom you could feel comfortable about delegating important responsibilities. But not all of us work with the ideal.

So, first of all, look around for people who are functioning properly and productively in their present positions and who are demonstrating some *capacity for additional responsibility.*

One of the most obvious situations, and yet one that is not used well in most churches, is the delegation of important administrative responsibilities from a Sunday School superintendent to his or her assistant.

Another thing to look for is whether the subordinate shows *initiative* in his present job. Is she an "idea person" who frequently suggests ways that the organization could be improved? Does she rise to a challenge? Does she get the broad picture of how the whole educational program functions, rather than just being excited about her little chunk of the pie?

The third guideline has to do with *self-discipline*. A person who can discipline himself has a fair chance of disciplining others. He ought to show organization in his own life, in his home, and in his work at church. Others should show a responsiveness to working with him and under his leadership.

In project delegation, you should have a fairly accurate picture in advance of the goals and procedures involved in accomplishing the project. In such a case, you will want to select the best person for that particular job.

Leaders have to understand how delegation provides value to the subordinate in the process. Obviously, the central purpose in your mind is to get things off your desk so that you can function more creatively and productively. Yet certainly one of the constant tasks of a leader's ministry is to train other leaders, and delegation is one of the key ways to do it.

How Does an Effective Leader Delegate?

Timing is important in effective delegation. Though delegation is always in order and always produces positive benefits for those who do it properly, there are times when it is virtually crucial. For example, a pastor who has made a decision to leave his church within sixty days should (unless the church board does this) parcel out duties to others who can carry them on after his departure. A Christian education committee chairman whose tenure of office is about to end ought to focus heavily on delegation in the remaining months of his term.

On the other hand, it is also a good time for delegation when a person has just been appointed to office. Before people get accustomed to the superintendent going to each room to pick up the records and the offering, that task could well be assigned to somebody else. Before the departmental superintendent gets into the swing of checking the roll and distributing visitation cards, he might delegate that task to a class member.

A leader who delegates well also focuses on desired results and not methodology. That is, he tells the one to whom he is delegating a task *what* he wants to have achieved and perhaps *when* he needs it done, but he does not spell out exactly *how* to do it. One value of delegation is getting some new light on methodology and approaches to doing things, which will never happen if we prescribe every move the subordinate must make.

On the other hand, it is necessary to provide adequate information for the task being delegated. We need to share with the subordinate whatever we can regarding the background of the problem or task, controls that we hope to build in, expectations, the extent and limitation of decision-making privileges, what he may expect by way of problems and pitfalls, and so forth. He also needs to know what your role will be in relation to this project or task you are assigning to him.

It is probably also safe to say that good delegating leaders never ignore protocol. In an issue of the *Hillsdale Report,* Dr. J. Donald Phillips reminds us of this common problem:

> It is often easier and quicker to go to one of your immediate subordinate's men to get a job done at the lowest level of competency. However, nothing can upset the organization faster. If in an emergency, this must be your procedure, have it understood from the beginning by all parties that you will report this activity to his supervisor as soon as humanly possible. This will permit the supervisor to take any measures that need to be taken to handle problems that might have been created.

WHAT PROBLEMS CAN BE ANTICIPATED IN DELEGATION?

Most problems will be those which we create ourselves, but even they can be largely alleviated if we learn to look for them and guard against them in advance. Here are a few problems we can expect:

1. We may hesitate to delegate tasks that we *like* to do, even though they are tasks that could be done by other people. Maximum efficiency and effectiveness in an organization does not necessarily mean that each leader does what he

likes to do.

2. Failure to learn more about people in the organization can produce real problems. If we are going to find the best people suited to certain jobs, we are going to have to know our people well. What are their interests? What are their skills? What are their spiritual gifts?

3. Another common problem is a failure to follow through in the delegation process. It is easy to sweep a job off our desks and forget it. Yet the subordinate who now has it may need our continuing help and guidance to get the job done right, at least the first few times around.

Remember that delegation works best in an organization that fosters security, a deep respect for individuality, and a minimum of fear and competition among its workers.

How to Make Good Decisions

Many Christians shy away from leadership precisely because they don't like to make decisions. Yet it is quite obvious that anyone who is in a position to lead other people in an organization, no matter how large, will be forced to make some decisions regarding his own activity and the involvement of those other people.

One of the problems with decision-making is that it frequently draws criticism from others whose lives the decisions affect. This natural fallout, part of the total leadership pattern, is not too pleasant for the leader.

David made thousands of decisions during his years as leader and king, and many of them were hailed by his people as wise choices. The point is that one can never know in decision-making whether he will gain popular support or unpopular criticism; that is what makes the position of the decision-maker tenuous and sometimes undesirable.

Nevertheless, we just can't get out of it; so we had better examine how to do the job well. In this chapter we explore some of the elements of decision-making and how the process can be understood and improved. Like most of the aspects of administration, decision-making is a skill which can be studied and developed, not some innate ability that one either has or doesn't have.

WHY DO WE MAKE INFERIOR DECISIONS?

As already indicated, one of our problems is a failure to see that decision-making can be learned. Consequently, we do not make an effort to study the process and improve our own decision-making skills. Of course, the opposite of being afraid of the decision-making process is taking it too lightly and thinking that anyone who happens to be promoted or elected to a position of leadership automatically has the ability to make the right decisions in that position.

The type of leadership style one utilizes is also a major factor in decision-making. It is possible, for example, to be too "receptive" and pass off the decision-making responsibility to others. There is a fine balance between encouraging maximum input from your colleagues (which is good) and giving the decision-making role by default to them because their ideas and personalities may be stronger than yours (which is bad).

Other leaders suffer from the opposite problem in that they seek to make decisions purely on the basis of their own opinions. Sometimes such a leader is called a "hoarding executive" because he will not release any of the authority or responsibility connected with making decisions for the organization. This kind of individual will soon drive away from him creative people whose ideas can really help the church or Sunday School, people who probably have capacity for leadership. Sometimes a hoarding executive acts as he does just because of ego and sometimes because he really believes that only he has the insight and the wisdom to make the right decisions.

Erich Fromm describes the ideal decision-maker as a productive man who is chiefly interested in using his capacities to the full and is guided by reason in doing so. We might add to that the ancient words of Machiavelli: "A prince should be a great asker of questions."

COMPONENTS OF DECISION-MAKING

There are a number of ways to identify the components of the decision-making process, but they all seem to come out about the same. Certain steps must be followed in studying decisions, other steps in making the decision, and still others in testing the decision.

Let's call the first step *understanding the decision*. It is necessary for the leader to get familiar with the background of the problem. He needs a certain amount of general experience in the area, an ability to master the information available to him, and a bit of administrative intuition, intelligence, and training. He dare not be led into thinking that he will have *all* the facts, but he nevertheless needs to accumulate whatever information he can.

Obviously the asking of questions is important, but the leader needs to know whom to ask and how to sift the answers. Scripture speaks directly to this phase of a decision-making process when it says, "For lack of guidance a nation falls, but many advisers make victory sure" (Prov. 11:14).

A second step in studying decisions is the *identification of the major problem*
or problems. The word "cause" is important here. If the Primary Department attendance has been consistently dropping for the last six months, what is the cause? If there seems to be unrest among the Junior High young people in the evening training group, what is the cause? Decisions that seek to solve problems need to get to the root of the cause, not just deal with the symptoms.

In making the decisions it becomes necessary first of all to *propose some possible alternatives*. The alternatives will be better both in number and quality if you have first studied the problem properly. There may always be a different alternative from those which are obvious; so a bit of delay, if you have the time, is sometimes wise. Of course, it is possible that you will not be able to identify an absolutely foolproof alternative; so *select the best one you have* by comparing the validity of all of them.

Ed Dayton reminds us that "some of the things that you might want to compare are the *risks* involved, the *cost* of the alternative, the *people available* to implement the decision, the *past effec-*

tiveness of using this type of alternative, the amount of *time* that this alternative will require, and how it will be received within the organization" (*Christian Leadership Letter,* October, 1974).

In the actual making of the decision we *test the alternative* twice–just before we implement it and just after we implement it. When we think we have the best answer to the question or the best solution to the problem, we test it in theory against possible outcomes. Even when it appears that all systems are go in implementing the decision, it may be wise to wait just a bit longer, pray just a bit more, and think through the best way to announce the decision and put it into action.

Then we also test the decision in *evaluation* after it has been implemented. Much of the literature in management science indicates that once a decision is made, one should never look back on it. I disagree. It seems to me that there are sometimes good reasons for changing a decision unless we assume infallibility, which is a most dangerous position. I don't think one has to vacillate to honestly evaluate a decision or solution which he has implemented. If the evaluation comes up positive, he will know that much more about making a similar decision the next time.

WHAT ARE THE SPECIFICATIONS FOR GOOD DECISION-MAKING? It seems that one of the basic characteristics of good decision-making is the *recognition as to whether a certain decision is policy-setting or an adaptation*. In other words, what kind of decision is this? It is possible that the decision has already been made for you by standard policy in the organization. If, for example, there is a clear-cut salary scale under which all employees fall, then the application of the data already available may almost automatically lead to the decision.

On the other hand, if this is something completely different, a unique event which calls for the establishment of new policy, the decision must be approached in a different way. It is probably wise for the leader to assume in the initial stages of decision-making that his problem is generic, that is, that there is already some inherent logical answer within the functioning of the organization.

A second specification is to *identify exactly what the decision must accomplish*. These are sometimes called "boundary conditions," a reference to the minimal goals which a decision must attain. A Sunday School superintendent who has the responsibility of appointing a substitute teacher to a certain class for a period of a month had better know in advance exactly what that teacher is expected to accomplish in that class during that month. The general rule is that the more clear-cut and concise the boundary conditions are, the more effective the decision will be.

A third specification of good decision-making is the *initial selection of what is best or right*. Invariably decision-making must carry with it some compromise and adaptation, but we don't begin there. We begin with an identification of the best thing we could do and then work back from that in the compromise process.

For example, the best answer for the growth and effectiveness of your boys' club program might be the erection of a half-million-dollar gymnasium. Even if that is completely out of the question, start with that and work back to something less rather than start with what you have and work up to the first level of acceptability.

A fourth specification for good decision-making is the *clarification of what is to be done, when, and by whom*. Practically, no real decision has been made unless carrying it out in specific steps has been assigned to a specific person with a specific time factor built in. Up to that point we have only good ideas or intentions. Who has to know of this decision? What action needs to be taken? Who is to take it? What authority or resources does he need to do it? How will I know whether or not it has been done?

The process of decision-making is one of the most important, yet one of the most difficult, aspects of Christian leadership. But it is not one in which we stand alone. As a matter of fact, Christian leaders have a great advantage over their secular counterparts in this process. As the Scripture says, "If any of you lacks wisdom, he should ask God, who gives generously to all without finding fault, and it will be given to him" (James 1:5).

How to Recruit Workers

Teachers should know better. James made that quite plain. The tremendous educational task of the church can be accomplished only through an army of lay workers performing various duties under the direction of a few professional workers and educators. The adequate fulfillment of the task requires more than willingness; it requires training.

To become a teacher in the youngest grades of the public school system, one must study content and methods for several years after high school. In contrast, many church teachers who deal with eternal truths week after week are asked only to "read over the quarterly" a few minutes before class. Often willing workers in our churches assume posts of responsibility without even knowing what is expected of them, much less having training for the job.

This pressing need for adequately trained persons in the educational ministry of the church has come into focus even more clearly as the relevance of the church in today's sophisticated society has come under closer scrutiny. Better materials, more adequate programs, and development of a genuine interest are characteristics of improved church attitudes toward the need for worker training.

RELATE RECRUITMENT AND TRAINING TO BIBLICAL OBJECTIVES

The Apostle Paul laid an early church groundwork for the importance of interpersonal communication in a system of worker development, saying, "You then, my son, be strong in the grace that is in Christ Jesus. And the things you have heard me say in the presence of many witnesses entrust to reliable men who will also be qualified to teach others" (2 Tim. 2:1-2).

Those are Paul's words to one young Christian worker, but to a group of pastors, he said, "For I have not hesitated to proclaim to you the whole will of God. Guard yourselves and all the flock of which the Holy Spirit has made you overseers. Be shepherds of the church of God, which He bought with His own blood" (Acts 20:27-28). The heart of teacher training in the Apostle Paul's pattern is based on mature Christians teaching others.

D. Campbell Wyckoff has said:

> Leadership is a function of the church. Leadership training is basically a matter of making the nature and mission of the church clear, establishing the functions of leadership in the light of the nature and mission of the church, and selecting and educating persons to know those functions well and to perform them skillfully (*The Gospel and Christian Education*, Westminster).

The purpose of training workers is obvious, though many of the fringe benefits of a training program are often overlooked. In a thorough training program, the worker will also learn to understand the entire program of the church and to see his place in such a program—this is in addition to the course's basic content and concentration in Scripture, church history, personal evangelism, doctrine, and educational methodology. Many individual problems facing teachers should be dealt with during the training sessions. There is also a certain fellowship which is experienced as teachers learn side by side in training programs. An adequate program provides for discussion and understanding among teachers which may not be possible in other ways.

These are days of specialization, and the educational program of the church is no exception. A student (regardless of age) probably will sense when the quality of the instruction he receives in the church is inferior to what he receives in public or private school. If the church is to demonstrate sincerity in methodology and procedure in its efforts to communicate a superior message, it is necessary for teachers and leaders to be trained for an effective ministry.

Churches with ministers of education should certainly look to these professionals for training impetus. Of course, all departmental superintendents and coordinators of various aspects of the program must line up to support the training sessions.

Securing personnel to handle training sessions continues to be one of the biggest problems most churches face in structuring a satisfactory program. Of course, if there is a Christian college or seminary in the area, the church can employ its faculty in the training program, and perhaps even mature, advanced students can serve in this capacity. Many churches have college graduates in their membership who could serve as teachers in special fields. In situations where a church is too small to conduct a thorough program on its own, cooperation with other churches or use of denominational specialists could improve the value of the program.

RECRUITMENT IS TIED TO TRAINING

Starting a training program is the easy part. Once the program has been structured, the real trick is to get the constituency to make use of it. There are several things that must be considered in recruiting leaders for any training effort:

1. The board of Christian education should begin by making a survey of every task in the church and a compilation of job analyses for the task. Every potential leader should be listed, and interests, as well as aptitudes, should be considered.
2. The training program must be "sold" to the people. The need for training, its value, and each worker's responsibility to improve himself have to be motivating factors in securing the sacrifice of time that a worker must make to attend a fully

developed training program. Connected with this kind of motivation is a dignifying position of church leadership.

3. A high standard for the teachers and leaders of a church is the best incentive for the program. A printed certificate or diploma is often helpful in building recognition. Appreciation of workers in the form of annual workers' banquets and appreciation dinners can contribute to the incentive.

4. Church leadership must not back off from the importance of the leadership training program when the standard objections of "No time," "Not interested," and "We have never had it before and have gotten along OK" begin to pour in. The development of a satisfactory training program may take several years, and they must be years of patience and perseverance.

The benefits of a properly functioning leadership training program are sufficient to outweigh the difficulties involved. As O.L. Shelton argues:

> Opportunities for training and improvement should be made available to all who accept the responsibilities of a church school teacher. It is unfair for a church to enlist a person to teach, and not provide materials and equipment for the task and guidance in the work....Many teachers become discouraged, and valuable leaders are lost because proper introduction was not given to the work. Encouragement and financial help should be given to teachers to attend institutes, conferences, and schools. People enjoy doing the thing that they feel they are doing well, and the church should give every assistance in aiding teachers to enjoy and improve in performing their tasks (*The Church Functioning Effectively*, Bethany Press).

Too long the church has floundered in its educational program, using inadequate facilities and unskilled workers. Most churches today can well afford the necessities of a training program. Obviously such a program is no substitute for spirituality, but is, as a matter of fact, a spiritual supplement to the ministry which the workers are doing at the call of God. A proper recognition of their ministry is foundational to any good system of leadership training.

FOLLOW PROPER GUIDELINES

Whatever system we use, certain guidelines should be observed if we want success at the other end of the line. This is not an exhaustive list; it is merely representative.

1. Teachers teach as they have been taught. To quote Richard Graham, director of the Teacher Corps, "If teachers are taught in conventional classrooms, sitting in neat, silent rows, reading texts and listening to lectures, they are likely to inflict the same horrors on their pupils." Perhaps the leadership of our teacher training classes is more important than the content.
2. Proper recruitment is essential from the start. Let's junk the universal platform appeals dripping with the aphorism, "Anybody can do it." The key is to approach a specific person, for a specific job, for a specific period of time.
3. Recognition and reinforcement are primary motivating factors and progress is based on the principle of setting achievement goals for all local church workers.
4. Leadership training should be home-related. Most evangelical teachers and leaders in local churches are not now doing anything to relate their ministries to Christian homes. To divide church and home is perversion of both Old and New Testament principles. But if there is to be cooperation, we must teach our teachers and lead our leaders to see how such implementation can be made.
5. Confront veteran teachers with new methods and insights. What do your teachers and leaders know about upgraded departments, the inquiry method, team teaching, and simulation gaming? Rather than hide from trends and technology, the evangelical educator should explore them and, if possible, capture them for Christ.

What Richard H. Brown wrote in *Change* (March-April, 1970) concerning college teachers may well be applied to church teachers:

We need teachers who are capable of being leaders in inquiry, who have an urgent sense of the processes and possibilities of human growth and a realistic sense of and respect for the mutuality of the teaching/

learning process. Above all, we need teachers with a higher and clearer sense of purpose as teachers than many now have; a confident awareness of what they themselves have to offer in terms of maturity, experience, knowledge, and skills; an awareness that students can avail themselves of what the teacher has to offer only if they—the students—sense and feel and understand what is available; but they will do none of this unless they respect the teacher and the situation in which they encounter him.

How toTrain Other Leaders

For years a large paper company spent eighteen to twenty-four months training each new packaging salesman. As the company's managers evaluated what it was doing and took a much closer look at what the man actually needed to know, they concluded that the training program could be greatly condensed. Now that company's salesmen assume an account responsibility within ninety days after starting to work, and the general reaction on the part of customers, salesmen, and the company has been favorable.

Perhaps the church has just the opposite problem. Rather than pouring too much time, effort, and money into training leadership, we have a tendency to equate willingness with competence and to press into service anyone who can be persuaded to say yes.

If you are an administrator in your church, one of the single most important tasks you have is the development of people. In doing so you will be following a biblical pattern set many years ago by such godly leaders as Moses (who trained Joshua), Elijah (who trained Elisha), and Paul (who trained Timothy). Of course, the classic example of leadership training in the Bible is the work of Jesus with His twelve disciples. A careful study of the life of our Lord indicates that He was not primarily concerned with big mass meetings and a ministry to the multitudes. Most of His time was spent with the Twelve and building His life into them.

TRAINING IS BASED ON EVALUATION

A constant evaluation is extremely important in the process of administration. A progressive leader evaluates himself; he evaluates the goal achievement of his organization; he evaluates the subordinates who are already working under his supervision; and he evaluates potential leaders with a view toward recruiting and training them for the expanding ministries of his church or Sunday School.

Such evaluation is based on records and reports made available to the leader through the proper channels of the organization. For example, a Sunday School superintendent should constantly solicit from his departmental superintendents quarterly reports on their activities. In turn, he submits quarterly written reports to the Christian Education Board or Committee .

In addition to reports, there should be clear-cut records such as attendance figures, number of calls made, faithfulness at attending meetings, and so forth, which give clues to the commitment and competence of the workers.

It is also important to note that evaluation is based on objectives. We need to identify exactly what it is we want from people before we analyze whether or not they have done effective jobs. Henry A. Singer, executive director of Human Resources Associates in Westport, Connecticut, spelled it out:

> A common complaint is "I'm not sure that's my responsibility," or "I never know how I'm doing on my job." Both of these comments reflect a lack of job definitions and appraisals. Every employee should have a clear idea of the dimensions of his job, his responsibilities, and the extent of his authority. Once these are well defined, there is an objective basis for evaluating his performance ("The Impact of Human Resources on Business," *Business Horizons,* April, 1969).

Let's be clear about the fact that the evaluation of human resources in business or in a church is both objective and subjective. It is objective to the point, as Singer notes, that we can identify exactly what a worker is supposed to have achieved and then measure that achievement. It is subjective because there are so many other important elements in job performance besides goal achievement. For example, we must evaluate attitude, relationship with other workers, willingness to respond to leadership, potential for advancement, and many other qualities.

The leader must learn how to measure the qualities of other people in order to select the right persons for the right positions at the right time in the church's educational program.

TRAINING CAN TAKE VARIOUS FORMS

Perhaps we can say that training *should* take various forms. Some workers respond to certain kinds of training programs and are completely turned off by others. A variety of offerings in the training program gives us an opportunity to capture the attention of a potential worker as well as regain the interest and excitement of one who has been on the job for a long time. Here are ten different ways to go about training leaders in the local church. All of them are proven and all of them will work if implemented with competence and care.

Training classes. Some churches offer a leadership training classes for one quarter each year as a part of their regular Sunday School curriculum. For thirteen Sundays potential teachers are invited to take a special class for the development of leadership. Quite obviously, training classes could also be held on weeknights, Sunday evenings, and other times of the week.

Special seminars. A special weekend seminar in leadership development is a fine way to initiate a training program or to carry out retraining of workers already on the job. Usually the seminar is most effective if you bring in an outside expert rather than staff it with your own people.

Cadet teaching. In college Education departments this is called "student teaching" or sometimes "practice teaching." I dislike the latter term because any time we are working with real people it ought to be more than just practice. But here we put a potential teacher under the care of an experienced and competent teacher for a period of time so that the student teacher can learn by taking part in actual instructional situations. This training method is effectively used in addition to whatever other plans we might have available.

Conventions and conferences. Perhaps your church is located close to a major city where Sunday School conventions are held annually. It is always a wise thing to get as many of your teachers as you can to attend such a convention and even offer some kind of incentive or reward for doing so.

There are other kinds of conferences, such as annual denominational meetings or perhaps educational conferences at a nearby Christian college or seminary which could be profitable as training tools for your staff.

Monthly workers' conference. Many churches are effectively using the monthly workers' conference as a training tool. Of course, it does not have to be monthly; a quarterly workers' conference would be helpful too. What really counts is whether the two hours or so which your workers spend together at the conference really offer the kind of information and inspiration which will help them do a better job.

The Timothy approach. This method is so named because it is patterned after the way Paul personally trained Timothy to do many of the tasks which Paul had previously done. Pastors ought to use the Timothy approach with assistant pastors, superintendents with assistant superintendents, and so on. Again, the Timothy approach is effective when coupled with other teacher training methods, and it functions well on its own too.

The leader-elect plan. One national organization always refers to its vice-president as the president-elect, because the bylaws call for the vice-president to automatically succeed the president. There is some real merit in this, and we might use it in the church in such positions as assistant Sunday School superintendent, vice-chairman of the Christian education board, and similar posts. One takes a much more serious view of training for a certain task when he knows that he will hold that task within the next two or three years.

In-service training. Of course, in-service training could take any of the above forms, but the emphasis is on refresher programs which have new levels of expertise rather than going back to the elementary fields. It is a good idea to pull every Sunday School teacher out of his teaching post for at least one quarter every three years and put him or her in a special in-service training class.

Refresher courses. The refresher course is also a sort of in-service program in which we provide an opportunity to retool for people who have been doing a job for a period of time. Perhaps it could be used for former teachers and workers who have been out of teaching for several years but want to get back in.

A reading program. Coupled with any other kind of leadership training should be a careful reading program. We live in a day when more books and articles are available than ever before, and we should take advantage of the resources God has made available to the church in this age.

TRAINING REQUIRES SPECIFIC GUIDELINES

We need to ask some hard questions about our training programs to make sure they are really productive because productivity is the goal.

First, are the trainees expected to do something tangible and specific as the result of the training they receive? Does the training culminate in the ability to teach? Does it prepare people for personal witnessing? What specific performance is supposed to result?

Second, will what the trainees are going to do result in a genuine advancement of the church's educational program? We need to train people to do things that really need to be done. If it is teachers we need, then training programs ought to be geared toward teaching. If our concern is visitation, we will want to develop practical field education experiences.

Third, have we varied the training methodology in recent years, or is it the same old thing each time we announce a program? If the answer to the first part of the question is no or not much, we probably are not taking advantage of the recent technology and media available to the church. Films, slides, video cassettes, filmstrips, simulation games, and numerous other devices are valuable for enhancing training at the local church level.

Finally, are the training leaders really geared to produce what you need in the training? If training is effective, it produces measurable, sought-after changes in individual performance. Objectives are important in all education, but they are *critical* in training.

Training must not be confused with telling. To be sure, we need telling in general communication to keep our workers informed. But training is more of a two-way operation. It requires feedback from the trainee in order to see whether the objectives have been achieved.

How to Work with People in Groups

Christians seem to be constantly involved in group work of one kind or another. That is especially true of those who are active in various ministries in the educational program of a local church. The church is by definition "plural," that is, it emphasizes that new life in Christ is not isolation but rather involvement with other people of "like precious faith" (2 Peter 1:1, KJV).

Yet, many people talk only about the individual aspects of biblical Christianity. Quite obviously, the Bible teaches that a person's salvation is *individual*—it is a direct relationship between himself and Christ, unaffected by what others may think of him or do to him. To be sure, many other people may have been influential in his coming to a decision for Christ, just as many may have urged him to avoid commitment to Christ and the church. At the time of conversion, however, an individual stands alone before God.

But that is the last time he is alone. He is baptized into the body of believers and becomes a member of a group. The writer of the Book of Hebrews urged us to continue meeting together · and not to forsake it as the Day of the Lord approaches (Heb.

10:25). Believers should admonish one another (1 Thes. 5:14) and encourage each other by being concerned for the interest of others in the group (Phil. 2:1-4).

The largest group the Christian is involved with is the universal church, consisting of all believers of all times and places. Another large group is the local representation of the church, which may be just a dozen people or may run in the thousands at its regular meetings.

Experts in Christian education and church renewal remind us that these large groups do not meet all the needs of growing Christians. A dynamic church, really interested in serving its people, will structure adequate small-group experiences to provide for interpersonal exchange.

To achieve the level of edifying relationships described in the New Testament, smaller groups are almost essential. Often the open and honest sharing and the growth process which begins in small groups can overflow into a larger body. Small groups offer an opportunity to know fewer people more deeply. This leads to the mutual trust that allows us to share our lives with one another. Then we can truly bear each other's burdens and encourage and even admonish each other when necessary. This is what small groups are for: knowing ourselves and each other better through Bible study, prayer, and sharing, so that we can grow to be like our Lord and to know Him more fully (Michael Wiebe, *Small Groups*, Inter-Varsity Press).

But what is a "group"? Strictly speaking, there are five characteristics of a group which help us to arrive at a usable definition. For example, a genuine group has *purpose*. The purpose may not always be understood by every member of the group, but it nevertheless exists and at times becomes dominant.

Groups also offer *interaction*. Usually the interaction is verbal and face-to-face; but even if those two commonly found ingredients are absent, some kind of interaction (letters, tapes, and so forth) is found among group members.

There generally is also some level of *interdependence*. Group members look to each other for reinforcement of ideas, for criticism, protection, and encouragement. A small prayer cell which meets weekly would be a good example of this kind of interdependence.

All of these lead to a *perceived unity*. Members see themselves as part of something. In some cases, that "something" may be very formal and rigid (such as a service club where dues and attendance are required). At other times it may be loose and informal. But the group members generally know who's in and who's out.

A fifth idea or characteristic of groups is *boundaries of inclusion/exclusion*. Again, in a very informal group, members may come and go; and there may not be any formal way of distinguishing the "ins" from the "outs." But there are "ins," and there are "outs"; and some indication of the boundaries of participation is usually found.

Consider a family Bible study which meets Tuesday evening as a part of a local church's Christian education ministry. Do you see its purpose? Do you see its role of interaction? Do you see the interdependence of its members? Do you see the perceived unity of the group? Do you see the boundaries of inclusion/exclusion? You probably can answer yes to all of these questions if you have had experience with such a group.

But our primary question is how to enhance group work. Or perhaps there is an even more primitive question: How do you get group work started?

REALIZE THE VALUES

Groups are the result of concerned people. That's why so many good small groups are informal—they have not been rigidly structured by some formal organization in the church but have just sprung up out of needs. And that is one of the values of small groups which we have hinted at several times already in the preceding paragraphs—a group *uncovers and meets needs*. Dr. Clifford Anderson writes in an unpublished monograph:

> While a structured curriculum is valuable, an experience in a group where the group writes its own agenda can be most helpful. If a group wants to explore the implications of Christianity in relation to some area of

daily life, this is good. Even in groups with a structured curriculum, there should be time for sharing of burdens and joys and prayer for one another. If any institution should be noted for its genuine human concern, it should be the church. This was once the case ("The Use of Group Dynamics in Our Ministry").

A good small group also *prompts change.* Though the changes developed by small groups are not always positive, massive nationwide revolutions begin with small groups. Like the revolution itself, the change in the lives of the group members may be good, or it may be bad; but the very dynamic of verbal interaction carries with it a swirl of change in the lives of the people who are willing to interact with others.

One reason some churches are resistant to change is that they are unaccustomed to openly sharing their ideas and to listening to the ideas of others in a small-group setting.

A good group also *provides support.* In the setting of an evangelical church a small group serves as a sort of "sinners-saved-by-grace anonymous." The familiar buddy system can become a system of group support to hold up struggling believers' hands.

Finally, a good group *demonstrates love.* The Bible teaches us that the exercise of any spiritual gift, including the gift of exhortation, is worthless without love (1 Cor. 13). Group members learn to love each other in spite of faults and failings, and such love is spiritually therapeutic for both the givers and the receivers.

RECOGNIZE THE PURPOSE

This is where some good groups go awry. I have indicated that not all group members always understand the purpose of their group—but they should. It becomes the responsibility of the group leader (or perhaps the collective responsibility of the group members) to clearly affirm a purpose which is common to all. This is sometimes referred to in the jargon of leadership literature as "mutually agreeable goals."

Why does this group meet? Why do we give up two or three hours a week to be here together? What precisely do we want from this experience?

Committees often fail as group experiences because their purpose is not clear to the members. Three qualifications of purpose can be stated with respect to a small-group ministry: it must be common to all; it must be clearly understood; and it must be clearly stated.

REGULATE THE CLIMATE

Small-group experts talk a lot about group "climate." In the church some of the qualities of climate may be dignity, mutual respect, openness, and submission. Group dynamics can be unleashed only in a nonthreatening, nondefensive, and nonembarrassing climate.

The dynamic of a group is developed through certain exercises, such as name-tag games and other fun types of experiences which stimulate creativity and interaction. Positive climate is further developed by interaction methodology, such as having group members tell about their memorable family traditions.

Though the leader's example in warmth and openness is essential, he must also be willing to be vulnerable and to emphasize clearly his equality with other group members rather than an autocratic dominance in the group.

Group leadership is surely the key to successful group activities. But the leader can't do it alone.

The physical setting of the group is important to its climate. A cozy family room with a crackling fire is much more likely to develop a positive climate for group experiences than the pews in the sanctuary.

Informal activities help too. They loosen people up a bit, and that informality and willingness to participate tend to carry over into the serious study activities of the group.

RESTORE THE COMMUNICATION

If you want to see how important communication is in any group work, notice how small groups gather together in the parking lot as members talk with each other after a tense and controversial board meeting. If they *could* have or *would* have said in the board meeting what they are now saying to each other in the parking lot, the formal meeting probably would have been much more successful.

Of course, size and time are factors. A good group should be relatively small and have an uncrowded schedule. The actual size and time relate to the purpose of the group; so I can do no more than suggest a model with a defined purpose.

A home Bible study group that wants to do more than just hear a speaker expound certain portions of Scripture should be no larger than twelve to fifteen members and meet about two hours a week at one sitting.

Group members need to learn the practice of self-disclosure while being willing, like their leader, to be open and vulnerable. This does not mean telling the group all about your sordid past or sharing all your personal problems, but it does mean responding at any moment as you honestly feel, but with grace and discretion.

Once the patterns of group interaction are established, we need to examine them further. Is the verbal communication really getting at meanings instead of just words? Is everybody participating? If Bible study is the focal point of the group, are people willingly submitting their own viewpoints to the authority of the Scriptures?

You can try it too. Maybe God wants you to be leader of a small group, or at least one of its active members. Check that little booklet by Michael Wiebe from which I quoted earlier. His last paragraph pinpoints the values that await us in small-group ministry:

> Is it all worth the work? Is it worth the risk of being known? One might just as well ask, is it worth it to become more like Christ and help others do the same? God desires His people to be built up. He has chosen small groups as one major way for us to be edified and to help others move closer to "the measure of the stature of the fullness of Christ" (Eph. 4:13, KJV).

How to Equip Others

The word "equip" in *Webster's New Collegiate Dictionary* (G. & C. Merriam) carries a simple definition: "To furnish for service or action: make ready by appropriate provisioning." That is precisely what we mean when we talk about equipping God's people for ministry in the local church.

In the text of the New Testament the concept best emerges in the use of the word *katartizô,* translated variously by such English words as "render complete," "mend," and "repair." Four classic New Testament passages contain this term: "We are glad whenever we are weak but you are strong; and our prayer is for your perfection" (2 Cor. 13:9); "To prepare God's people for works of service, so that the body of Christ may be built up" (Eph. 4:12); "May the God of peace ... equip you with everything good for doing His will, and may He work in us what is pleasing to Him, through Jesus Christ, to whom be glory forever and ever" (Heb. 13:20-21); and "The God of all grace, who called you to His eternal glory in Christ, after you have suffered a little while, will Himself restore you and make you strong, firm, and steadfast" (1 Peter 5:10).

To study these passages is one thing; to develop a practical program for equipping the saints in a local church is quite another. Implementation of an equipping ministry requires several things of church leaders who are responsible for its effectiveness.

A BIBLICAL PERCEPTION OF THE NATURE AND MINISTRY OF THE CHURCH

This is so basic that I hesitate to spend time reiterating it, but flagrant violations of basic principles still abound in our enlightened day. We have a tendency to gravitate toward glamour ministries, particularly those which will produce visible and immediate results, such as "decisions." But Frank Gaebelein well reminds us that the long-term, sometimes tedious, always essential ministry of teaching is central to the church's biblical ministry:

> Among priorities for the local church today, none is more urgent than teaching. A church that fails here is delinquent at the heart of its mission. During His earthly ministry, our Lord was the Master Teacher; in His post-resurrection appearance on the Emmaus Road, He expounded the Scriptures (Luke 24:27); the central emphasis in His Great Commission is upon teaching (Matt. 28:19-20). And in Paul's list of the gifts of the Spirit, teaching is indissolubly united with pastoral work—"He gave some...pastors and teachers" (Eph. 4:11) ("The Teaching Church," *Christianity Today,* January 31, 1969).

A LEADERSHIP STYLE THAT ACKNOWLEDGES THE BODY-TEAM CONCEPT OF CHURCH MINISTRY

It is one thing to talk about secular leadership characteristics such as ambition, confidence, integrity, justice, objectivity, flexibility, and creativity. A Christian leader ought to possess all of these, but even possessing them all in abundance (a rare find) is inadequate when measured against the biblical focus on leadership style.

The New Testament clearly identifies the task of the church as a group ministry. Consequently leading the body or the group requires a team-oriented leadership style. There should be little room in an evangelical church for a leader who suffers from a recurrent Napoleonic complex. Recent decades have clearly shown us what obsession with power can be and do, so every local church should be determined to avoid putting autocratic monarchs in key positions.

The church leader (pastor, Christian education director, elder, superintendent) must also have solid theological credentials. Former Congressman Walter Judd once remarked that a man who has gotten hold of bad ideas is dangerous in direct proportion to the amount of his education. As we develop (equip) church leaders let's never forget to lay a solid biblical base. Above all, our people need to be men and women of the Word.

The effective church education leader must take a broad view of what is included in his ministry. The concept of Sunday School has long since proved too narrow. More recently the limitation of the field to a study of church education alone is also restrictive. A thorough understanding of Christian education includes all programs and experiences which supplement the maturation ministry of the Christian home, the Christian church, and the Christian school. This is a broad view of equipping; it can be carried out only by a person who wants to reproduce his life and leadership in others.

A NEED-MEETING PROGRAM GEARED TO THE TIMES

When we talk about equipping, we mean giving people something they do not have and yet obviously need. In some cases, that could be basic Bible study; in others, an understanding of learning theory and teaching principles; in still others, a commitment to biblical motivation for ministry. The equipper must understand how to integrate individual needs with church goals so that harmonious service results. There will be a constant resolving of conflicts and adaptation to the turbulent environmental change which we all experience from year to year.

When we talk about a need-meeting program and about equipping people, we are clearly focusing as well on the identity of the institution—the church. Equipping must be unshakably church-related.

Second only to the home, the gathered church provides the foundation for all of the other forms of Christian service and fellowship. Other organizations as parachurch organizations, find their authentication only insofar as they relate to the functioning of the local church. Not only is God not finished with the church, but He never will be. People who are equipping leaders know how to concentrate their energies on the positive task of being the church in the world.

A false veneer of methodology without the solid bulwark of biblical construction is to a church worker what credit-card spending is to a family without any real money. It may look good for a while and it may even pass the inspection of the experts. But in time stern reality will catch up and will destroy its effectiveness.

A CLEAR SORTING OUT OF THE DIFFERENCE BETWEEN SPIRITUAL ISSUES AND ORGANIZATIONAL ISSUES

One of our biggest problems is that we fail to see the church both as an organism and as an organization. Many articles limit their discussion to only one of these aspects of the church. But it should be obvious that the church partakes of the characteristics of both. Until we understand this concept, we will continue to supply organizational answers to spiritual problems (and vice versa).

Equipping means knowing our people well. We need to understand whether the problems of a given leadership candidate are primarily spiritual or organizational. If he doesn't know how to utilize his time and if he cannot set goals which can be fulfilled, no amount of praying or Bible study is likely to solve those problems for him. On the other hand, if he is not walking closely with the Lord and is guilty of hypocrisy and perhaps has an unloving attitude toward his brothers and sisters in Christ, five years of study in the best business school may not change his deficiencies of spirit which create those nagging difficulties.

A Sensitivity and Skill in the Tasks of Administration

The tasks of administration are many, but they center primarily in things such as organization, delegation, motivation, human relations, control, and planning. Not every church leader has the gift of administration, but everyone who carries an administrative role must learn to function within the demands of that role. To a degree at least, these are basic skills which can be learned, and they must be learned if they are to be transferred to others in an equipping ministry.

In my opinion, chief among the nagging administrative tasks in the Christian organization is human relations. A group of teachers were rather surprised by the results of a questionnaire they sent to more than 2,000 employers. As a service to students, they asked: "Will you please look up the records of the last three persons dismissed from your business and tell us why you let them go?" In two out of three cases, regardless of the type of work or section of the country, the answer was the same: "They couldn't get along with other people."

The application of human relations techniques in the administration of organizations is a complex and professional skill. It does not just happen because they are "good people," or because they happen to be Christians.

Peter Drucker says, "There are no good people; there are only people good for certain things." Of course, such a statement comes out of a theological vacuum but it does legitimately express the truism that everyone must find his proper niche in an organization in order to function effectively and happily.

But the biblical truth is that there *are* good people, at least in their standing before God, and those good people ought to become *better* people each day in the process of sanctification. But this does not happen accidentally. It is a carefully calculated design of spiritual growth on the part of an individual, and of warm human relations and a team spirit on the part of his organization. "Now we ask you, brothers, to respect those who work hard among you, who are over you in the Lord and who admonish you. Hold them in the highest regard in love because of their work. Live in peace with each other" (1 Thes. 5:12-13). The carrying out of an effective equipping ministry demands that the church leader be committed to it. He or she must perceive the biblical thrust of the involved body, which occupies so much of the New Testament text. Once we find our function within that body and commit ourselves to its progress by sharing what God has allowed us to learn with other people, we can begin to implement in our own particular places, and then perhaps in a wider sphere, the kind of ministry which equips others for the tasks God has called them to do.

How to Disciple Leaders

What Robert Frost once said about students may be even more accurate when applied to church leaders: "Education is hanging around until you've caught on." In teaching the concept of job control, I have frequently stated in classes and seminar groups that any kind of job control at the administrative level takes a minimum of one year. When we look at positions in the upper levels of church administration, one year is hardly long enough to "hang around" if one really intends to produce and reproduce in the New Testament sense of discipleship.

Our key word is "disciple," and it needs definition or at least description right up front. First of all, the word is hardly used exclusively for the twelve original followers of Jesus. It appears over 260 times in the Gospels and Acts and is used most often to include Christians other than the original Twelve. In the Book of Acts, Luke used the word "saint" three times, the word "Christian" twice, but the word "disciple" twenty-six times when he referred to the believers. Every true Christian is a learner; therefore, every Christian is a disciple.

So much for the denotation of the word, but the connotation

today is considerably more narrow. We are talking about how a leader influences those with whom he comes in contact on a regular basis to move them toward an intensely biblical and personal commitment to Jesus Christ, marked by obedience and a uniquely Christian lifestyle.

It is tempting to generalize the subject with respect to both disciples and discipler, but the greater value seems to rest in a much more narrow focus. I direct my attention, therefore, to the pastor or minister of education, since those are the administrative offices that dominate the program. The general principles of discipleship which pertain to them certainly apply in varying ways to superintendents as well as to various managers and directors at different levels on the organization chart.

We often say that the pastor sets the spiritual tone for a church, and in some vague way that notion may be true. But we really need to break down the process of spiritual influence to indicate precisely who it is the leader is discipling and how he goes about carrying on such a ministry with various groups. Any educational administrator with a reasonable record of "hanging around" can identify with the groups I have chosen as focal points for discipleship—deacons and elders, fellow administrators, teachers, and students.

Before we examine these groups, let me identify a unifying thread of structure that I hope will be visible in the tapestry of these remarks. It is the modeling behavior of Paul the apostle, who of all the people in the Old and New Testaments, except our Lord Himself, is surely the discipler's model. Paul is the quintessential demonstration of education and experience combined, a gem of brilliance who made a great impact on the world, the like of which has never been seen since.

THE BOARD OF ELDERS OR DEACONS:
DISCIPLING THROUGH COOPERATION

Let's begin right at the top, for if a leader does not relate properly to his board, he will not have the opportunity to hang around until he has caught on. And whatever time he does hang around will be characterized by agony, frustration, and tears rather than a mutuality of ministry that leads to reaching goals. The key word I have chosen here is "cooperation," and the particular example from Paul's life occurs in Acts 15, when he appeared with Barnabas to argue the case for a Gospel of grace for Gentiles, at what we call "the council at Jerusalem."

Though scarcely having returned from the first missionary journey back to Antioch, the sending church, Paul had already attained a stature among first-century Christians that made him a leader to be reckoned with in any decision. His ability in public debate surely could have cowed some of the less-educated disciples and other leaders in the church at Jerusalem. Yet they were in reality the "governing board" of the mother church to whom he was responsible. He was their servant; he understood that relationship, and he behaved in accordance with it.

It surely could be argued in the structure of a church setting that the board members should set a model for the leadership behavior they want to see in their "employees." But the simple fact is that many educational leaders have advanced beyond some of their board members in educational, spiritual, social, emotional, and intellectual maturity. Therefore, the employer-employee relationship dissolves into greater commitment—remember the words of Jesus: "From everyone who has been given much, much will be demanded; and from the one who has been entrusted with much, much more will be asked" (Luke 12:48).

Perhaps over the long haul of ministry, a church leader reaps the greatest benefits from a passive yet effective discipling of board members through cooperation.

Fellow Administrators:
Discipling through Camaraderie

One of my favorite passages in the New Testament occurs toward the end of Acts 11, where Barnabas, the "Son of Encouragement," goes to Tarsus to bring Saul the scholar back to Antioch so that the local church there may have more in-depth Bible study than Barnabas himself could provide. Together they ministered to the church at Antioch, and together they shared the encouragements and discouragements of the first missionary journey until a sharp disagreement regarding the status of John Mark led to a separation at the beginning of Paul's second missionary journey.

One could very well ask who was discipling whom in the Barnabas-Saul relationship at Antioch. Obviously, both together were edifying the believers, much in the way that administrators join hands to provide educational programs for college students. But I suspect that if you walked into the Antioch church during those years, you would have had a great deal of difficulty ascertaining who was "in charge," so great was the camaraderie among the co-workers.

Leaders must constantly be on guard against jealousies that can immediately destroy the discipling process. It is at least as difficult for a pastor to count other staff members his friends as it is for a college president to maintain similar relationships with his faculty. But it is not impossible; and without compromising the dignity of the office, it is certainly desirable to develop a relationship in which the pastor can say to the members of a multiple staff just what Jesus said to His own disciples: "I no longer call you servants, because a servant does not know his master's business. Instead, I have called you friends, for everything that I learned from My Father I have made known to you" (John 15:15).

Conflict is more likely to happen at this level than at any of the others which we are discussing. Control involves correcting, regulating, monitoring performance, and other actions generally threatening to subordinates. There is a significant balance between power and authority in administrative relations.

TEACHERS: DISCIPLING THROUGH COMMUNITY

It is somewhat difficult to draw an accurate analogy with the ministry of the Apostle Paul when trying to describe a leader's relationship to teachers and workers. Surely, however, we can look at Aquila and Priscilla as they assisted the total missionary cause, but were not leaders on a par with Paul and the other apostles, or even junior instructors, such as Timothy, Epaphras, and others. Yet they were constantly a part of the total team ministry, a part of the community of believers who served together. They were people to whom Paul referred as "my fellow workers in Christ Jesus" (Rom. 16:3).

There are few things more nagging than trying to think great thoughts of institutional development, curriculum design, and overall long-range planning, and being brought back down to earth by arguments regarding parking places, a few dollars miscalculated in salary, or whether the secretaries have been overusing their quotas at the copying machine. Nevertheless, these are the "stuff" of which community is made; therefore, these are the points at which discipling must begin (Phil. 2:1-5).

Students: Discipling through Communication

When speaking of the students of the Apostle Paul, one is tempted to quickly identify Timothy and Titus and others with similar New Testament fame. But perhaps the most dynamic demonstration of communication to a listening group appears in Acts 17, where Paul offered an apologetic for the Christian faith on the Areopagus in Athens with the result that "a few men became followers of Paul and believed. Among them was Dionysius, a member of the Areopagus, also a woman named Damaris, and a number of others" (Acts 17:34).

It is probably true that church leaders do not speak often enough to students. But we all share the task of communicating Christian values and a distinctly biblical world view to our congregations. Like Paul on Mars' Hill, we must speak with clarity and an alertness to contemporary issues, demonstrating our willingness and ability to blaze a trail through the wilderness of contemporary pagan society's moral mishmash.

We cannot be excused. God will not allow it, and our own spirits will condemn us if we do not lead our churches to be the Christian consciences of their respective communities. Leadership in Christian education has the privilege of developing a perspective on contemporary social issues that is far broader than that which can be seen by the parishioner.

The privilege of that perspective brings a commensurate responsibility to bring to bear the white-hot spotlight of God's

Word on the many pressing and distressing problems of contemporary culture. That is practical discipleship.

How to Solve the Absentee Problem

Figures released in 1980 by the Bureau of Labor Statistics show that in an average week, 2.4 million of the 56.5 million American nonfarm wage and salary employees who normally worked full time were on unscheduled absences part of the week, for an average of two days. This amounts to 1.4 million absent because of illness and another million for miscellaneous reasons, including vacations and personal time. That's an increase of some 15 percent in just five years. Unscheduled leave of more than a week went up by about 10 percent in the same period.

White-collar theft drove retail prices up nationwide during the seventies, and now absenteeism is having the same effect. It's always easy to slide over percentages and statistics, but we're talking about real people and lost productivity.

Obviously absenteeism is a problem in the church as well as in business and industry. Sunday School teachers don't show up. Committee members are absent in such a percentage as to make a quorum incomplete and thereby waste the time of others. Church members attend morning and evening services, Sunday School, and prayer meeting on a hit-and-miss basis.

As with business and industry management, church leadership needs to check into the causes of absenteeism and then take specific measures and institute controls to prevent or at least minimize disruptions caused by the absentee problem. As soon as we do that, we'll discover that we run smack into "people problems" in the church.

SUPERVISION THAT FOSTERS ABSENTEEISM

Obviously all the people talked about in the earlier statistics have supervisors or bosses to whom they are responsible. Their absences not only complicate the tasks of these managers at various levels, but they are also closely related to the managerial behavior shown by the supervisors. In short, voluntary absenteeism generally indicates a lack of cooperation with one's supervisor or a lack of concern for the organization or church ministry for which one is responsible.

James K. Van Fleet, well-known management consultant and lecturer on managerial motivation, authored a book entitled *The 22 Biggest Mistakes Managers Make and How to Correct Them* (Parker). Of the twenty-two items Van Fleet lists, seven have to do with any kind of leadership role and can be applied to Sunday School superintendents, departmental superintendents, deacons, elders, and other church officers and leaders. Remember, he is identifying "biggest mistakes."

Trying to be liked rather than respected. A supervisor errs by accepting favors from his subordinates or doing special favors in order to develop friendly relationships rather than building respect for the office he holds. Anyone responsible for leadership will have to make unpopular decisions on occasion, and discipline will have to be rendered. It is nice to be both liked and respected, but if there must be a choice, leadership requires respect first.

Failing to ask subordinates for their advice and help. Wise leaders allow subordinates to have "a piece of the action." The problems of the church are their problems as well, not just the problems of boards and committees. A good superintendent makes it easy for people to communicate their ideas and their personal problems to him. He follows through with answers and, if possible, solutions. Such communication can go a long way toward cutting down absenteeism, often caused by an employee's feeling that his supervisor doesn't understand his problems.

Failing to develop a sense of responsibility in subordinates. How often we see this in the church today! But developing a sense of responsibility is not just a matter of constantly scolding regarding one's "Christian duty." We must allow freedom of expression, give people a chance to learn other jobs (particularly the jobs of their superiors), and always accompany responsibility with authority.

Emphasizing rules rather than skill. This is simply a matter of good delegation, which calls for allowing an individual to use his own creativity to get a job done.

Failing to keep criticism constructive. We must never assume that the subordinate is always at fault when something goes wrong. A good supervisor whose employees are less likely to be involved with absenteeism attempts to get as many facts as possible, controls his temper at all times, praises more than he criticizes, listens to all sides of the story from all employees, and makes sure that an employee's dignity is always protected.

Not paying attention to employee gripes and complaints. Every church should have a normal process of what managerial science calls "grievance procedure." People need to be able to voice their complaints and expect that their superiors will listen and either do something or explain why nothing can be done.

Failure to keep people informed. Communication is absolutely essential in all organizations, especially among voluntary workers as those in the church. People need to know as soon as possible of any changes that will affect them, and one must try to squelch rumors (or at least ignore them) when they have no basis in the organization's actual progress or plans.

An Absenteeism Checklist

There are a few simple practical guidelines we can use in the church to cut down on nagging absenteeism. A supervisor should

always insist on *prompt notification* when someone in his department must be absent. In some cases, that notification can be
quite advanced. In other cases, there will be last-minute emer-
gencies. But notification should nevertheless be given.

It is important too to *try to deal with the absences before they
happen* rather than listen to explanations after the absent worker
returns to the job. Unwarranted or "phony" absences will often
show up fore and aft of holidays or weedends.

We cut down on the crisis caused by absenteeism if we *have
backup personnel available.* Every department should have
standby substitute teachers. It is also good to have alternate
committee members who can be called to complete a quorum or
discuss an important issue when a regularly elected committee
member cannot be present.

Good records must be kept on attendance or lack of it. Good
supervisors make periodic checks to see which workers are
frequently absent. When these people are isolated, they can be
the targets of special counseling sessions to further probe the
cause of the chronic absenteeism. Sometimes a *public group
confrontation is useful,* in which a given department or perhaps
the entire staff is faced with the problem and asked for their
suggestions on how to deal with it. A good supervisor also *looks
for inadequacies in the work situation* that lead toward
absenteeism.

ULTIMATELY IT'S A QUESTION OF QUALITY CONTROL

How this common term of managerial science ought to ring out
in a Christian organization! Of all "businesses," the church ought
to be the most concerned about quality control. Poor teaching,
poor committee work, and poor record-keeping all cut the quality of the church's ministry and reflect on the person and work of
Jesus Christ, the Head of the church.

Business and industry are now facing more than half a million
suits a year with respect to product control liability. According to
figures compiled by Assembly Engineering, purchasers of manu-
factured products filed more than 50,000 product liability suits
regarding injury. With today's consumer protection, these suits

now have much better prospects in the courts. Since 1960, the number of such suits has risen from fewer than 30,000 to the present number, and an estimate by the Aluminum Association says it will soon be over a million.

But who protects the consumer at the local church against poor teaching, boring preaching, and disorganized programming? How does he sue? Obviously, what he does is leave the church and try to find a more satisfactory situation elsewhere. But in most cases that does not help the individual, his family, and certainly the church he is leaving. The only way to solve the product liability problem is to exercise quality control right up front.

In the final analysis, the subject must be dealt with as a spiritual problem. People who have committed themselves to certain responsibilities have covenanted before God and His people to follow through. They are certainly under obligation to do the best they can in those responsibilities.

Scripture tells us that it is required in stewards above all things that "those who have been given a trust must prove faithful" (1 Cor. 4:2). That negates unwarranted absenteeism by the same principle that covers our work. But, remember, it is also a spiritual problem on the part of the supervisor, if he has not made a personal effort to investigate the cause of the staff member's absence. Are there really problems at home with which the church should be helping? Is the task we have asked this individual to do greater than he or she can handle? Is fear of failure causing the absence? The concept of teamwork and genuine togetherness must prevail if we are going to lick the problem of absenteeism in the church as well as in industry.

Paul wrote to believers: "Therefore, as God's chosen people, holy and dearly loved, clothe yourselves with compassion, kindness, humility, gentleness, and patience. Bear with each other and forgive whatever grievances you may have against one another. Forgive as the Lord forgave you. And over all these virtues put on love, which binds them all together in perfect unity. Let the peace of Christ rule in your hearts, since as members of one body you were called to peace. And be thankful" (Col. 3:12-15).

How to Serve under Fire

It happens to all of us. And the higher the leadership post, the more common the experience of serving the Lord under fire. Every church has fair-weather workers, soldiers who are willing to do battle as long as things are going well and the enemy isn't too tough. We all desperately need more soldiers who know how to serve under fire, people who can stay at their posts even when the rockets of criticism are exploding around them.

David learned early in his life about leadership and about how bitter a pill criticism can be. The Philistines with whom he had been living while on the run from Saul had gathered at Aphek to battle the Israelites, and David was planning to make the trip with them. But King Achish dismissed David, probably suspecting his real loyalty to Israel, and sent him and his men back to Ziklag, their headquarters in exile.

First Samuel 30 begins with these words: "David and his men reached Ziklag on the third day. Now the Amalekites had raided the Negev and Ziklag. They had attacked Ziklag and burned it." The passage goes on to say that all the women and children had been kidnapped and that the situation was so desperate that it brought David and his men to tears "until they had no strength left to weep" (30:4).

Then an amazing thing happened. Rather than making plans immediately for liberating their wives and children, the faithful few who had followed David in his flight from Saul turned on *him* and even spoke of stoning him, so great was their grief over the disaster at Ziklag.

Imagine David's predicament! His wives and children had been taken captive too; his help had just been refused by the Philistines after he had graciously offered it; and now the few loyal friends he had left in the world were talking of killing him as though the attack on Ziklag had been entirely his fault!

No doubt David learned that day some very important lessons about taking criticism. These lessons came back to his mind many times during his long years as a king.

The word "criticism" does not have to be negative. The first definition in Webster's *New Collegiate Dictionary* defines criticism as "the act of criticizing, usually unfavorably." But it can also mean "the art of evaluating or analyzing with knowledge and propriety works of art or literature" and "the scientific investigation of literary documents (as the Bible) in regard to such matters as origin, text, composition, character, or history."

In the highest sense, criticism can mean trying to learn things about ourselves, our ministry, and the world around us. But it can be a bitter "low blow" given at a most inopportune time from a most unexpected person.

I am not particularly concerned in this chapter with the art of *giving* criticism, though that is important for all Christian leaders. What is more to the point, however, is the ability to *take* criticism, to handle it properly, and make the most of it in a positive way, even when it was not intended positively. In order to focus on that aspect, we need to study something about the types of criticism, the sources of criticism, and the handling of criticism.

TYPES OF CRITICISM

Immediately, two adjectives come into our minds when we talk about categorizing criticism—*constructive and destructive*. Destructive criticism does not necessarily mean that the motive of the critic is to destroy the object of the criticism, since it is often offered in ignorance. One writer uses an alliteration on the letter "C" to attack destructive criticism:

> Captious criticism takes note of trivial faults; its author is usually unduly exacting or perversely hard to please. Carping criticism is a perverse picking of flaws. Caviling criticism stresses the habit of raising petty objections. Censorious criticism means a tendency to be severely condemnatory of that which one does not like ("On Criticism," *The Royal Bank of Canada Monthly Letter,* November 1976).

Constructive criticism is most often offered verbally, which leads to a second distinction of type, *spoken criticism and implied criticism.* Again, as in all of the four types we will deal with, the former is preferred. Implied criticism can more easily be misunderstood, even when its intentions are noble. It often takes the form of a sarcastic comment when the intentions are not noble and can quickly fester into open conflict, leading to the disruption of friendships and perhaps even to the division of a church.

If you intend to criticize someone with the objective of building him up in a positive sense, it should probably be done face-to-face with good manners and honesty in an atmosphere of spiritual dignity.

Still a third category to be considered would identify both *fair criticism and unfair criticism.* The former could be referred to also as criticism which is deserved; whereas the latter would be criticism which is undeserved. It is extremely important to identify these types of criticism (if possible) when one becomes the object of a critic's words. We shall return to that subject a bit later.

Finally, we can talk about *good and bad criticism.* Obviously, bad criticism is probably destructive, implied, and unfair. Good criticism, on the other hand, takes great concern for the feelings of the other (Phil. 2:1-4) and adds a solid dose of kindness to its judgment. Also, good criticism gives the criticized person an opportunity to make personal adjustments, that is, it gives the other person the benefit of the doubt.

SOURCES OF CRITICISM

Criticism can come to us (or at us) from superiors, peers, subordinates, the general public, friends, and even from ourselves. Perhaps the best way to analyze all of these is to use one single example, that of a Sunday School teacher in a local church.

Criticism from a *superior* might be a word from a departmental superintendent that our teacher has been arriving consistently late for Sunday School. That would be a necessary and even good piece of criticism if it is fair, spoken, and constructive, which it definitely could be.

The same teacher also could receive criticism from another teacher at the *peer* level. If spoken in love and with a genuine concern, that friend is really exercising a Christian duty to offer constructive criticism about some aspect of the other's ministry.

Criticism from a *subordinate*, perhaps a student, is more difficult to handle. Often it doesn't come person-to-person because the subordinate is afraid of facing the superior and speaking with him about the matter. So this criticism often takes the form of complaining to other subordinates until little cliques form, some of which think the critic is right and the leader unfair; while others, taking the side of the leader, rush to tell him what one of his subordinates is saying about him.

This creates a most difficult situation in a Christian organization and is the kind of pot Satan likes to stir. John W. Alexander, in a helpful booklet titled *Practical Criticism* (InterVarsity Press), suggests that this is one kind of situation in which the writing of criticism is important.

A Note to Leaders: If one of your supervisees is unhappy with his relationship to you, insist that he express his grievances—*in writing*—so that together you can go through them prayerfully with hope for solution. This can enable you to transform destructive negative criticism into constructive criticism.

Criticism from the *general public* is to be expected. There will always be people who do not understand or agree with what we do or why we do it. In the case of our teacher, such criticism might come from the parents of one of the Sunday School students or perhaps from a member of the church who has not been supportive of the Sunday School program and seizes every opportunity to say something negative about its organization and quality.

Criticism from *friends* is most difficult to take, as David discovered in the passage referred to earlier. Nevertheless, it should be a valuable kind of criticism if we can trust the person who offers it.

Finally, *self-criticism* is of utmost importance and ought to be going on continually. The danger is that we can push it too far so that we become perfectionists, demanding more of ourselves than we can deliver. An overdose of self-criticism can diminish self-worth and create feelings of inferiority when they are not necessary.

HANDLING OF CRITICISM

Perhaps the first guideline in handling criticism in the Christian community is to *consider the source*. Criticism from a superior or a friend certainly would be more valuable than criticism from the general public. Nevertheless, even "enemies" can help us if we're willing to extract the value from their words.

The second guideline is to *maintain your security*. The natural reaction when we are criticized is to fight back and become defensive, offering reasons or even excuses for the behavior under attack. The problem is that defensiveness almost always leads to emotional reactions rather than rational responses.

Don't counterattack. This is again an irrational response based on the assumption that the other person's motives are improper and his information inaccurate. Even potentially constructive and "good" criticism can quickly degenerate into a fight if the object of the criticism insists on an immediate counterattack.

It is, of course, important to *validate the data*. Try to find out whether what the critic is saying is really justifiable. Alexander suggests that we actually ask for evidence.

> If the critic's evidence is adequate and his conclusions valid, then he has done you a favor by providing guidance for making corrections.

He may have called your attention to a weakness that you knew nothing about, to a mistake which you did not realize had occurred, to oversights of which you were not conscious, to flaws which you had not noticed. "Why didn't somebody tell me?" we often ask. A negative critic may be endeavoring to do just that: tell us!

A fifth suggestion in the handling of criticism is to *learn what you can.* I indicated earlier that even in the most negative and unfair situations of criticism something can be learned. Perhaps it is only a greater humility before God and a greater dependence upon the Holy Spirit to handle all things in our lives. And while we're talking about the control of the Holy Spirit, it is in order to add a sixth suggestion: *Answer with kindness.* Scripture says, "A gentle answer turns away wrath, but a harsh word stirs up anger" (Prov. 15:1). This is an axiom which every Christian leader should internalize and use often.

Finally, *pray.* The words of an old hymn suggest this helpful guideline in handling criticism—"Take it to the Lord in prayer."

> Do thy friends despise, forsake thee?
> Take it to the Lord in prayer!
> In His arms He'll take and shield thee,
> Thou wilt find a solace there.

How to Grow a Sunday School

You mean your church isn't listed among the ten largest Sunday Schools in the United States?

Too bad. But don't give up, for two reasons. First of all, size is certainly only one measure of a church's success. There is very little evidence, either in New Testament theology or contemporary educational research, to argue that a church of 5,000 has a more effective teaching ministry than a church of 500 or even 200.

Is it not possible that the law of diminishing returns works at both ends of the scale? Of course the argument "quality rather than quantity" can be a cop-out used to excuse our uninterest in evangelism and outreach. It can open up a credibility gap in a church which loudly proclaims its lack of interest in numbers.

The other reason you should not be discouraged is that you *can* grow both numerically *and* spiritually; after all, that's what life is all about—growing. It is not coincidental that the Bible uses the pictures of "birth," "eating," "growth," "hunger," and "death" to describe spiritual realities.

The dynamic of a growing church is evidence of the life

principle, providing that the growth is more than just numerical. Just be sure to measure that growth by the proper yardsticks both in the areas of quantity and quality. Let me suggest six concepts, or "keys," which can unlock the door of growth in your Sunday School and your total church program.

PREPARATION

Peter in his second epistle urged believers not to be myopic (1:9). Evangelical churches, however, have a tendency to look only to the things that are at hand while sacrificing a strong emphasis on occupying until the Lord returns. Preparation for Sunday School growth begins with paying attention to long-range objectives.

Obviously there is also the preparation of adequate facilities. Too many Sunday School contests look effective in March, but their success becomes questionable when the September figures show a striking similarity to the preceding year.

There is also the preparation of adequate administrative control. Someone has to organize a pattern for growth and demonstrate how the long-range plans and the prospect of facility expansion fit into the objectives of the program for the next few years. Preparation consequently focuses on plans, plant, and people; and if any one of them is omitted or slighted, the prospects for growth begin to fade.

PLANNING

I have already suggested that we plan long-range goals and the utilization of facilities. But we also need to plan a satisfactory organization and departmentalization of the educational program. This includes proper use of records and reports, clear delineation of channels of authority, the development of job descriptions, and a complete system of follow-up to any formal effort at evangelism and outreach.

In that highly philosophical book, *Alice's Adventures in Wonderland,* Alice comes to a fork in the road and asks directions of the Cheshire cat. The Cheshire cat informs the little girl that since she has no particular place she wishes to go, it really doesn't matter which road she takes.

And wasn't it Socrates who said we have a much better chance of hitting the target if we can see it? What kinds of written plans are available at your church right now for five or ten years from now? How many classrooms will you need? How big should they be? How many teachers will be needed to carry on the program? What kind of training should they have?

Talking about teachers leads us to a third key to Sunday School growth.

PERSONNEL

Among the many approaches used successfully in recruitment and retention of workers in local church programs, one of the most significant is an elevation of the teaching ministry. We want to attract committed people. Furthermore, we want that commitment centered in the highest order of command, Jesus Christ Himself. Therefore, when we recruit personnel for growth, we sell the privilege, not the predicament; and the task of love, not the tyranny of legalism.

After we have the workers recruited, we have to make sure they are properly trained and thoroughly reliable for the task. Leadership training programs can be of varying types and lengths, but the crucial factors are their availability and level of quality. Since it is not the purpose of this paragraph to deal with leadership training, let's leave the subject with the suggestion that any church beginning a training program should consult its denominational Christian education office, the Christian education department at an affiliate or nearby evangelical college or seminary, or some professional organization such as the Evangelical Teacher Training Association (110 Bridge St., Wheaton, IL 60187).

PROGRAM

The growing Sunday School of today is one with a biblical curriculum, life-related teaching, and an evangelistic emphasis. It is really rather foolish to argue about whether a Sunday School should be primarily evangelistic or primarily nurture-centered. Either one that excludes or deemphasizes the other is a perversion of New Testament Christianity.

The command of the Great Commission is to disciple all nations. But the discipling of nations is more than sharing the Gospel with them, or even making them members of local churches. It is the continuing process of welcoming new believers and teaching them the depths of the Word.

There is surely no greater example of educational evangelism than the ministry of the Apostle Paul, particularly his work at Ephesus and Thessalonica. To the Ephesian elders he said, "For I have not hesitated to proclaim to you the whole will of God. . . . Remember that for three years I never stopped warning each of you night and day with tears" (Acts 20:27, 31). And to the Thessalonian Christians he wrote, "Our Gospel came to you not simply with words, but also with power, with the Holy Spirit, and with deep conviction. You know how we lived among you for your sake. You became imitators of us and of the Lord; in spite of severe suffering, you welcomed the message with the joy given by the Holy Spirit. And so you became a model to all the believers in Macedonia and Achaia" (1 Thes. 1:5-7).

We need to be reminded that "program" is a great deal more than some words on a bulletin. In the fullest sense of curriculum and nurture, "program" refers to the systematic inculcation of the dynamics of Christian living in order to produce mature and Christlike members of the Saviour's body.

PUPIL

We must enlist each pupil in the process of *church growth* by involving him in the process of his *own growth*. One of the most common principles in salesmanship is the welcome testimony of a satisfied customer. Certainly we want the pastor to visit that new family in the area, and it is important for a Junior Department teacher to contact eleven-year-old Jim. But it may be even more effective if eleven-year-old Bill, a regenerated and growing member of the body of Christ, plays the role of biblical Andrew in bringing Jim to the truth.

The use of students in Sunday School growth can take many forms, such as group visitation, personal faith-sharing evangelism, and the general enthusiasm of peer-group influence. We want everyone in the vital church program committed to capturing the community for Christ.

PROMOTION

The word promotion is used here, not to describe an exercise of advancing from one class to another, but rather in the communications context of "public relations." Advertising pays not only in industry but also for a growing Sunday School. Special days and events, mailings, posters, radio spots, and other means should be used to get the message out to people. At the heart of the process, however, is the training of the church to go out and genuinely share the message of the Gospel on the job, in the school, and across the back fence. This is not the kind of visitation that says, "Will you come to our Sunday School next week?" It is, rather, the kind of visitation that puts the primary emphasis on an individual's relationship to Jesus Christ and a secondary emphasis on his attending a particular kind of meeting at a given geographical location.

It is interesting to observe that, though Jesus Christ never went to Sunday School, almost all the principles just listed for application in a growing Sunday School are principles exemplified in the ministry of the Lord.

First, He exercised great care in personal preparation for His own ministry and the preparation of His disciples. There was no hasty "crash program" of training. He spent time discussing the responsibilities of the disciples.

Second, Christ exhibited the highest leadership level of administration in that He could get things done through other people. The involvement of the disciples in their own learning process was only one example of our Lord's careful attention to personnel development.

Third, the pagan society in the first century felt the impact of the early church because of the promotional thrusts of Christ and

His disciples as they shared the message with all who would listen.

Can this be done today? The obstacles are many, but the victory is ours because "the One who is in you is greater than the one who is in the world" (1 John 4:4).

PART TWO

UNDERSTANDING

TOTAL CHURCH

PROGRAM EDUCATION

How to Advance Christian Education in the Church

The best-selling book *The Power of Positive Thinking,* by Norman Vincent Peale, has a theological base that would not agree with or appeal to most evangelical Christians. Nevertheless it has had an enormous sales record which indicates that it has struck a responsive chord in the minds and lives of millions of its many readers.

In a society which is filled to the brim with negative pessimism, it is good for us who are God's children to look on the bright side. As a matter of fact, for a Christian it is not only good but it is also biblical. I do not refer to some kind of idealism which is unwarranted by the facts but rather to the genuine recognition that because our God is in control, we are serving on the winning side.

Sometimes a critical evaluation of our ministries is helpful, even necessary. Negative responses show us areas of need or neglect so that we can redirect our efforts. But all of the suggestions that are in this chapter are positive, representing things which we *should* be doing to upgrade and improve our Christian education programs.

STUDY AND PRACTICE THE DOCTRINE OF THE PRIESTHOOD OF BELIEVERS

There are only five passages in two books of the New Testament which refer directly to the priesthood of believers. They are reproduced here from *The Living Bible*:

And now you have become living building-stones for God's use in building His house. What's more, you are His holy priests; so come to Him [you who are acceptable to Him because of Jesus Christ] and offer to God those things that please Him (1 Peter 2:5).

But you are not like that, for you have been chosen by God Himself—you are priests of the King, you are holy and pure, you are God's very own—all this is so that you may show to others how God called you out of darkness into His wonderful light (1 Peter 2:9).

All praise to Him who always loves us and who set us free from our sins by pouring out His lifeblood for us. He has gathered us into His kingdom and made us priests of God His Father. Give to Him everlasting glory! He rules forever! Amen! (Rev. 1:5-6)

"You are worthy to take the scroll and break its seals and open it; for You were slain, and Your blood has bought people from every nation as gifts for God. And You have gathered them into a kingdom and made them priests of our God; they shall reign upon the earth" (Rev. 5:9-10).

Blessed and holy are those who share in the first resurrection. For them the second death holds no terrors, for they will be priests of God and of Christ, and shall reign with Him a thousand years (Rev. 20:6).

In *Search*, a journal published by the Southern Baptist Convention, William E. Hull derives five basic principles of church polity and practice from the composite picture of the biblical evidence about the priesthood of believers:

1. The priesthood of the believer must be held in healthy tension with other basic concepts; it is not absolute.
2. The believer can delegate some of the authority of his life and ministry to other believers.
3. The priesthood of the believer is conditioned by the gifts and roles

in the life of the fellowship.
4. The priesthood of the believer implies shared responsibility and ministry as well as shared authority.
5. The priesthood of the believer is the basis for decision-making in the church (Winter, 1972).

The point is that the work of God moves forward on the basis of a group of involved people, not only on the basis of individual leadership. Such a statement does not minimize the importance of gifted leadership but rather tends to put into healthy and dynamic tension the idea of the key leader and the importance of democratic participation in the life of the local church on the part of all its membership.

PAY MORE SERIOUS ATTENTION TO
THE CHRISTIAN SCHOOL MOVEMENT

In the past two decades biblically committed Christians have been waking up to the fact that the incipient paganism of public education is a handy tool for the secularization of our society. This is not a new observation; it has been described by many competent educators through the years. Mark Fakkema, writing in *An Introduction to Evangelical Christian Education,* quotes Luther A. Weigle, a former dean of Yale Divinity School:

> When the state, through the Supreme Court, threatens to take all religion out of tax supported schools and colleges and commit them to atheism, the religious freedom of American citizens is gravely endangered.

However, it is not the absence of Bible reading and prayer or any form of "religion" in the public schools which poses the problem. It is the systematic inculcation of secular humanism as a philosophy of life to which Christian boys and girls are exposed almost every day of their school careers. The problem is obviously greater in some school systems than in others. But one who is actually aware of the issues could challenge the conclusion that parental voice, commitment to absolute truth, establishment of a biblical morality, and an atmosphere of relative purity have been erased from most public school systems America.

The development of genuinely Christian schools at the elementary and secondary levels may not be the final answer. They should, however, make some progress toward offering our children and young people an education that takes God into acount and develops the learning process within a framework of faithfulness to His revelation. Not all of us can do this because of economic pressures, size of church, or other locally prohibitive factors. But there are many churches today with excellent physical facilities which could launch a very positive program of quality education with relatively little additional monetary investment. What it takes, besides a qualified and dedicated faculty, is a genuine understanding of the issues at stake and a sincere desire to do the job well.

STRENGTHEN A COMMITMENT TO THE INSTITUTIONAL CHURCH

Since the days of the so-called Enlightenment the message and status of the church have been severely criticized. Then it was almost entirely external criticism. But today even many Christians ask questions about the institutional church's validity.

It seems that our response to this type of criticism has to be a flexibility which is rooted in commitment to the continuity of both biblical and historical patterns of the church. To put it another way, we must be ready for change and willing to change when it is necessary and when it helps fulfill needs and meets contemporary objectives. But we must resist change for the sake of change and, in the final analysis, we must question any person or movement which doggedly refuses allegiance, not to any given denomination or organization, but to the principle of local churches as representatives of the total, universal body of Christ. With respect to the role of the church in our society, we need to be relevant but reverent and accept no substitutes.

SUPPORT CHRISTIAN HIGHER EDUCATION

Christian colleges and seminaries face a two-pronged problem and get "pricked" with regularity by each prong. Enrollment decline and financial difficulty keep presidents and board members up at night. Experts continue to prophesy the death of small private colleges.

Unless the evangelical public develops a much greater commitment to its colleges than it has shown to this point, many of those funerals will be held on the campuses of Christian colleges. The commitment I am calling for must strike in at least two dimensions: financial support and theological analysis. Any denomination supporting a college or seminary has every right to force theological adherence to the denomination's doctrinal standard. The history of liberalism has shown that its roots take hold at the college and seminary levels which eventually spread its poison to the churches.

GET SERIOUS ABOUT LEADERSHIP TRAINING

Statisticians estimate that over 45,000 people are permanently injured or killed every year by poorly trained ambulance personnel who handle them improperly before they get to the hospital. Translated into spiritual terms in the church, one has to wonder how many children, young people, and adults have their Christian maturity stunted each year because of incompetence at the teaching and administrative levels in church education.

Getting serious about leadership training for some churches may mean hiring a professional minister of education. A person properly trained for this post should possess the spiritual gifts of teaching and administration and have spent some time in formal development of those gifts. It is his or her task to be a teacher of teachers and a leader of leaders in the local church. Other churches, unable to afford the services of a professional, will develop programs and/or procedures of leadership training geared to produce better classroom teachers, better counselors, better witnesses, and generally better leadership to carry on the work of Christ through His church.

How to Understand the Total Church Program

Have you ever noticed the sign at the point where a two-lane highway divides into a four-lane superhighway with a median strip? It is usually placed at the beginning of the median strip, on the left side of the road, so that any motorist who veers left instead of right will have his thinking jarred in time to correct his mistake before it becomes a catastrophe. The bright-red sign is calculated to be a lifesaving device and no doubt has served its purpose well many times.

Maybe we need some signs like that in church education during this confusing decade. So many voices are saying so many things that it sometimes is quite difficult to decide what direction to take in fulfilling the biblical injunctions of nurture and instruction in our educational programs. At the risk of being just one more of those confusing voices, I would like to suggest five negative propositions with regard to church education. To put it another way, here are five warnings (or at least warning signs) which point to what I consider to be an inadequate conception of our role. I know that a negative approach is not always the best one, and perhaps it is not as welcome as encouragement or reinforcement. But sometimes it is helpful to warn, so here are five "stop" signs.

In my judgment, in order to adequately fulfill Christ's commands regarding the discipling ministry of the church, evangelical churches in our day must:

STOP PLAYING AT ADULT EDUCATION

Adult education is big business in the United States today. The average American adult changes jobs seven times and careers three times in his life. One of the three major purposes of a junior or community college (the fastest growing aspect of higher education) is continuing education. This is an attempt to keep the people of the community abreast of certain phases of the knowledge explosion in which they are interested and to provide a retooling of skills which rapidly become obsolete in our advancing society. Also, many adults in American society have learned to appreciate the enjoyment as well as the necessity of continuing education.

But much as society in general tends to think of school as an experience for children, so the evangelical church has too often placed its educational emphasis on children and youth. We also need to focus on adults, particularly providing biblical training for parenthood and the developing of an adequate Christian home. Our adult classes need to be tuned in to modern teaching methods. Our teachers of adults need to recognize that adults need visual aids and interaction groups at least as much as children do and perhaps more.

The most important condition for satisfactory adult education is motivation of the students. Adults need to recognize the importance of learning and to be convinced that *they can learn*. Christian adults need to feel that their learning experiences at church are really meeting genuine needs in their lives. They need to understand that the content of their classes is an honest attempt to show how the Bible relates to the issues of contemporary living.

Let's remember, too, that an adult Sunday School class is by no means the *only* educational experience we should be providing.

It can be supplemented by home Bible classes, the instructional nature of preaching, informal discussion groups, leadership-training classes on Sunday evenings or weeknights, serious Bible study at prayer-meeting time, and carefully guided reading programs which urge adults in our churches to read *at least* one good book per month.

STOP DEFINING CHURCH EDUCATION AS SUNDAY SCHOOL

The current movement of church education certainly began with Sunday School, and the importance of this largest educational agency of the church should not be minimized. But times have changed, and the emphasis has changed too. Despite its size and prominence, Sunday School is only one of the many things that we do in church education. In some cases, Sunday School has been considered a less-than-satisfactory approach to fulfilling the educational goals of the church. Some Christian educators are reevaluating their interest in and dependence on Sunday School.

Do not misunderstand my point. I am not suggesting that we should do away with Sunday School or that anyone has given us a satisfactory substitute. It is just unwise to "put all our eggs in one basket," as the old cliché warns. We need to develop a well-rounded and well-balanced program of church education which will help our people see the total nurturing task of the local representation of the body of Christ. Sunday School is not to be equated with church education, and anyone who still forces that equation has been left behind in the progress of the field of Christian education.

STOP CHEATING THE FAMILY

One helpful and hopeful trend in church education in the last fifteen years has been a renewed emphasis on, indeed almost a revival of, the importance of the home and family. Most books taking an evangelical stance on the issue of family living have been published within the last decade. Churches are holding family conferences. Sunday School publishers are emphasizing family sections in their literature. Pastors are preaching series of messages on the Christian home. All this is as it should be, and we can be most thankful for the emphasis. What has been a very low level of quality in family-life education in our churches may now be on the rise.

But we still tend to do two things which militate against the values which can accrue from these good approaches. One is a fanatical preoccupation with youth emphasis. Addison Leitch has spoken out against what he calls the "youth cliché" as follows:

> Although the accent on youth is nowhere in holy Writ, in our churches today it has become almost the essence of what we are about. If one wants to argue this point he is welcome to do so. Insofar as the programs produce and nurture Christians we can give nothing but three cheers; but what concerns me is a queasy feeling that apart from the false emotionalism so often involved, and the popularity hunger of the youth leaders, and the fact that "everybody's doing it," the real problem is the adults' "cop-out." They would like to throw the emphasis on the "youth" program so that they won't feel the pressure of the "adult" program (*Christianity Today,* December 3, 1971).

A second continuing problem is the tendency of evangelical churches to "program out" family activities. Check your church. If the bulletin advertises some activity for every night of the week, you may discover that some member of a thoroughly involved family may be tied up at church all of those nights, thereby distorting and disintegrating family unity at home. This doesn't have to be the case, and a future chapter will offer some suggestions on "Family-Cluster Programming."

STOP WILDLY FOLLOWING EVERY NEW LEADER OR TREND

Our failure to utilize supernatural resources leads to a sort of spiritual hero worship in evangelicalism. Whenever we think we are failing in our programs, we cast about for someone who is "successful" and attempt to model our programs after his success. Maybe what we need is a fleet of buses to bring in Sunday School students. After all, many churches have been successful with that. Or perhaps we need to restructure our Sunday evening service to make it much more informal and provide for the interaction of the members of the body. Maybe we need a personal evangelism training program patterned after some church that has built a large congregation by this method.

It may well be that one or all these ideas will work. It may also be that we do not need any of them and that the importing of somebody else's success to our area could actually hinder and deter our program rather than help it! Rather than grasp for a handful of ideas used by somebody else, we should identify our own local objectives in the light of biblical commands, make sure our programs and ministries are leading toward those objectives, and "plug in" spiritually gifted people to work together in fulfilling those objectives.

STOP MINIMIZING THE PASTORAL ROLE AND IMAGE

Not too many years ago *Christianity Today* reported that there were about 35,000 pastorless churches in America. Anyone who works consistently with pastors, both in their own churches and at pastors' conferences, knows that there are many discouraged pastors in evangelicalism who have often thought of joining the ranks of the dropouts. In his research for the book *Ministerial Man in the Middle,* J.B. Colburn identified four professional burdens of the ministry:

1. The tension between the minister's image of his work and that held by the laity.
2. The tension between the minister's responsibility to his work and his responsibility to his family.
3. The tension between saying what the congregation wants to hear and what he believes God wants them to hear.
4. The tension between the perfection expectations of some parish-ioners and the honest acceptance of himself as he knows himself to be.

The pastoral role is a biblical one and one which continues to be extremely essential in our churches. Liberal denominations may play down the importance of preaching and depict their ministers as agents of social change. But an honest commitment to the New Testament honors the gifts of proclamation and teaching which must be in the spiritual repertoire of an adequate pastor.

Well, I've said it, and I'm glad. Perhaps this chapter is merely an attempt to point out some of the deficiencies that abound in many of our programs of church education in these desperate days when biblical approaches to Christian nurture are absolutely essential.

How to Operate a Christian Education Committee

Many churches are insufficient in size and financial resources to hire a professional Director of Christian Education. There is, however, no church too small to operate a properly functioning Board or Committee of Christian Education. Two pertinent organizational characteristics of church education are *correlation* and *unification*. These important functions must be performed by some centralized person or group. Most church educators agree that they are best performed by a Board or Committee of Christian Education.

WHAT SHOULD A CHRISTIAN EDUCATION COMMITTEE DO FOR THE CHURCH?

First of all, it makes little difference whether the group is called a board or a committee. In technical management science there is a distinct difference between the functioning of boards and committees but as we use these terms in popular conversation that difference becomes obscured. Some church boards prefer having all other decision-making groups labeled "committees," to distinguish them from the "official board." But the name of the group should not detract from its functioning capabilities.

One of the major tasks of the Christian Education Committee is to serve as a recruiting agency for teachers and workers. It is a central "employment" clearing house for all the agencies and ministries in the church. No superintendent should recruit teachers for the Sunday School without the approval of the Committee of Christian Education. The youth sponsor should not ask a new couple in the church to help with the youth program without the approval of this committee. Deliberations about the recruitment and appointment of personnel occupy a significant proportion of the Committee's meeting time.

Long-range planning for the church education program is another responsibility of the Christian Education Committee. The Committee is constantly reviewing the present and the future in the light of what has been done in the past, both negative and positive. In 1990 the Committee is asking itself the question, "What do we want to be doing in this church educationally in 1995 and what resources will be necessary to do it?" There are a number of aspects of the educational program which need to be kept in constant balance: curriculum, personnel, finance, calendar, and physical plant. The correlation and coordination of these kinds of factors now, and a planning for what they will be in the future, represent a major responsibility of the Committee.

The Committee is also an educational agency in itself. As it promotes and extends the work of other agencies, it is constantly informing the congregation of the church's needs, plans, and progress in educational ministry. By the use of posters, bulletin promotion, coverage in the church newsletter, and numerous other ways, the Committee instructs and encourages the congregation about the church's educational program.

WHO SHOULD SERVE ON THE CHRISTIAN EDUCATION COMMITTEE?
Here there is a difference of opinion among church educators. Some contend that the membership of the Committee should be detached from the actual functioning of the educational agencies. Only in this way, they say, can the Committee be impartial and

objective about its decision-making. My opinion is that such detachment only serves to remove the Committee one step farther from the actual trench-line activity of the agencies it is administering. In fact I think *representation* is the key feature of a good Committee of Christian Education. Every functioning agency of Christian education should be represented on the Committee of Christian Education by its head.

A typical Committee, for example, might be made up of the Sunday School Superintendent, director of Children's Church, committee chairmen of club programs, superintendent of the Vacation Bible School, coordinator of training hour groups, and the director of music or chairman of the music council. To this representative group would be added the pastor as an ex-officio member, at least one deacon or elder, and possibly a member elected by the congregation. If there is a Director of Christian Education, of course, he would be an ex-officio member as well, as most DCEs prefer not to chair the Committee.

It is quite obvious then that the size of the Committee will vary with the size and activity of the church but, generally speaking, a Committee with under five members is limiting its resources of ideas and a Committee with over fifteen members is asking for trouble with regard to attendance at meetings and sufficient time for discussion.

If Committee members represent educational agencies, they become Committee members by virtue of their leadership roles in those agencies. For example, the Sunday School Superintendent is not elected to the Committee of Christian Education but is an automatic member of the Committee because he is Sunday School Superintendent.

There is a possible negative feature here in that, if the Committee is constantly appointing all of the workers and leaders in the educational program, it tends to appoint its own membership and becomes therefore almost a self-perpetuating body. Actually, this doesn't happen in function since the member-at-large and the deacon/elder representative are always appointed or elected by sources outside the Committee. Furthermore, all of the membership should be approved annually by the official Committee or the congregation.

WHAT DOES THE CHRISTIAN EDUCATION COMMITTEE DO AT ITS MEETINGS?

The business conducted by the Committee will be determined by the constitutional definition of its operation. As already indicated, there will be a strong emphasis on planning of a long-range educational program with accompanying personnel and finance considerations. The Committee will also deal with leadership training and the supervision of all educational workers. Correlation of curriculum, calendar, finance, and personnel is the constant task of the Committee; it alone has the ability to handle this. The Committee is regularly evaluating the present needs and assets of the church and determining whether educational objectives are being achieved. The Committee serves as sort of a collective educational conscience for the entire church.

WHAT ORGANIZATION GUIDELINES DOES THE COMMITTEE FOLLOW?

Like all functioning boards and committees, this one needs a chairman, possibly a vice-chairman, and certainly a secretary. If the church is large enough, there may be the need for structuring subcommittees to deal with such things as missionary education, camping, and Vacation Bible School. The Committee chairman calls monthly meetings and prepares the agenda for those meetings. He also writes reports to the official Board of the church regarding the educational activities of the quarter or year.

WE DON'T HAVE A COMMITTEE OF CHRISTIAN EDUCATION WHAT CAN WE DO ABOUT IT?

Actually the Committee and its duties should be defined by the constitution. However, it is not necessary to have a constitutional revision before the Committee actually begins its work. The leaders of the various educational agencies should be appointed as members of the Committee probably by the official Board, and one of the members designated chairman. Perhaps after the Committee has functioned for a year or so, a constitutional amendment can be proposed. Remember, however, that the

Committee should *represent* all the educational agencies, and its primary task is to provide correlation for the educational program. Give it a job to do and authority to do the job. Don't let it be just a fact-finding group to service the official Board of the church.

The Committee of Christian Education should have a collective job description to guide its activities and provide a pattern for future members. Regular minutes should be kept so that a permanent record of deliberations and decisions will always be available. A good Committee chairman prepares a written agenda and distributes it to all members. A good secretary makes sure that orderly minutes are reproduced and given to each member within one week after the meeting.

It is helpful to produce a total organizational chart to pinpoint the lines of authority in which the Committee works. The chart shows the Christian Education Committee's responsibility to the official Board of the church and the former's key role in overseeing the total educational program. A good "org chart" also clearly depicts the representative nature of the Committee's membership.

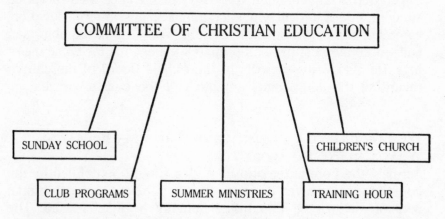

The Committee chairman should also take the initiative in preparing reports and recommendations for the congregation. At least quarterly, a brief but thorough report of the Committee's activity should be forthcoming.

It should be obvious from the nature of the Committee's business that a frank and honest atmosphere of discussion must prevail at all times. If a nominee for a certain position does not possess the spiritual and/or educational aptitude for a job, this should be aired in the meeting and not complained about three months later. Such a responsibility to discuss the spiritual qualities of a brother requires that the Committee members themselves possess the highest caliber of spiritual and emotional maturity.

Such maturity, coupled with a devotion to Christ and the ministry of His church, is what makes a CE Committee work.

How to Design an Effective Children's Church

Not many Christian educators, even in this day of revolt against traditional patterns, question the wisdom of a graded Sunday School. But graded worship has always been under attack, and the popularity of Children's Church has waxed and waned in the wider fortunes of church education for the past two decades.

I have always taken the view that Children's Church is a positive learning experience and a valid part of the total church education program—if it is carried out properly. Unfortunately, many times it is not, and it is these negative examples that people point to when they question this ministry. So let's take a look at the values, problems, and patterns of Children's Church.

VALUES OF CHILDREN'S CHURCH

It is simply a fact of life that parents *are* disturbed by young children in the regular church services—not only the parents but also other persons around them. We also know that children learn better on their own levels. I have heard many pastors indicate that they can keep the attention of children with no problem; a few even claim that Children's Church is not necessary because they can shout louder than the kids!

Of course the issue is not volume or disturbance. Rather it is the necessity of a worship experience which can be cultivated on a gradual basis through the childhood years, preparing our children to participate meaningfully in corporate worship during their teen and adult years. Furthermore, there is the necessity of meeting the spiritual needs of children, teaching them responsibility and participation, and training tomorrow's church today.

I don't doubt that many pastors can shout louder than the kids, but I seriously doubt whether they can minister effectively to children at the elementary level and feed the adult flock in a strong preaching ministry at the same time. We know that Jesus and Paul rarely tried it; they ministered almost exclusively to adults.

OBJECTIONS AGAINST CHILDREN'S CHURCH

In addition to the common claim that one's preaching can reach adults as well as children, there are four other objections which I have commonly heard regarding Children's Church. The first goes something like this: "Families belong together in church, and Children's Church programs just break them up." I rather think this claim is more sentimental than educational since, in such a family, six days often go unused as far as family togetherness is concerned. One hour or so on Sunday morning is hardly going to change a pattern if it is already negatively established in a home. Also, there is the evening service for family togetherness, and even the most widely expanded Children's Church programs do not reach into junior high age, allowing many years for a family to be together even after Children's Church experiences have finished.

A second complaint is that Children's Church is too often just a glorified baby-sitting hour. Of course, that criticism is often justified, and where it is true, there is no genuine value in the Children's Church. But, of course, it should *not* be a baby-sitting hour but a learning experience founded on worship.

Closely akin to that objection is the one that claims "too much play—too little order" in Children's Church. In some cases this could also be said about adult church, Sunday School, club programs, and other things that we do. It is hardly fair to single out one particular educational ministry and fault it for a problem which could be common to all of them.

Finally, we often hear that Children's Church is not valid because it's just like another Sunday School. Such a complaint is frequently grounded in fact. But it needn't be because Sunday School ought to focus on pedagogical experiences whereas Children's Church should focus on worship experiences. To be sure, there is worship in Sunday School and learning in Children's Church, but it is the point of emphasis that makes the difference.

PERSONNEL FOR CHILDREN'S CHURCH

Just as in any other important educational ministry, workers in a Children's Church ought to feel distinctly called to this ministry. As a matter of fact, if they do not feel so called, we will have some difficulty in getting them to serve. There is usually a good deal more hesitancy on the part of Christian adults to accept a responsibility which will keep them out of the morning service than there is to miss their appropriate adult Sunday School classes in the earlier hour.

In addition to commitment, we should look for the qualities of initiative, creativity, willingness to work, contagious enthusiasm, and general organization. There are various types of ministries within the framework of Children's Church, and not everyone needs to be a director.

If your church operates more than one unit of Children's Church, it is wise to have a coordinator who ties together the activities of all the levels and also represents Children's Church on the Christian Education Committee or Board. This latter responsibility is of great importance, because Children's Church will get lost in the maze of activities if not properly represented in that decision-making body.

The coordinator or director of each unit should make quarterly reports which include a summary of the activities, attendance, offerings, needs, and results of the Children's Church ministry.

FACILITIES AND EQUIPMENT

Usual space requirements related to Sunday School can be applied to Children's Church. Guidelines for color, light, and sizes of chairs and tables are all applicable to both groups.

A chapel is ideal for the two older groups (primary and junior church) because anything we can do to make Children's Church look more like adult church will enhance the transfer value of their learning experiences.

If children are required to meet in the same room for Children's Church as for Sunday School, the room should be rearranged so that even the physical outlay connotes a change of objective and program.

The usual equipment items such as supply cupboard, worship table, books, offering plates, usher pins, chalkboard, flannelboard, bulletin board, projectors, and so on are useful to carry out an effective program. Financing should be arranged in the regular church education budget, handled by the Christian Education Committee.

PROGRAMING CHILDREN'S CHURCH

In various size churches I have seen effective Children's Church programs run from one unit to four. When there is just one, the focus is usually on primary-age children (grades 1, 2, and 3) with some allowance for younger children. The other three divisions in a full-scale Children's Church line-up are nursery church (ages two and three); beginner church (ages four and five); and junior church (grades 4 through 6).

Shorter periods with more activity are necessary in nursery and beginner church, but we can begin to develop more formal programs with a higher degree of instruction and participation at the primary and junior church levels. Certainly by the time we get to the junior church, we want to pattern the program as closely as possible after the adult worship service, including such usual elements as a call to worship, a hymn, Scripture, a prayer, meditation, announcements, an offering, special music, and a message. But all of it, including the music, needs to be at the children's own levels.

THE IMPORTANCE OF PARTICIPATION

The children themselves should be used as much as possible in Children's Church programs, especially at the primary and junior levels. They can serve as ushers, trustees, deacons, junior ministers, song leaders, choir members, and so forth. It is preferable to elect these participants at least twice a year so that their terms do not get too long for their interest spans and also to secure greater involvement throughout the group.

We can emphasize the importance of such ministry with a formal installation service and can even train the children to do the job properly. Children who will not fit into some of these more sophisticated duties can still be involved in putting up pictures, straightening chairs, putting away toys, holding up posters and charts, and similar activities.

GUIDELINES FOR EFFECTIVE CHILDREN'S CHURCH MINISTRY

One of the deficiencies often noted in a Children's Church program is the failure to plan for the children during the brief time between Sunday School and church. This is often complicated by the utilization of the same educational areas for both sessions. Nevertheless, it is important for us to have our staff on hand and functioning so that those who come early have something to occupy their minds and hands before the formal program starts.

In thinking through the relation of Children's Church to adult church, we should not overlook such things as the distribution of the Lord's Supper, special speakers, a missionary emphasis (and perhaps a missionary project), the use of bulletins, and serious ministry of the Word of God by a teacher or even at times by one of the older children. Children's Church provides a great in-service training ground for our high school young people as they prepare and minister to the younger children in many ways.

It is also important to take the primary and junior children into adult church on occasion. Some churches do this once a month; others do it only on the fifth Sunday, four times a year. But generally speaking, we need to expose them to what is going on in adult church. Remember that no young child is allowed out of the room until someone calls for him.

We really need to have a contact person who can tell us when the adult service is about finished.

It is difficult for a pastor to end his message exactly at a certain time; but it is also important for the Children's Church workers to know how to draw their program to a close. An alert usher who will signal the Children's Church director at the appropriate time for a five-minute warning is most helpful.

Finally, let me suggest that the Children's Church ministry is an excellent place for the service of a couple. It's good to have at least one man in each department, and he should have a significant role at the primary and junior levels.

So let us not discount Children's Church or criticize it unduly. Rather let us recognize the importance of worship and learning experiences at a child's own level throughout all the years of his childhood and develop effective Children's Church programs which really will teach these values and minister effectively to fulfill carefully planned objectives.

How to Plan a Successful VBS

Planning for Vacation Bible School should have begun early last fall as you evaluated the program and results of last year's school. But if that has not been done, late winter is past time to get to work in earnest. The Board or Committee of Christian Education has no doubt appointed a superintendent and assigned her/him a committee to carry out the various planning steps.. In thousands of churches each summer children, youth, and adults are won to Christ; teachers are "discovered" for the church's educational program; Christians of all ages take part in concentrated Bible study; Sunday School impact is reinforced; and homes are reached through the ministry of Vacation Bible School. Best of all, your church can be among them if you remember and follow through on several aspects of careful planning.

PLAN YOUR DATES
There is no *best* time of the summer to have Vacation Bible School. Factors such as school schedules, weather and climate,

family vacations, church conferences, and camp programs influence the calendar placement of Vacation Bible School. Actually, most progressive churches already have their VBS dates set when they put together a long-range yearly calendar based either on the calendar year (January-December) or the curriculum year (September-August). The impact of VBS is not dulled by conducting it in June, July, or August. Most educators would argue simply on the basis of time that two weeks are better than one, but certainly one week is better than none. In scheduling any school two things are important: (1) Select the dates which are most adaptable to your location and program. (2) Don't be afraid to change from the pattern of the past.

Plan Your Personnel

Once the director and assistant director have been selected they gather around them departmental superintendents and chairpersons of key committees such as transportation, publicity, and recreation. The only way to adequately determine personnel needs is to project the enrollment by departments. Allow the departmental superintendents to have a voice from the earliest stages of planning and depend on them to a great extent in selecting personnel for their departments.

Don't forget that in all education the focal point of planning learning experiences is the teacher. Direct contact with the children is basic to learning so don't let anyone slight the importance of being "just a teacher." Try to use people who are not now regularly teaching. Perhaps college students home for the summer can bolster the ranks of your VBS staff.

Plan Your Recruitment

The biggest problem in most Vacation Bible Schools is the recruitment of workers. There will be churches all over the country wanting to conduct Vacation Bible School this summer but not able to do so because of a lack of workers. In most cases the lack of workers stems from poor recruitment procedures. Consider the following suggestions:

1. Emphasize the need, not the predicament.
2. Spread the work load among as many people as possible.
3. Ask departmental superintendents to approach people personally rather than making a general announcement from the pulpit.
4. Hold a special recruitment Sunday showing a filmstrip related to whatever curriculum you have chosen.
5. Emphasize service for Christ.
6. Use senior high teens if you do not have a study department for them.
7. Pray that God will give you all of the workers you need.

PLAN YOUR STAFF TRAINING

Regular staff meetings should be scheduled in which basic plans and policies are formulated. A significant section of time should be allocated to departmental meetings directed by the departmental superintendent. Samples of all handcraft projects should be prepared well in advance and sufficient materials ordered to meet the projected attendance. (Unused materials can probably be returned.) Space allocations and specific program responsibilities should be determined at least two months before the school is held.

Job descriptions are just as important for Vacation Bible School workers as they are for Sunday School teachers. Remember to include a statement of what the workers may expect from the church as well as defining what you want them to do.

PLAN YOUR CURRICULUM

Several evangelical publishers produce excellent curriculum materials for Vacation Bible School. The best way to make an intelligent choice is to clearly determine the needs of your community and the objectives which you have designed for your school. Then order the introductory kits and filmstrips from several publishers. Evaluate their materials and themes in the light of your needs and objectives. Ask the various departmental superintendents to carefully review the materials for their departments and report their evaluations in a staff meeting. Most curricula now being produced for VBS have built-in flexibility, that is, they can be adapted to a one-week or two-week school, a school scheduled on alternating days, or various other formats or patterns now being experimented with in Vacation Bible School programming.

PLAN YOUR SCHEDULE
Here again, flexibility is the key. It may be that the traditional morning hours are best for your area. On the other hand, perhaps an afternoon or even an evening school may produce better results and reach more people. If your church is unusually small and it just doesn't seem workable to carry out a school on your own, you might give serious consideration to entering a cooperative effort with another small evangelical church in your area. In a two-week school one week could be scheduled at each church. Or, if the churches are close enough together, both buildings could be utilized to obtain maximum space.

PLAN YOUR PROMOTION
Every legitimate means of communication should be used to let the community know that Vacation Bible School is going to happen. Pulpit announcements, bulletin reminders, posters, mailings, church newspaper, radio broadcasts, and eyeball-to-eyeball invitations should bombard all the prospects for several weeks before registration day. And don't forget the parade! I was an unbeliever regarding Vacation Bible School parades until we tried one a few years ago. It works!

PLAN YOUR CONSERVATION
Follow-up is one of the most important parts of Vacation Bible School. One church casually thumbed through its cards at the end of a two-week school and discovered that its VBS had contacted *ninety* new families in the community during those ten days.

All prospect cards should be correlated with the central record system so that Sunday School teachers as well as the regular visitation workers can immediately begin tracking down new people for Christ. Of course, those who have trusted Christ as Saviour during the school should receive special follow-up attention.

Plan Your Financing

There are a number of different ways to secure the funds for an effective Vacation Bible School but here are some general suggestions:

1. Budget the school as a regular part of the annual Christian education program.
2. Plan on approximately a dollar per student per day. Costs may run slightly above or below that estimate, depending on materials used, but this will serve as a general budgeting guideline.
3. Don't use VBS offerings to pay the cost of the school unless absolutely necessary. This is an ideal time for the children to become involved in missionary giving. Plan a special project within reach of the expected income so that the satisfaction of achievement will reinforce the experience of giving to Christ.

PLAN YOUR EVALUATION

Most curricular materials have an accompanying guidebook which deals with matters of evaluation as well as preparation. After a school is over evaluation ought to take place on at least three levels: the departmental level, the interdepartmental level, and the administrative overview by the Christian Education Committee. One of the things you will want to check carefully is how well the Vacation Bible School program related to the total program of church education. You should be able to determine how it related organizationally as well as its careful correlation in personnel and follow-up. Be sure to keep written records of all evaluative comments so that next year's committee will have even better information to work with than you had this year.

These ten planning ideas are basic but by no means exhaustive. Don't forget all of the miscellaneous items which make an *acceptable* school really *great*. I am thinking about things such as a photographer to shoot action pictures, checking with the police for safety patrols and clearance on the parade (nothing helps a VBS parade like a squad car in the lead), careful delineation of all duties according to position, a dedication service for workers, careful planning of the closing demonstration program, a picnic, and a well-programmed refreshment time each day.

But who is responsible for all of this? The pastor? The DCE? The Board of Christian Education? The VBS superintendent? Yes—all of these and many more! The principle of mass participation is basic in church educational programming. As one pastor put it, "VBS is the only thing around here that everybody does!" VBS doesn't have to be a drag; it can be a boost. And the difference between the two is largely related to how well and how early you plan.

How to Carry Out Biblical Evangelism in the Sunday School

Lauded by all, but understood by few, biblical evangelism continues to be one of the major tasks of the church and yet one at which few of us are satisfactorily efficient. We hold seminars and conferences; we dream up contests and gimmicks; we emphasize numbers and rewards; but when the dust has settled, the haunting question still remains: Are we really practicing *biblical* evangelism?

It is impossible to talk about evangelism in the biblical sense without looking at the word itself. It appears quite often in the New Testament, and the English word itself is little more than the transliteration of the Greek word *euangeliz* ōr *euangelizomai.* The word literally means "to announce the good news." A few times in the New Testament "good news" is a general term meaning "happy tidings," but the predominant use of the verb focuses on the *kerygma,* or proclamation of the Gospel.

The Scriptures not only give us many examples of how the early church practiced sharing the Good News but also set forth some timeless principles which must be applied to any program of evangelism we undertake.

BIBLICAL EVANGELISM MUST BE BASED
ON THE PATTERN OF CHRIST

In a nontheological sense, it is possible to say that Jesus Christ was the first foreign missionary. He bridges the gap between the Old and New Covenants, having come from heaven to earth to share the Good News His Father wanted announced to Adam's race.

Perhaps the key verse is John 20:21: "As the Father has sent Me, I am sending you." The key word is *sent*. The sending process began with Jesus and has been perpetuated over almost 2,000 years of church history. Jesus sent the disciples, they sent other disciples, and the church has sent bearers of the Good News to almost every nation, tongue, and tribe in the world.

The last concept is the second ingredient of the pattern of Christ: He was sent *into the world*. The prepositional phrases of John 17 are extremely important. Here our Lord prays to the Father that He does not want His disciples to be taken "out of the world" (v. 15) but rather that they are to be left "in the world" (v. 11). Nevertheless, they are not to be "of the world" (v. 16), in order that through unity and holiness they might be witnesses, as He sends them "into the world" (v. 18).

There is a subtle but important issue at stake here. Evangelism is done *in the world* rather than *in the church*. We must recall that after the disciples believed and followed the Lord, He did *not* continue to preach the Gospel to them. Sharing the Good News has to do with the proclamation of regeneration and the new birth; it is not the development of a ministry for Christian growth and maturation.

Jesus was sent into the world to *seek*: "For the Son of man came to seek and to save what was lost" (Luke 19:10). But He also came to *serve* (Mark 10:45). The seeking ministry and the serving ministry should not be confused. One was salvation and the other servanthood. To be sure, one must be a servant before he can properly be an evangelist. But if we confuse the proclamation of the Gospel with service to needy people, we end up with a social gospel that is *not* biblical evangelism.

Of course, that is not to say that the church does not have a social ministry or that there are no social implications to the

Gospel. The social implications are enormous, as James reminds us. The point is that we are not to confuse social service, ministry to the needy, and sacrificial labors among the saints with evangelism, which is the proclamation of the Good News in the world.

BIBLICAL EVANGELISM MUST NOT FOCUS ON A BUILDING OR A SCHEDULE

To talk about "biblical evangelism in the Sunday School" is to create a temptation to box the task of sharing the Good News into a certain physical structure at a certain hour of the day. Of course we are entirely pleased whenever anyone trusts Jesus as Saviour, wherever that decision might be made. Not only that, but sharing the Good News with students in general sessions as well as class sessions certainly should be a part of the task of the Sunday School.

Having said that, let me hasten to add that evangelism cannot be viewed as the primary task of the Sunday School. Many or most of the people who attend an evangelical Sunday School are already believers, *and you cannot evangelize believers!* (However, we should not take it for granted that any child or adult is a believer.) The primary task of the Sunday School in all of its departments is *to nurture*. Birth is not the main issue—growth is!

So we look then at the New Testament patterns. Though we cannot find the structure and schedule of Sunday School as we know it today, we do see the New Testament church reaching out into the world to carry on its task of sharing the Good News.

The message of the Gospel is absolute, but the methodology is not restricted. God must surely be pleased with every honest and ethical effort to communicate His truth to lost people.

In the eighth chapter of the Book of Acts, we have the interesting account of the apostles confining their activities to Jerusalem. Meanwhile, the entire church (presumably almost exclusively a lay movement) "preached the Word wherever they went" (v. 4).

So biblical evangelism in the Sunday School is not something that we do in a certain place or at a certain time. It is rather a pattern of life—a faith-sharing life—which is taught to Christians of all ages as a part of a total program of nurture for which the Sunday School primarily exists.

BIBLICAL EVANGELISM CANNOT BE MEASURED IN TERMS OF RESULTS

How often we make this tragic error! How often we think that evangelism is soul-winning, putting an emphasis on the number of people who make decisions, come forward, or sign cards. To be sure, the very concept of evangelism implies that something ought to be happening as a result of the spreading of the Good News. But this result is not implied or contained in the Word itself.

However, the proclamation of vital Good News should bring results. "The war is over!" brought joyous relief to millions in 1945. That news meant that sweethearts, husbands, sons, and brothers would soon be coming home. Families would be re-united, and the long months and years of worrying and suffering were over at last. The news brought its own immediate rewards of relief and thanksgiving.

Moreover, that good news did not go around soliciting adherents. Its bearers did not wait anxiously for people to render their decisions or reactions. It was proclaimed, and the magnitude of its content was self-evident. That kind of good news does not go pleading for acceptance—it is worthy of itself.

This is the news of salvation: "Death is defeated! The grave is beaten! Your sins are forgiven! God reigns among people!" That kind of news is good; in fact, it is Gospel. The Gospel does not go begging for subscribers. Those who welcome it are blessed; those who refuse it are still blind to their greatest needs. As Christians we are not salesmen and women offering a product and pressing for a sale. We are heralds of a glorious Word. Salvation has come! Salvation has come for you!

As soon as one speaks in this manner, he will invariably be accused of opposing the church's important task of soul-winning. Such accusation is nonsense. Every genuine Christian is interested in seeing other people come to Christ. But even the term "soul-winning" distorts the biblical message of evangelism because it implies too great a role for the human instrument.

You and I do *not* "win souls." That is the exclusive task of the Holy Spirit. It is our task to "evangelize," that is, to communicate the Gospel in such a way that it can be understood.

BIBLICAL EVANGELISM MUST CENTER ON THE MESSAGE, NOT THE EXPERIENCE

In classes on personal evangelism both in the local church and in Christian colleges and seminaries, we teach people how to witness. Frequently what we mean by "witness" is to provide an explanation of what God has done in our lives. The classic biblical illustration is the blind man who simply said, "One thing I do know. I was blind but now I see!" (John 9:25)

That simple testimony, spoken by a man who was minutes (or at the most, hours) old in his newfound faith, is hardly a comprehensive model of biblical evangelism. The Good News is at the same time a simple and a complex message. At the least it contains an intelligent declaration of the incarnation, crucifixion, and resurrection of our Lord and the application of those historical events to the lives of people.

We may very well *begin* the process by explaining what God has done for us, but an account of our own experiences alone is not biblical evangelism.

By the same token, biblical evangelism must not center on the experience we hope an unbeliever will have. *It is the message, not the experience, that constitutes the Good News*. Biblical evangelism concentrates on what God has done, not on what we have done. It is grounded in propositional truth and the facts of history.

In Peter's evangelism (Acts 2), he spent a good bit of time in building up the case for God's working in the history of the nation of Israel before he began to talk about the implications of the death and resurrection of Christ. Never does he mention his own call as a disciple, though such an approach was frequently used by the Apostle Paul.

In both cases the use or nonuse of personal experience was not the focal point of the evangelism—that place was reserved for the message of the Gospel itself.

So let us get on with the task of biblical evangelism in the Sunday School. Let us have all of it that we can. But in the process, let us make sure that what we are doing is distinctly *biblical* rather than some cultural adaptation or contemporary dilution of what God really intended.

How to Bathe Church Education in Love

Twenty-five years ago both secular and Christian educators were being told that the wave of the immediate future in the classroom process was programmed instruction and teaching machines. There was no question about their popularity in those days. Almost every school and college built into its budget a large block of funds for this new medium's hardware and software. Today, thousands of dollars' worth of that equipment sits unused, gathering dust in teachers' closets all over the country.

Of course, there was a great deal to be learned from our brief love affair with teaching machines, and many of the ideas and concepts which were generated by the research put into programmed instruction are a valuable part of education today. Every once in a while one can still see a teaching machine being used in some exotic way, a reminder that the investments of earlier decades were not entirely misplaced.

But the greatest lesson we learned was that the gimmickry and gadgetry of educational research can never replace the impact of people on a student's life. Especially in Christian education is that axiom so basic.

What a teacher is to his students, how he relates to them in nonclassroom as well as classroom contexts, really makes the difference between life-change and pedantic pedagogy. In short, love is the oil for the machine of teaching.

LOVE REFLECTS THE SPIRIT OF JESUS

Jesus wanted His disciples to live as He did and to impart the love of the Father to those they would be discipling. Consequently He said to them during the last week of His life on earth, "A new commandment I give you: Love one another. As I have loved you, so you must love one another. All men will know that you are My disciples if you love one another" (John 13:34-35).

In a real sense, the teacher is the representation of Jesus to the student, whether that student is a child, youth, or adult. The key to unlocking the door of teaching is to win the hearts of students by showing genuine love. This is true in the home as parents relate to their children and in the classrooms of the church and the Christian school.

Dr. Gilbert Peterson once pointed out the significance of love relationships to the overall process of teaching and discipling:

> What was unique and very special in the caring-reaching ministry of Jesus was His teaching through human relationships. He mixed into a rainbow blend the living language of relationships and the spoken language of words. The remembered teacher is the one who lives, loves, and demonstrates care. When most of the words are forgotten, the memory of one or two teachers who really cared for us still lingers ("The Ministry of Teaching," *Insights,* Scripture Press).

LOVE FOLLOWS THE COMMANDS OF SCRIPTURE

The same Bible writer who recorded Jesus' words to His disciples admonished all believers to relate to each other in love. "Dear friends, let us love one another, for love comes from God. Everyone who loves has been born of God and knows God. Whoever does not love does not know God, because God is love" (1 John 4:7-8).

I have never met a Christian teacher who did not want to be biblical. No Sunday School teacher or church worker has ever told me that he deliberately set out to disobey or ignore the commands of Scripture regarding the ministry to which God had called him. Yet the primary command of Scripture is to love God, and the second, according to Jesus, is like unto it, to love one another.

In the broad sense of the word "neighbor," Jesus spoke in the Gospels of love for anyone who had need, thereby encompassing vast hosts of people all around us. In the Epistles and the early life of the church, we see a special focus on love for other believers as the demonstration of Christian behavior.

The name Etienne de Grellet is not a household word in contemporary American society. But he is remembered to the present hour because of the thousands who have been challenged by words he wrote more than a century ago: "I shall pass through this world but once. If, therefore, there be any kindness I can show, or any good thing I can do, let me do it now; let me not defer it or neglect it, for I shall not pass this way again" (*Familiar Quotations,* Little, Brown and Company).

Love Demonstrates the Reality of the Church

The writer of the Book of Hebrews said it succinctly and yet with impact: "Keep on loving each other as brothers" (13:1). Not *let it start,* or *let it be expected,* or *let it have a chance of survival,* but *let it continue.* Love is to be the mark of the church's collective relationships.

The kind of love that binds the congregation together has thousands of threads in the relationships among the people of that group. One is reminded of Gulliver in Jonathan Swift's *Gulliver's Travels* who was bound by Lilliputians. There was no one single thread that held the giant to the earth, but thousands of strands which the busy little people tied over his body in every direction.

Such is the role of a Christian teacher. He himself weaves as many threads as he can into the total fabric of the church. Then he helps his students understand how they can love each other and thereby further bind the giant of disharmony and division that always threatens the people of God.

But it all begins with the relationship of the teacher to his students. He should be a living demonstration of love—not a machine which spouts information and programs students to respond appropriately to certain stimuli.

Of course, this is not to say that love in any way substitutes for communication of the truth. When Jesus came, He was full of both grace and truth, neither to the exclusion of the other. And this leads us precisely to the next thrust in our consideration of the importance of love in teaching.

LOVE ENABLES US TO SHARE THE TRUTH OPENLY

Paul admonished the Ephesians to speak the truth in love (4:15). He might well have said that the *only* way one should speak the truth at all is in love, which is the proper way for the truth to be communicated. One is tempted to say that the truth can be shared only "in love," but other passages of Scripture give legitimate indication that it is possible to communicate the truth without having a motive of love (cf. Phil. 1:15).

Jude (vv. 20-23) urges Christians to always begin their ministries to other people with love, but if necessary, to use the fear of hell as a motivating impulse to spur people to action in spiritual things. But that is only after love has been rendered unsuccessful.

A Christian teacher should assume that the Holy Spirit can use love as the primary motivating tool of his ministry. The use of other motivational techniques (such as fear) ought to be only a last resort. We understand, of course, that the love we attempt to show students may not always be returned in the spirit with which it is given. The key is not in the balance of our own human compassion, but in what the Holy Spirit is able to produce in us through His supernatural power. That's why Christian teaching is so completely different from any other kind of teaching.

Perhaps a word of warning is in order here. Sometimes we masquerade under the umbrella of love in order to cut down other people. We say things like "I'm only telling you this for your own good" or "It's only because I love you that I'm telling you what Mary said about you last week." There will be times when we have to share with friends as well as with our students the direct truth as we understand it, and in those times we will want to do it in a spirit of love and concern for the object of our sharing. But let us never be hypocritical in allowing our own critical natures the excuse of behaving improperly under the banner of false love.

LOVE MEETS THE SPECIAL NEEDS OF VOLUNTEER WORKERS

The church leader has a task unlike that of the business executive or even the administrator in a Christian organization which employs a staff. He is working, for the most part, with volunteers who must be motivated apart from monetary incentive.

A Sunday School superintendent, for example, cannot get his teachers to perform more adequately, to prepare more thoroughly, or to attempt innovative teaching techniques, by raising their salaries. He can appeal to their sense of duty and perhaps stimulate them with suggestions of loyalty to the Lord. But he is much more biblical if he seeks to involve them in a more acceptable ministry through love. The point is that his love for them meets a need and therefore produces a basis for positive response.

Relational teaching, as described by Dr. Peterson earlier in this chapter, and relational leading stem from the same basic thrust—the willingness of people to respond positively to someone who has helped them or ministered to them.

LOVE GIVES MEANING AND POWER
TO THE GIFT OF TEACHING

There are only three reasons for inadequate teaching in the church: no gift, no development of the gift, or no power in the use of the gift. Here we focus on the third reason.

The first three verses of 1 Corinthians 13 are a part of the total fabric of chapters 12 through 14, which form a unitary truth on the subject of the edification of the church. In chapter 12, Paul wrote concerning spiritual gifts and the unity of the body. He pointed out that the diversity of gifts is in keeping with the diversity of the body. Within the body of Christ or within a local representation of that body are many different kinds of people with many different kinds of gifts, called to do many different kinds of tasks.

Paul opened the thirteenth chapter by clearly stating that the exercise of any spiritual gift apart from love is worthless to God. That is true of teaching as well. A Christian teacher who goes about his task without love for his students is not only betraying his call, but also rendering his gift (if, indeed, he has the gift of teaching) completely valueless to the church. His lessons become like clanging bronze, noisy and raucous, but of no lasting value.

Just as love gives meaning to a marriage relationship, so love gives power and meaning to the teaching task. Multiplied stories could be told about students who seemed to pay little attention to an earnest but frustrated Sunday School teacher, causing grief and turmoil in the class week after week. But because of the loving patience of that teacher, coupled with the dynamic of the power of the Holy Spirit, those students later became outstanding leaders.

And it's still happening today. You have in your class or your church people whom God will call to important positions of Christian leadership, even though they may not give much evidence of that now. For the time being, it is your task to let the oil of love flow through the machinery of teaching as you equip present and future leaders for the work of the church.

Never forget Paul's words in Philippians 1:9: "And this is my prayer: that your love may abound more and more in knowledge and depth of insight." That is a prayer which we can pray for ourselves and share with our students. May they someday reflect the love they see in us.

How to Use Testing in the Sunday School

In my first graduate course in educational measurement, the professor began the first class period by saying, "Any teacher who signs a contract to teach, signs a contract to evaluate the results of his teaching." He was speaking strongly against the tendency of those times, mitigated a bit since then, to decry and denounce testing and evaluation in American education.

To be sure, teaching without testing would be more fun for both student and teacher. But it would not provide the best learning atmosphere, and it would certainly not offer that essential ingredient of measurement whereby we analyze whether or not we have achieved our goals.

Sunday School teachers do not sign contracts in the same sense that professional teachers do (though more and more churches are going to different kinds of written service agreements), but the same principle applies. The Sunday School teacher who agrees to teach a class ought to understand that he or she thereby also agrees to evaluate whether learning has taken place.

One book, whose title and author I've forgotten, talks about the teacher's role in the formal educational process in four steps:

1. The teacher must identify the educational objectives sought.
2. He must determine what educational experience the students must have in order to achieve the objectives.
3. He must design the educational experiences and arrange their order of presentation.
4. He must evaluate the degree to which the desired changes in student behavior have taken place.

I do not see a great deal of difference between that kind of process used by professional teachers in the school system and what a good Sunday School teacher should be doing.

PURPOSE OF TESTING IN THE SUNDAY SCHOOL

In one of my books I talked about testing as a *teaching technique.* That is certainly one of its purposes, and in church education, it may be the primary purpose (see chapter 24 in *24 Ways to Improve Your Teaching,* Victor Books). Testing is a viable and significant teaching technique, if we seek creative ways to test and also keep the stated purpose in mind.

Another purpose of testing in the Sunday School is the one I have just written about—*measurement of learning.* In order to achieve this purpose, it should be clear that the stating of educational objectives has to be very specific, usually in terms of what we call "student behavior."

But one of the problems we face in evaluating the achievement of educational objectives is that many of the objectives are difficult to translate into observable behavior. This is especially true in Christian teaching where so much of our content is in the "affective domain"; that is, it has to do with such things as attitudes, emotions, and volition, *rather than* observable behavior. Not only that, but in many instances the total desired change in a student may not be observable until months or perhaps even years after the educational experience we are evaluating. But it is important to remember that unless we have clear objectives at the start, we cannot possibly have a clear measurement at the end. Let's look at it one more time: Educational evaluation is directly based on clearly and specifically stated educational objectives.

A third purpose for testing in the Sunday School is the *evaluation of teaching proficiency*. Every test we give measures us as well as our students. I have little patience with a teacher who considers his presentation so perfect and his tests so accurate that any negative results clearly place the blame (in his mind) on the students. Such an exaggerated view of our own teaching abilities minimizes the complexity of the teaching task and runs contrary to the warnings of James 3:1.

Students may do poorly on a test in school or Sunday School, not so much because they are slow learners or have not done their studying, but because we have not been competent communicators or perhaps the test itself is so horrendously confusing that it genuinely does not measure what we were supposedly teaching.

For example, we might teach the names of the books of the Bible and then test to see whether our students can repeat those names. So far so good. We are operating purely in the cognitive area and at the level of knowledge alone. But if we have taught only basic informational data about those books and not interpretative understandings, it is unfair to ask for interpretative understanding on a test at the end of the quarter or year.

PROCESS OF TESTING IN THE SUNDAY SCHOOL

Testing or measurement is a process that attempts to obtain a specific (usually quantified) representation of the degree to which a student has "learned." A test is a measurement instrument which gives us information on the student's progress. If it does not serve the purpose for which it is intended, we say it "lacks validity." If a test is so deficient that it does not measure consistently, we say it "lacks reliability."

The test itself is usually just a group of questions or tasks to which a student is asked to respond. In *24 Ways to Improve Your Teaching* I explain how to use certain kinds of tests. But here it may be valuable just to list the various kinds of tests which can be used in a Sunday School setting. We will set them in couplets of contrast to easily identify the differences.

1. *Individual and group tests*. Obviously, individual tests are

tests given to one student at a time, whereas group tests are administered to a group.

2. *Teacher-constructed and standardized tests.* Informal tests that we prepare ourselves are more likely to relate specifically to our own students, but standardized tests prepared by a publisher may have greater validity and reliability. I prefer the former because I am more concerned about relevance than reliability in the informal educational nature of the Sunday School.

3. *Subjective and objective tests.* There will be some subjectivity in all of our tests, particularly those which are oral or essay. Generally, such tests require more time on the part of both teacher and student, but they do probe more deeply into a student's knowledge of the subject matter. Objective tests, on the other hand, are more difficult to prepare, but carry less risk in analyzing the accuracy of the responses.

4. *Speed tests and mastery tests.* A speed test is one in which a student has a limited amount of time to answer a series of questions. Our purpose is to see how fast he can work through the questions and how many he can accomplish in the allotted time. The mastery test, on the other hand, is more concerned about the student's thorough knowledge of the material presented. Its major function is to measure the knowledge and skill that every student in the class should have acquired; so ample time for completion of such a test must be allowed.

5. *Readiness and diagnostic tests.* Readiness tests are designed to determine the ability of a student to undertake a certain type of learning. Entering college students frequently take tests in language arts or grammar to determine whether they need "remedial English" courses. Diagnostic tests, on the other hand, are administered after the formal instruction in order to discern what the student has learned. Most of the tests we work with in Sunday School are diagnostic in nature, though we should probably be doing more with readiness testing than we do.

PLANNING FOR TESTING IN THE SUNDAY SCHOOL

Good evaluation of learning does not just happen; it is carefully planned. There are three areas which run parallel in the construction of a test. All of them represent concerns of the teacher throughout the educational experience, not just at evaluation time. The items are learning objectives, course content, and desired behavior.

A good test balances an emphasis on course content, in conjunction with the objectives of the course, with a view toward the measurable behavioral outcome in the lives of the students.

That elusive quality of validity which we talked about earlier rises and falls in accordance with the accuracy of the balance of teaching and the degree to which the test items accurately reflect the balance of content and skills which we have taught.

All of this is not as difficult as it sounds. Any Sunday School teacher can do it with a little practice and a willingness to put in some time in the testing part of the job as well as the teaching part.

PROBLEMS WITH TESTING IN THE SUNDAY SCHOOL

The most obvious problem is the *threat* that testing poses to many students who think Sunday School is just fun and games. My experience has shown that in the early days of testing, students at all levels (particularly adults) are threatened by the "school-like" atmosphere of the class. Then later, as they get turned on to the serious study of the Bible and related subjects of Christian living, they can actually become enthusiastic about the testing dimension. In a Sunday School setting there are no grades; so testing can be more of a teaching situation without the threat of permanent negative records resulting from the evaluation.

A second common problem with testing, particularly among nonprofessionals, is what we might call *the myth of absolute standards*. This sounds good, but it can be misleading. If a test is intended to discriminate between the learning levels of students, something has to be sufficiently different to be noticed. If every student can score a perfect paper on a mastery test, there has been no discrimination, no measurement of the varying levels of achievement.

Another common problem is *testing for trivia*. We ought to be aiming, especially at the senior high and adult levels, at a high degree of comprehension or understanding in our Sunday School classes. If we test only simple references, names, and places, we tend to put the emphasis on "grocery lists" and rote memorization rather than on the thinking process.

Still another problem with many tests is *deliberate trickery*. This is unfortunate since one of the purposes of a test is to be a teaching technique. Test questions ought to be geared to help the student *understand* the point. Sometimes we include trick questions intentionally but more often unintentionally. Poor wording of test items can confuse students who really do know the answers, with the result that they answer incorrectly, ending up confused and discouraged about the test rather than reinforced in their learning experiences.

Yes, testing can be an extremely valuable technique in a Sunday School. But it takes courageous teachers, who are willing to put some time into learning how to test, explain the value of testing procedures to their students, and follow through with other kinds of informal evaluation to supplement the formal written measurement. Like everything else, we can partially measure a test's productivity by the kind of effort we put into it.

How to Counsel Your Students

Perhaps no other professional field is as attractive to students today as the field of counseling. No doubt the anxieties and pressures of modern life account for the sharp increase in the need for psychologists, psychiatrists, and counselors. This great need has attracted many prospective professionals as well as lay persons.

One of the interesting trends in counseling is the expansion of lay participation. This is a movement away from the practice of requiring people to rush immediately to a professional counselor or psychiatrist at the first threat of emotional difficulty.

In the first place, fees for professional counseling are usually quite high. Beyond that, psychiatrists who can blend Christian insight and biblical understanding with professional expertise are scarce. Some gifted counselors are so overloaded that prospective clients sometimes wait weeks—even months—for appointments.

Part of the answer rests in the interested lay person. Laymen who are willing to devote time to learning basic counseling skills and who are willing to spend time with other people are a big part of the solution to emotional suffering. The implications of Dr. Jay Adams' influential book *Competent to Counsel* (Presbyterian and Reformed) lead us to consider the vast potential for counseling which resides in the members of a local church.

Dr. Henry Brandt, well-known Christian psychologist and conference speaker, has indicated that his own ministry now centers much more in the realm of lecturing and teaching. His object is to impart basic therapeutic principles which can be applied to people's problems.

Dr. Larry Crabb, a Christian psychologist in Indiana, suggests that many of the problems people bring to a professional psychologist could be cared for by skillful lay leaders. Such leaders can be trained to help another person recognize his problems, understand them, and make headway toward solving them.

The purpose of this chapter is not to discuss the types of counseling or to determine whether counseling ought to be directive or nondirective. My intention is to consider the practical potential of a Sunday School teacher as a counselor.

DESCRIPTION OF A COUNSELING TEACHER

Any good teacher is at the same time a mentor and friend: he leads his own life before his class in an exemplary fashion; he learns continually so that he may teach with freshness; and he relates to his pupils with genuine care and compassion. Dr. Gilbert Peterson indicated the significance of such an attitude in the first release of a series of teaching pamphlets titled *Insights*:

> Care, as normally defined, means a disquieted state caused by a burdensome sense of responsibility. Compassion is a sympathetic, tender responsiveness. When we combine the two concepts, we can see what a teacher ought to feel for those God has entrusted to him or her. He has a sense of responsibility for class members that is demonstrated by a sympathetic, tender responsiveness ("The Ministry of Teaching," Scripture Press).

Often college students interested in psychology as a major seem to have obvious emotional or psychological difficulties. Many study the science of human behavior with the goal of solving their own problems as well as ministering to other people. Yet the counselor must be a person who is in control of his own emotional difficulties. An emotionally disturbed counselor may perpetuate the problems of the counselee and complicate them by adding his own frustrations to the situation.

There is a great deal of difference between teaching and counseling. Even though a teacher may be in contact with emotionally disturbed people, he might not be ministering on a personal level.

A teacher studies for the purpose of transmitting information. Even though a teacher may lean heavily on participatory classroom techniques, he is primarily an information-giver.

A teacher ordinarily talks to groups (small or large), whereas a counselor is often in a one-to-one situation. A teacher is primarily a talker, whereas a counselor needs to be primarily a listener. This is not to say that a teacher shouldn't listen, but rather that listening is critically important in counseling.

However, there are some ways in which the characteristics of a good counselor are *like* those of a good teacher. One is the maintenance of contact on a friendly and loving basis. A teacher's primary task is not to convince a student or force him to agree, but rather to bring about understanding. A counselor's task is to help the counselee identify his problems and search for ways to solve them. A counselor does not demand that his client implement the solutions that he has proposed.

In both cases, a student will frequently choose a direction different from that which his teacher or counselor would have suggested. At that point, as a loving parent who keeps the front door open and the light burning in the window, the teacher or counselor continues his friendship and openness with the hope of having some redemptive opportunities in the future.

In addition both teacher and counselor need to be perceptive questioners; that is, they need to learn the technique of asking appropriate questions. A teacher uses questions to discover whether he has communicated clearly. His students' responses reveal whether they have understood and can feed back what has been taught.

A counselor needs to understand the counselee's problem. Some of his questions may be for his own information; others may be for the benefit of the counselee. The latter type of question is almost always reflective. It is used as a device to help the counselee gain insight into his problem.

DUTIES OF A COUNSELING TEACHER

One of the chief qualities of a counselor—one that disqualifies many of us at the outset—is *availability*. The kind of availability which attracts counselees is an elusive and somewhat ambiguous thing.

I have discovered that people who make effective counselors are not necessarily those who publicly announce their availability and willingness to "meet with anybody at any time." Effective counselors are people who seem unhurried and are willing to spend time with other people. They function almost like a tight end in football who manages, play after play, to "get in the open" where the quarterback can see him and throw the ball in his direction. Such a play seldom accounts for long yardage, but it is essential in the steady downfield drives which produce touchdowns.

In the same way, a counseling teacher will not often make obvious and dramatic breakthroughs with one who has deep-seated emotional problems.

In the first place, he should not be counseling people whose problems are severely traumatic. Second, the kind of people he will be dealing with are not, for the most part, severely neurotic. A counseling teacher should be on the preventive end of the process.

An effective teacher quickly establishes *rapport* with his class, so an element of the counseling process is built into a properly functioning teacher-student relationship. However, don't be discouraged if you don't achieve counseling contacts with all of your class members. You may see some of them drawn toward other teachers or adults in the church for counseling simply because they feel that those people's personalities fit more comfortably with their own. By the same token, if your counseling is helpful to members of your class, you will discover that other people in the church will be coming to you with their problems.

Mutual confidence is a basic quality for effective counseling. Sometimes it takes a while to establish a relationship based on this kind of trust, but this is one of the responsibilities of a counseling teacher.

Sometimes a student may "smoke-screen" you in a counseling session. He may discuss a lesser problem (perhaps even something fictitious) before feeling secure enough to deal with the real issue. Here God-given patience is crucial. A teacher may wait for the real problem to surface, or he may probe for it using carefully worded, nonthreatening questions.

Don't take lightly the concept of mutuality in the confidence between counselee and counselor. You must trust if you wish to be trusted. Since you are the more mature party in the relationship, expect to have your trust violated even though you will never violate that confidence yourself.

There is the matter of *listening and watching carefully*. Be alert to hear and see what there is about the counselee—his words, his manner—which will give you clues to facilitate your helping him.

You do not have to be a trained psychiatrist to pick up information by observing a counselee. Learn to watch for facial expressions, repeated statements, and other significant behavior.

Finally, there is the issue of *referral*. It is the duty of a teacher-counselor to refer those problems which are beyond the area of his own capability. Cases of severe emotional trauma or neurological impairment should be quite rare in the experience of an average Sunday School teacher. However, if they emerge he must know enough about the counseling process to know when he has reached the end of his ability. Then the counselee must be referred to someone with more professional training.

If God leads you to this added dimension of the teaching ministry, or if you sense in yourself the gift of exhortation, begin to pray for God's providence in directing your way those people whose lives you can touch and help.

In the meantime, inquire at your local library for books on counseling. Your pastor certainly would have some good books to recommend. Prepare carefully to be able to help your students in this vital area of your ministry.

How to Teach Students to Walk Spiritually

Walking is one of the basic activities of human life. It actually represents life in the New Testament record of the ministry of Jesus. Three times He broke up funerals by bringing the corpses back to life and all three times walking was involved in the activity immediately following the resurrections.

A good example is the daughter of Jairus, ruler of the synagogue at Capernaum. In Mark's account we read that Jesus said to her, "Little girl, I say to you, get up! Immediately the girl stood up and walked around" (Mark 5:41-42).

In the Scriptures, particularly in the New Testament, the concept of walking takes on significant spiritual meaning. The word is often used not to describe a physical activity but rather a state of life, or behavior pattern. A number of different Greek words are represented by the English word "walk" and various levels and attitudes toward spiritual behavior are represented. Even in the English text there are different kinds of walking, or different emphases with respect to a Christian's walk.

Certainly, one of the major tasks of a Christian teacher is to teach his students how to "walk" by themselves. As quickly as possible, growing Christians of any age need to throw away their crutches and step out in strength dependent upon the inner vitality of the Holy Spirit and the outer support of the Word of God.

Let's consider some of the ways that a Christian teacher wants to see his students progress. As the characteristics develop, we then will be able to say with John, "I have no greater joy than to hear that my children are walking in the truth" (3 John 4).

WALKING IN NEWNESS OF LIFE

Like the persons raised from the dead during the time of Jesus' ministry, so new believers today, the Scripture teaches us, should walk in the pattern of the resurrection of their Lord: "Just as Christ was raised from the dead through the glory of the Father, we too may live a new life" (Rom. 6:4). Christian teachers introduce their students to a genuinely new life. The initial entry into that new life is called *regeneration* and the process of bringing people to that point of life is called *evangelism*.

But that's just the beginning. From that point on every day should produce a greater awareness of that new life. So Paul reminds us (Rom. 12:2) that the transformation of life comes about by a renewing of our minds. Let's never forget that a Christian teacher works on the heart through the mind. Conformity to the world represents "oldness of life." We are to encourage our students not to allow the world to put its mask on them, but rather, as a cosmetic commercial says, to let "the new you" show through—the vibrant inner person of the nature of God implanted by the Holy Spirit.

This speaks to the first part of a teacher's task in teaching students how to "walk." One can't walk until after he is born and walking is a decisive sign of growth.

WALKING BY FAITH

In one of those famous Pauline parentheses the apostle raises a significant truth about this basic New Testament concept, the Christian walk. I am referring to 2 Corinthians 5:7 where, in the middle of a treatment of the contrast between being alive physically in this body and spiritually present with the Lord, Paul reminds us, "We live by faith, not by sight."

It sounds highly theological but it's a practical kind of theology. Our students from the early primary classes right on through the oldest adult classes need to recognize the role God should play in leading and controlling every area in our lives. For example, children in elementary school and young people in high school need to understand that they study and take exams by faith—a trust in God's willingness and ability to help them in their lives. Adults need to recognize the role of God in family financing and in the major decisions of life.

These are days of tempestuous confusion in the world around us so it is certainly as important now as it ever was in the history of the church to recognize that God knows what He's doing and why He's doing it. One of the greatest temptations Satan puts before Christians is to give up, to quit, to "throw in the towel." Discouragements come and there are times when we cannot find it within ourselves to meet them. In those times Paul reminds us (and we must remind our students) that "we live by faith, not by sight."

Surely it would be much easier if we could see everything God was doing for us—if we could know what lies just around the bend or how God was going to solve the problem that seems unsolvable at the moment. But this is not God's plan because it would lead to faithless living. People who walk in newness of life are able to walk by faith as well because the witness of the Holy Spirit within guarantees God's control and concern for their lives.

WALKING WORTHY OF OUR VOCATION

This is a phrase taken from Ephesians 4:1. The word "vocation" (KJV) is the common Greek word *klēseōs* which means "calling" (NIV). Paul is not referring to any particular profession or type of work, but rather the glory of being called into the family of God. Every Christian has a "call" from God whether he is a plumber or pastor, a merchant or a missionary.

That calling requires a life of humility, meekness, long-suffering, sharing with other believers in love, concern for the unity of the spirit in peace, and the relationship of the members of the body of Christ. All of this is described thoroughly in the early verses of that fourth chapter of Ephesians.

But how do we walk "worthy of the calling"? The Holy Spirit produces in us (and in our students) the kind of evidence of His Spirit that identifies us as belonging to God. This gives a new kind of self-worth, not dependent on what we have become in our power and strength, but one based on the value of the redemptive blood of Christ and the status of membership in God's family.

WALKING WORTHY OF THE LORD

Here again is a most interesting Greek word. It is the word *axiōs* from which we get our English word "axiology." Axiology is a branch of the field of philosophy which has to do with the study and science of values. In other words, a Christian who is walking worthy of the Lord is one who considers spiritual things valuable. We would say he has a value system which places such things as family loyalty, love for Christ, faithfulness in church, study of the Word of God, prayer, witness, and spiritual growth as high priorities in his life. Paul identifies three ways that a worthy walk pleases the Lord: by bearing fruit, by growing in the full knowledge of God, by being empowered or strengthened by His might (Col. 1:10-11).

A person who is allowing those things to happen in his life is demonstrating the productivity of Christian education in the church because that's what it is all about. Can we really be worthy of the name of the Lord? Yes, we can if we take these verses seriously, but only on God's terms. The integrity, honesty, faithfulness, dependability, and loyalty of a good Christian brings glory to the name of Jesus Christ and that is the worthy walk.

WALKING HONESTLY

Here's the integrity issue pinpointed for the Thessalonian church. The *New International Version* says it clearly and relates closely to the Greek text:

Make it your ambition to lead a quiet life, to mind your own business, and to work with your hands just as we told you, so that your daily life may win the respect of outsiders and so that you will not be dependent on anybody (1 Thes. 4:11-12).

It's one thing to be recognized by believers. Perhaps we may say that's the second step of the Christian walk. The first one is to be recognized by God, placed into His family by faith in the finished work of Jesus Christ in accordance with God's great grace. Then having been recognized by God, we are next recognized by other members of His family. God has also ordained that people who are outside of the fellowship of believers have opportunities to judge the credibility of Christianity by the behavior of Christians.

Obviously, this third level of evaluation is in some ways the most difficult. God can see our hearts and understand what we really intend, even when our outside actions do not reflect those good intentions accurately. Christian brothers and sisters, if they are operating in the patience and grace of the faith, can forgive us our failures, allowing love to make up for a multitude of sins. But the world has a tendency to take the claims of Christianity at face value and even to examine us with special severity. That's why the Bible reminds us and wants us to remind our students to give no offense in any aspect of our lives so that the Gospel is not blamed.

WALKING IN THE LIGHT

John, the Apostle, is one of the primary users of the word "walk" in the New Testament. In one passage he admonishes us to "walk in the light, as He [Christ] is in the light" (1 John 1:7). This kind of walking also results in fellowship with each other.

The verbs in this verse are present tense, indicating a state of life or an ongoing behavior pattern. The walk is to be continual, not occasional or repetitive. The cleansing from sin is not an event, but an ongoing process in the life of a committed believer. Granted, we're not perfect; we do sin. But as we believers walk in the light, God produces *koinonia* (fellowship) among us.

WALKING AS HE WALKED

This is another of John's phrases (1 John 2:6): "Whoever claims to live in Him must walk as Jesus did." The point is simple: Jesus' pattern of life was a model for the believers, not just a demonstration of God-life here on earth.

But, we must ask, how did Jesus "walk"? What characteristics marked His lifestyle during those three and one half years of earthly ministry?

Certainly *humility* marked our Lord's relationships with others. He walked humbly and displayed, in the great pattern of Moses, a godly meekness at all times—except when confronting sin.

He also walked singly with clarity of *purpose* and direction. One of the distorted pictures frequently given of our Lord's life is that of a confused martyr, never really sure of what was happening, never really in control of any situation. No more unbiblical image of the purposeful Lord could be imagined.

But the issue remains—how are we to communicate this lifestyle to our students? Perhaps the best word to identify the process is "reflection." As teachers and leaders live the life of Christ, exemplifying His character and grace, they provide models for others to follow.

Teaching students to walk is a process, not an event. It is a patient, often unrewarded, leading to the truth. Of course, it is assumed that a teacher will first be one who "walks" as Jesus did, in the light, honestly, worthy of the Lord, and worthy of the vocation of Christian living and teaching.

How to Serve the Servants of God

About 200 years ago there lived in Dublin, Ireland a brilliant theologian and writer named Jonathan Swift, the Dean of St. Patrick's Cathedral there. He is perhaps most commonly remembered for his classic tale, *Gulliver's Travels,* which was originally written as a satire on "little men" holding high public office.

We know the book, of course, as a children's classic describing the adventures of Captain Lemiter Gulliver, captain and ship's surgeon, who was the only survivor of the wreck of the good ship *Antelope.* His discovery of the Isle of Libit with its six-inch inhabitants called Lilliputians is one of the great fictional tales of all times.

The tragedy, however, is that Swift was right. There are "small" people. Perhaps not on an Isle of Libit and certainly not only in the world of fantasy. They exist in the real world and their smallness is in their character, not their stature. All of us have known political Lilliputians, moral Lilliputians, and social Lilliputians.

What concerns us most in the church, however, are spiritual Lilliputians. They concern us primarily because it is the task of

Christian education in a local church to help people grow up. This is clear throughout the New Testament, particularly in such passages as Ephesians 4:11-16 and Hebrews 5:11-14.

But from a divine viewpoint, that is, from God's way of looking at it, there are no little people and no unimportant places or ministries. There are only unconsecrated people who are unwilling to allow a very big God to fill their lives and to make them of sufficient spiritual size to carry out His work in the world.

Our task as leaders in the Sunday School and other educational ministries of the church is to help little people grow up, or to put it in more theological terminology, to prepare God's servants.

EQUIPPING GOD'S SERVANTS

When David went out to meet Goliath, Saul wanted to equip him with the king's armor. Paul used a similar analogy in describing spiritual warfare (Eph. 6). But what is involved in equipping? Apparently providing the kinds of tools, both spiritual and physical, which a servant will need to carry out his task properly.

Paul talks about the fact that Christians should "no longer be infants" (Eph. 4:14). The growth process begins at birth. One could even argue that the spiritual realm approximates the physical realm and that growth of some type is even being carried on before birth. Because of immaturity, many believers are tossed back and forth by different theological ideas, much in the way a ship is battered about on the waves of the sea. So one of our responsibilities in equipping is to provide a *stabilizing* ministry for God's servants. In dealing with this concept in Ephesians 4, Clarence Wulf writes:

> If I were to summarize Paul's analogy in one word I would use the term "instability." The Apostle is here speaking about the notion of a wave in the sea. One of the marks of a wave is that it never stays put. It is always on the move. There is undulation and fluctuation. It goes up and down, in and out, and becomes one of the most unstable things. So, too, the believer who remains a spiritual infant is going to have instability when it comes to doctrine—fickle in respect to truth ("Training People for Christian Life and Ministry," unpublished conference manuscript).

It is also necessary, according to Paul, to engage in the repairing of saints if we are to equip them adequately. In verse 12 of that same fourth chapter of Ephesians, the *King James Version* talks about "the perfecting of the saints." Probably the best English word we have to translate the original idea behind "perfect" is the word "repair." When Jesus found the first disciples, they were repairing their nets by the Sea of Galilee. That is exactly the same word Paul used in this passage to talk about equipping saints for ministry.

Some of the saints are broken; others are incomplete. Some are tired because of long service and hard work. It is the task of Christian leadership to put them into working order so their tasks of ministry can continue.

Still a third process in equipping the saints is what we might call the ministry of *developing.* A developmental kind of leadership is one that facilitates the work of others and makes it possible for them to carry out their tasks. A developmental leader values the differences in people and is nonjudgmental regarding their attitudes and approaches to things, particularly when they differ from his own. In order to actively carry out the developing task, we must also be patient, faithful, and above all, learn to be servants serving servants.

Enriching God's Servants

We hear a great deal these days about enrichment programs in education. The term generally refers to something a bit extra, a little beyond the minimal requirements, that margin of excellence toward which Christian ministry ought always to be striving. A leader who would engage in an enriching preparation of servants must help those servants understand *self-acceptance.* We might even call it self-love because that's how the Bible refers to it (see references four paragraphs later).

It is quite popular in evangelical circles to systematically and regularly put oneself down. Taking off from passages such as Philippians 2:1-4, we verbally and symbolically beat our chests, denying any self-worth and affirming our spiritual humility.

Sounds good! Too often, however, the end result is a Christian who wallows in insecurity, finds no real self-acceptance, and develops such a defensiveness about his own inadequacies that he cannot love other people! Collectively this illness of self-hate eats away at family relations, destroys contacts among Christians in churches, mission boards, and other Christian organizations. It is demonstrated daily in such little quirks as embarrassment at compliments. (Ever notice how difficult it is to respond to someone who says, "You look nice today"?)

The only really "Christian" reaction is "Oh, really? This old thing? I bought it on sale last year!" Such an attitude reflects a self-negation, a lack of acceptance of the way God made us.

The Bible teaches us to love ourselves (Matt. 22:39; Gal. 5:14; James 2:8; Rom. 13:9; Eph. 5:21-33). To be sure, biblical self-love is not *egoism*. It is rather a genuine self-acceptance in which, while recognizing our sin and perversion, we still see ourselves as "image-of-God" creations. Biblical love is *more* than self-acceptance but we must begin at a personal point of reference.

Being wanted is essential to security. Sometimes a search for security in a marriage partner, or even in friends and relatives may reflect a need for self-love. A person who has no love for himself cannot love others and is therefore a candidate for depression and self-centeredness (as Saul, 1 Sam. 9:20-21; 10:20-22). Only the loved (accepted) self can help other people learn to love themselves. But how?

The key to self-acceptance is a recognition and reception of God-acceptance (Rom. 15:7). God loves me so I can love myself. And if I can love myself, I can love you; and together we can affirm God's love for both of us—and for others.

It surely is clear that two other aspects of reflective relationship, namely *self-confidence* and *self-denial* depend on *self-acceptance*. All are important, however, and we need to help a growing servant understand how his accepted self can be a confident self and therefore a denied self.

ENCOURAGING GOD'S SERVANTS

The first thing we need to encourage in a developing servant is his willingness to serve. This demands a spelling out of the *requirements*. What is the need that he is to fill? What are the definitions of his job? How does his particular ministry relate to the broader ministry of the congregation? Research in business administration has shown that demonstrating to workers a larger significance of their work is a powerful motivator. We all try harder when we know we are needed!

A study of a gasoline company uncovered that their typical gas station attendant had a feeling of inferiority, resulting in an "I don't care" attitude and low productivity. The attendants were reminded that they were often responsible for the customer's lives so they should inspect cars properly, and that promptness and service could make the difference between a person's keeping an appointment or missing one. As the self-concept of the workers picked up, so did the quality of their work.

An understanding of *relationships* is also basic to the encouraging of God's servants. Again, self-concept is basic and this time it has to do with how an individual worker relates to other workers immediately tied to his area of responsibility and across the broad spectrum of the ministry.

He needs to learn to be himself rather than to play a strange role that is superimposed on him by the church or Sunday School. If our people can really find self-acceptance, then they can find a distinctive value in their own personalities. Just as you are emphasizing their strengths in the arena of ability, they need to emphasize their best qualities in the area of personality in order to work effectively with other members of the staff.

The emerging worker, the growing servant, must also realize his responsibilities. Andrew Carnegie said, "Take away my people but leave my factories and soon grass will grow on the factory floors. Take away my factories but leave my people and soon we will have a new and better factory." In a small Christian organization, whether a church, mission board, college, or publishing house, every individual is tremendously important. There is no room for foot-draggers or unproductive people who do not grasp a sense of significance and responsibility. Incompetence can be tolerated for a while if it is just a matter of the growing process. But if it is a lifestyle, the work of the Lord can be carried on better without some of His workers.

EXHORTING GOD'S SERVANTS

Paul talks a great deal about exhortation and indicates that he did it frequently. Exhortation has to do with our teaching the *meaning* of the ministry. How important is it to be a Sunday School teacher in the preschool department or a helper in Vacation Bible School? What does it mean to say to God and to His people in a local church, "I'll accept this responsibility"?

Of course, there is also the *manner* in which the exhortation takes place. Any Christian leader ought to know that more is achieved through reinforcement than scolding. Sometimes scolding is necessary, but it ought not to be the common order of every day. That kind of manner produces discouragement rather than encouragement.

Finally, there is the matter of *motivation*. What is it that gets God's servants moving in the right direction? Is it fear of what God might do to them or perhaps what their peers might say? Is it duress or a strong sense of duty that we want to impose upon their spiritual consciousness? Those are, without doubt, motivating factors, but they are not the best approaches. The really growing servant responds far better to persuasion, encouragement, and a patient but firm attitude toward eliminating his weaknesses and solving his problems.

How to Promote and Practice Fellowship

In a stimulating article which appeared in *Newsweek,* October 13, 1975, Ralph Keyes, a fellow of the Center for Studies of the Person in La Jolla, California, suggested that the many psychological hang-ups of our day may well be created by the organizations and ideologies that clamor to solve them. The article is titled "I'm Okay, You're Probably Okay." Keyes identifies the problem in the following paragraph:

> The paradoxical effect of those peddling self-improvement is that they can reinforce self-doubt. In an otherwise excellent report on encounter groups, three researchers recently have given as one of their premises, "It is essential that the experience be a *corrective* emotional experience."

In the conclusion of the article, author Keyes wrote: "Alternatively, we can reestablish control over our own spirit, unswayed by the therapy of the moment, unbelief, and self-contempt." His point is that choice is more important than therapy and that we're probably all a little better than we think we are.

So much for positive mental attitude and optimism. If we heed the words of the Bible regarding original sin and the corrupt old nature, we're probably all a bit *worse* than we think we are. Writing from a Christian point of view, Keyes might well have prepared an article which could have been called "I'm Rotten, You're Rotten."

What is happening, of course, is that the spiritual bankruptcy of this age is turning people to mysticism. Wearied by the old and impotent naturalistic rationalism which clearly has run its course in two world wars and a cynical Western civilization, many are resorting to Eastern religions to find some meaning in life.

Meanwhile, those who have been united to the Heavenly Father through Jesus Christ and to each other in the union of His body enjoy a relationship which is not only internal (between a Christian and his Lord) but also external (between a Christian and other Christians). This latter relationship we call "fellowship," and it is clearly one of the tasks of church education to produce and nurture fellowship within local congregations.

THE MEANING OF FELLOWSHIP
IN THE NEW TESTAMENT

The word "fellowship" (Greek, *koinonia*) is not easily defined. Often it refers to the mystical uniting of believers who have participated in the finished work of Christ and thereby have entered into a relationship with each other in His body, the church. But sometimes the word *koinonia* is synonymous with *ekklēsia* ("church"), referring to the body of Christ.

The church can respond to modern secular mysticism by demonstrating to the world that this relationship between believers is based on love and produces interdependence and spiritual mutuality. Of course, to understand the purpose and practice of *koinonia,* one must recognize and appreciate what it means to be the church.

How, we ask, can the members of a modern-day church understand and deal with the many problems which beset their congregations on every hand? One way is for believers to see their own lives, both individual and collective, mirrored in the churches of the New Testament. An expository preacher must take care to build a biblical basis for fellowship in his local church. Whenever God's anointed preacher or teacher enunciates the meaning of the church from the pages of the New Testament, the Holy Spirit illumines the minds of God's people to see themselves as the church in fellowship.

CHARACTERISTICS OF A FELLOWSHIP CHURCH

It is possible to identify churches by their emphases. One can talk, for example, about an evangelistic church or a missionary-minded church, or a prophetic church. All of these are labels to describe a certain specialty which a given congregation has carved out for itself in its own community and perhaps even in its denomination.

Certainly one of the types of churches which can be categorized by emphasis is what Lyle Schaller calls "the fellowship church." Such a church sees the developing of fellowship as one of its major objectives and prides itself on such things as friendliness, opportunities to be together, and sharing. Schaller enumerates some of the basic characteristics of a church that centers on fellowship:

1. The various fellowship and volunteer groups offer the opportunity for members to become better acquainted with one another.
2. There is a strong tendency to avoid controversy, conflict, and divisive conditions which often come to churches that take positions on controversial questions.
3. There is a lack of specific program goals, and congregational victories are few and far between.
4. The congregation as a whole tends to be conservative and anti-innovative in regard to change ("What's Ahead for the Fellowship Church?" *Church Management—The Clergy Journal,* February 1975).

Of course, Schaller's research is done across the theological spectrum. My own observation (not based on technical research) is that genuinely evangelical churches which place a high priority on fellowship (for example, the Peninsula Bible Church in Palo Alto, California) tend to defy many of Schaller's descriptive conclusions. He suggests that the fellowship churches in his survey tend to be neither evangelical nor evangelistic. I dare say, however, that if one surveyed exclusively evangelical churches which put a high premium on fellowship, he would find that they are also strongly evangelistic.

Fellowship is not a by-product of a church or a substitute for evangelism. On the other hand, fellowship should never run a poor second to an overemphasis on evangelism. Fellowship is what the church *is* when it meets together, creating that atmosphere of loving union and communion which offers an attractive option to the vacuum and futility of contemporary culture.

WAYS TO NURTURE FELLOWSHIP
IN A LOCAL CONGREATION

The following list is merely suggestive and certainly not exhaustive. It simply represents a place for us to begin (or to continue) an emphasis on fellowship in our congregations.

Preaching. In a church which concerns itself with the quality of fellowship, preaching can be central without pastor dominance. I emphasize that because a church in which there is a high degree of pastoral dominance is generally a church in which fellowship is minimal. In a journal article I tried to emphasize the importance of Bible exposition in every aspect of a church's ministry:

> We must never overlook the fact that the miracle of God through preaching is as great a miracle when it results in the edification of the saints as when it draws people into the church initially. As the people of God grow in the grace of God, they develop a perspective which can build their understanding of what it means to be the church. When they have seen this they begin to sense in practice the spirit of *koinonia* ("Preaching and the Fellowship," *Grace Journal,* Winter 1967).

Numerous passages such as Ephesians 4:12-16 emphasize the role of the preacher as being concerned with the maturity of the saints. That maturity, when developed, joins the body closely together in a resulting *koinonia.*

Planning. Perhaps the fellowship church needs to be a bit less existential—that is, a bit less focused on the here and now and what it is in its present form. By the same token, however, churches which have not experienced a satisfactory level of fellowship could well take their eyes off either the past or the future and focus a bit more on the present.

What is Jesus Christ to us *now?* Why has He redeemed us with respect to the *present?* To be sure, redemption from the sin of the past is a glorious blessing and one about which we testify frequently. Likewise, the expectation of His coming and the prospect of eternal life with Him in heaven is the blessed hope of the church. But what about *now?* What can we be to each other under God and before Christ in this present hour?

Programming. If Schaller is correct, a typical fellowship church is "program poor." After suggesting various deficiencies in the programs of fellowship churches, Schaller indicates that a wise approach is:

> to place at the top of the priority list in program development one or two areas in which the current program is reasonably strong and which are responsive to the needs of members and potential new members. These might include expansion of the ministry to mature adults or developing a specialized ministry to widowed persons or extending the fellowship circle to include more isolated and lonely adults living alone or increasing the number and variety of opportunities for corporate worship.

People orientation. In its building of preaching, planning, and programming, a church which already has a high level of fellowship ought not to lose its people orientation. That is the kind of New Testament philosophy which has made it what it is, and some of us could use a good dose of such an emphasis to increase the *koinonia* count in our own congregational blood. Often a fellowship-deficient church has placed too much emphasis on programming and too little emphasis on the needs and personality demands of its people.

Propagation. If there is a common weakness in a fellowship church, it is its lack of propagation and outreach. It is so "nice" to be together as believers that we forget about the millions around us who cannot experience fellowship because they are not in the body. Once again, it becomes a question of biblical balance. To borrow a phrase from Jesus, "You should have practiced the latter, without neglecting the former" (Matt. 23:23).

So let us get on with building a high level of fellowship in our churches. Let us design Christian education programs which will tune in children and young people to the importance of biblical fellowship. But let us sacrifice neither outreach nor nurture in the process of learning how to identify with each other in the context of our local congregation.

PART THREE

IMPROVING
CLASSROOM TEACHING

How to Understand Your Students

When we talk about child discipline in the home, the Old Testament passage most frequently quoted is Proverbs 22:6: "Train a child in the way he should go, and when he is old, he will not turn from it." There is no question that the writer's primary reference is to parental relationships with children in the home, since the home has always been God's primary place of nurture. However, the principle of the passage certainly applies also to a Christian classroom and to a church teacher.

There is, however, in both home and classroom, a common misconception of Proverbs 22:6. Some parents claim it as an absolute promise and wonder why God reneges on His word when children brought up in the way they should go do seem to depart from that way in later years. The best exegetes of the Old Testament suggest that "the way he should go" really refers to the child's own distinctive characteristics and implies that parents and teachers must deal with a child according to his own unique needs and abilities. The *Amplified Bible* renders our text, "Train up a child in the way he should go [and in keeping with his individual gift or bent] and when he is old he will not depart from it." In light of this emphasis on individual need and the uniqueness of students, what then is teaching? A multitude of definitions abound.

Teaching is the stimulation of a student's mind in order that he may grasp what the teacher wants him to know.

Teaching is the response whereby content is appropriated by a receiver from a source.

Teaching is the communication of experience.

Teaching is the process by which knowledge is imparted from one person to another person.

Teaching is an organized process of mental stimulation whereby a person's intellectual horizons are broadened.

Teaching is the process of introducing students to an understanding of truth.

Some of these definitions are only partly true, and all of them are inadequate. Indeed, if one were to write a thoroughly acceptable definition of teaching it probably could not be done in sentences or paragraphs but would require pages to identify all the variable components of the teaching-learning experience.

Certainly, effective teaching begins by understanding the various ingredients in that situation, among which are the teacher himself, the content, the role of the Holy Spirit, the methodology, and certainly the students. So in this chapter it is not my intention to provide a full definition of teaching or to deal with all the variables involved, but rather to focus on just one of those aspects—an extremely important one—understanding your students.

UNDERSTANDING HOW THEY FEEL

On July 24, 1732, Susanna Wesley wrote to her son John concerning the process of education she used in bringing up her children. After identifying the rigid family schedule maintained at the Wesley home, Mrs. Wesley wrote:

> In order to form the minds of children, the first thing to be done is to conquer their will and bring them to an obedient temper. To inform the understanding is a work of time, and most of children proceed

by slow degrees as they are able to bear it; but the subjecting of the will is
a thing that must be done at once, and the sooner the better.

While admiring the commitment of Susanna Wesley and some
of the products of her home, one tends to question the truly
biblical nature of the rigidity and force which characterized that
home. Indeed, after the historic fire in the Wesley home she
indicated that the children who were dispersed among other
families very quickly changed their behavior and became
involved with words and ways completely contrary to what they
had learned at home. There is a possibility, therefore, that the
order and design of the Wesley home were due to the iron rule of
the parents and not the internal commitment of the children.

In a moment I will discuss the nature of the student as he is,
but it is also important to recognize how he feels about himself.
The Scripture says, "As he thinks within himself, so he is" (Prov.
23:7, NIV marg.), indicating that external behavior is motivated
largely by internal self-concept. Phenomenological psychology
has built a whole system of understanding people and their
behavior on this basic premise without, of course, recognizing
that it was written by Solomon under the inspiration of the Holy
Spirit thousands of years ago.

It would be nice if we could teach students to feel the way we
want them to feel, rather than the way they really feel. It would be
ideal if they would always feel "good" and "highly motivated" and
"willing." The simple fact is they don't, so it becomes important
for a teacher to understand how a student feels about himself,
about his teacher, and about the learning situation before that
teacher can really deal with him effectively. Of course, those
feelings are sometimes negative and "bad." Wishing that a student's attitude were different does not, unfortunately, bring it to
pass.

UNDERSTANDING HOW THEY ARE

Philosophers call the study of human nature "anthropology."
That term has other definitions in the dictionary and in other
disciplines of learning, but for our purposes in this chapter we

want to focus on a "Christian anthropology of students" or what the Bible says people really are inside. Even secular educators recognize that understanding the nature of a student is imperative to teaching him effectively.

> Each theory of learning is linked to a conception of the basic nature of man. In basic moral inclination, is he initially good, is he evil, or is he neutral? Then, in relation to his environment, is he active, passive, or interactive? Each of the different conceptions has its adherents, and each has its own approach to learning (Bigge, "Theories of Learning," *N.E.A. Journal*, March 1956).

The Bible teaches us, of course, that man was made in the image of God but that the image was marred at the Fall. In his classic text, *What the Bible Teaches* (Revell), R.A. Torrey develops a series of propositions regarding "the present standing before God":

> They are darkened in their understanding, alienated from the life of God through the ignorance that is in them, hardened in heart (Eph. 4:18).

> The natural man receiveth not the things of the spirit of God, neither can he know them (1 Cor. 2:14).

> The natural heart is deceitful above all things and desperately sick (Gen. 6:5, 12; 8:21; Ps. 94:11).

> The entire moral and intellectual nature of unredeemed man is corrupted by sin (Titus 3:3; Eph. 2:3; Col. 3:5, 7).

Torrey develops seven other propositions and then concludes:

> The present standing or condition of men out of Christ is pictured in the Bible as dark and hopeless. One word will express it—*lost*, utterly lost....The more one has to do with men and women and the more one comes to know the depths of his own heart, the more convinced he becomes of the truthfulness and accuracy in every line of this hideous and repulsive picture.

But, of course, regeneration changes that because the Holy

Spirit produces a spiritual nature and directs the renewed mind toward the things of the Spirit (Rom. 8:5). Multiple references in Scripture refer to the change which comes about in the mind as well as in the heart. So a teacher who understands what his students *are* understands both their past (or their present, if they are still unregenerate) and what they have become because of the redeeming and life-changing power of Jesus Christ.

UNDERSTANDING HOW THEY THINK

In one sense, understanding how a person thinks s a lot like understanding how he feels. But I am using the word "think" in a more narrow sense, particularly with reference to learning and the mental process involved. In an interesting article which appeared in the June 1970 issue of *Traffic Safety,* published by the National Safety Council, T.K. Lawson and Arlene F. Tate remind us:

> Heads are not jugs. They have lids on the top, and when the lid is closed no amount of pouring will force an idea into the mind. People open these lids for themselves, but they do so only when the right climate has been established. Even after the lid has been raised, the idea must pass through a filter made up of such components as experience, habit, fears, and needs. The pouring communicator is totally unaware of this situation.

To be sure, the Lawson and Tate paragraph speaks more to adult education and does not take into consideration behavioral modification techniques. But it does make a central point—that *students must learn to think they can think* and to develop positive attitudes toward learning.

Many students think learning is unpleasant, impractical, and perhaps even a waste of time. The other extreme is to think that learning is just a fun time or that it somehow takes place automatically just by being in a classroom.

Too often church teachers are interested only in teaching students *what* to think rather than *how* to think. One could almost classify church educational programs and Christian schools into the what-to-think and how-to-think categories. Certainly, those who believe in the absolute truth of Scripture should take a much more serious view of teaching students "what to think" than those who believe that all truth is relative. But the "what" must be balanced with the "how," or we are engaging in nothing more or less than mind manipulation and indoctrination.

UNDERSTANDING HOW THEY RESPOND

In the famous seven laws of teaching developed by Gregory and popularized by a set of Moody Bible Institute filmstrips, two important laws view the issue of response. One is called "The Law of the Teaching Process" and states that a teacher should excite and direct the self-activities of a student by telling him nothing he can learn himself. This has to do with stimulating and thinking, as indicated earlier, requiring some kind of verbal or behavioral response, arousing the spirit of inquiry, and securing some kind of active involvement in the learning process.

The other relevant law, "The Law of the Learning Process," states that a student must reproduce in his own mind and life that which needs to be learned. Response is of the utmost importance because it also gives a teacher a chance to evaluate what learning has taken place. In communication theory we refer to it as "feedback," both verbal and nonverbal.

So understanding students is a multiple task which calls forth the best we have in us and requires a blending of philosophy and methodology to produce results in growing, maturing Christians who are being taught, each according to his own individual needs.

How to Create a Good Learning Environment

So often when we think of teaching we think of what a teacher does *for* students rather than what he makes it possible for them to do for *themselves*. Yet the bulk of research in education indicates that student experience, or the "doing" approach to learning, is by far the best. In the long run, it produces the most satisfactory and longest-lasting results. Even parents are admonished by child psychologists never to do anything for their children which the children can properly do for themselves.

The creation of a learning environment means that all factors in a given teaching-learning situation (not necessarily in a classroom) are arranged so that learning takes place. Emphasis is on the learning rather than the teaching, and on the learner rather than the teacher.

The creation of a good learning environment is not primarily an intellectual activity. The intellect is extremely important in the learning process and is a factor that affects both teacher and student. But I take the view that it is not the *primary* factor. Neither is a good learning environment primarily physical. That is, one could have a beautiful classroom with just the right lighting, color schemes, and square footage per student, and still not have a good learning environment.

By the same token, a good learning environment is not primarily related to equipment. Mark Hopkins did not have a filmstrip projector on that now-famous log, but he did a good job of creating a learning environment. Of course, that should not be taken in any way as negating equipment, any more than the physical or the intellectual. The point is, we are talking about the *primary* ingredient of a good learning environment.

In my opinion that primary ingredient is *attitude*. You have seen it as often as I have. A student with mediocre intellectual ability in an ill-equipped classroom with less than desirable physical surroundings somehow demonstrates a tremendous capacity to learn, and the teaching-learning process produces outstanding results. His attitude made the difference. But it is the attitude of the teacher that creates the learning environment and makes it possible for the learning process to get into gear.

ATTITUDE TOWARD THE SCRIPTURES

If it is true, as I shall soon suggest, that the attitude of the teacher is frequently reflected in the attitude of the student, then nothing could be more important than the way a teacher thinks about God, Christ, and the Bible. The Bible is absolutely indispensable in Christian education, both because of its role in the regenerative process (2 Tim. 3:15) and its provision of the absolute truth of God, which is the essence of what the church's educational program is all about. A *Christianity Today* editorial said it well: "Without clear recognition of this power [the power of the Bible] there can be no Christian education. Whenever education, even though church-sponsored, departs from a primary biblical frame of reference it becomes secularized" (November 22, 1963).

ATTITUDE TOWARD THE SPIRIT

A fine book for the church teacher is Dr. Roy Zuck's *The Holy Spirit in Your Teaching* (Victor Books). It is a beautiful balance of theology and pedagogy, emphasizing that ultimate learning in the Christian setting is an internal process carried out by the Holy Spirit. Nevertheless, that internal process is made possible by the way God uses Christian teachers to create a good learning environment. Zuck defines evangelical Christian education:

> the Christ-centered, Bible-based, pupil-related process of communicating God's written Word through the power of the Holy Spirit, for the purpose of leading pupils to Christ and building them up in Christ....Christian education is a divine-human task in which born-again teachers face the opportunity of cooperating with God the Holy Spirit as workers together with Him.

A teacher's attitude toward the Scriptures is shown by the way he handles his Bible in class, how he talks about it, and how he encourages his students to use their own Bibles. A teacher's attitude toward the Holy Spirit should be shown through prayer and the way he talks about the Holy Spirit's role in his classroom.

Every Christian teacher ought to frequently verbalize the importance of the Holy Spirit's control.

ATTITUDE TOWARD THE SUBJECT

Some lessons are simply more exciting than others. For example, it is much easier for a primary level teacher to get enthusiastic about teaching the biblical account of David and Goliath than a lesson from Leviticus 12. So he must constantly show that his attitude toward the subject does not reflect an opinion that the less exciting portions of Scripture are less important.

As my colleague Howard G. Hendricks is fond of saying, the very worst thing a Christian teacher can do with God's Word is to make it boring! Certainly equally dangerous, however, is conveying the attitude that a subject under study in a given passage is not really important.

ATTITUDE TOWARD THE STUDENTS

May we not think of our students only as a class. Of course, they have a collectivity, and we see them most frequently in a group setting. But the uniqueness of each individual student is not just a biological phenomenon. If a Christian teacher believes in "image theology"—that everyone is created in God's image and that even though sin has defaced the image, redemption can restore it and that the nature of God dwells within each Christian student—then he must demonstrate an attitude which recognizes each student's own developmental characteristics. As far as possible he teaches his students as individuals. As Peter Cousins put it: "Although he may reject many of the assumptions underlying 'progressive' education, [the Christian teacher] will approach each student as a person, and an individual of infinite value, created for love and community and with the God-given right to be treated as a person, not a school register number" (*Christianity Today*, October 9, 1970).

ATTITUDE TOWARD THE SELF

The teacher's own self-concept is a most important attitudinal factor in creating a good learning environment. Does he see himself as a great truth-giver who never errs, or as one to whom God has given the responsibility of assisting others to join him in his own search for truth and growth in maturity?

James put it bluntly when he said in the first verse of his third chapter, "Brothers, not too many of you should get excited about becoming teachers because I want to remind you that the person who is a teacher is under greater evaluation of God than other people" (personal trans.).

It is one thing to have an infallible Bible; it is quite another to have an infallible interpretation of the Bible. Dogmatism is an unpleasing posture for a Christian teacher. One teacher who puts on airs of superiority negates rather than sustains a good learning environment. Students depend on him and his words rather than learning to search the Scriptures for themselves.

ATTITUDE TOWARD THE SAINTS

Students in the various educational aspects of the ministry of the church should sense from their teachers and leaders a spirit of community rather than isolation. They should sense the love and union that join the saints together. They should hear about that love and union taught effectively by their parents at home and by their teachers at church.

ATTITUDE TOWARD THE SCIENCE

The science of learning is detailed, and in these few brief sentences we can hardly offer a satisfactory overview. Certain principles, however, can lead us to a better understanding of what actually goes on in the learning process. Here is a simple listing of some of those principles:

1. Learning must start where the student is. The whole concept of apperception—that is, going from the known to the unknown—implies that we meet a student at his present level of understanding and increase that level of understanding step by step in a developmental process.

2. Learning is based on interest. Is it easier to teach an eight-year-old child to ride a bicycle or to dry dishes? It is probably easier to teach him to dry dishes (especially if your table service is plastic), but he may feel considerably more motivated to spend time trying to ride the bicycle. The learning process moves ahead rapidly if we can demonstrate an interest element in the dish-drying task. Or to put it in popular terms, "In every job that must be done there is an element of fun" (Mary Poppins).

3. Learning is based on need. Students, particularly in their teen and adult years, tend to want a relevant application of what they are learning. When people are really involved in the learning process, they need to be helped to see how the activity relates to their needs and objectives. A teacher encourages more positive attitudes toward future learning experiences if he makes sure each individual involved sees this relationship.

4. Learning takes place through involvement. For small children involvement is usually physical—playing instructional games, building with blocks, drawing or coloring pictures. For older students the involvement is mental and verbal as they interact with information the teacher is offering. Teachers become guides in the inquiry process, and an environment is

created in which they can directly relate themselves to the learning process.

5. Learning takes place through seeing relationships. Professional educators refer to this as "differentiation." It has to do with recognizing how the parts of the puzzle go together.

Just as the body of Christ is one, so the geographical boundaries of that body which we call "local church" ought to be one, and each student will learn better and in a more positive setting if that environment is wholesome, positive, and loving. To borrow again from the article by Peter Counsins, "The Christian teacher is committed to an uncompromising assertion of objective standards and an equally unconditional acceptance of students. In so doing he is teaching the most important lesson of all. He learned it at Calvary."

How to Teach for Spiritual Growth

Wouldn't it be wonderful if Christian teaching, or any teaching for that matter, resulted in automatic behavioral change just because we had gone through the classroom exercise? But pedagogical research uncovered long ago the fact that application is not automatic and students do not "learn" merely because they're exposed to teaching for a period of time.

What modern educational study has confirmed was written centuries ago in God's Word, especially with regard to the spiritual perception of truth. First Corinthians 2:9 is clear: "However, as it is written: No eye has seen, no ear has heard, no mind has conceived what God has prepared for those who love Him."

Later on in the chapter we discover that it is impossible for a natural man to understand spiritual truth. But here we see that even a believer does not naturally see, hear, or understand spiritual truth. And having opened this section of his chapter with the statement that spiritual growth is not automatic, Paul goes on to explain how a Christian teacher, with the aid of the supernatural work of the Holy Spirit, can bring about spiritual growth in students through the teaching process.

SPIRITUAL GROWTH REQUIRES COMMUNICATION

First Corinthians 2:10 talks about God's revelation: "But God has revealed it to us by His Spirit. The Spirit searches all things, even the deep things of God." The word "revealed" should not be understood purely in the sense of the inspiration of Scripture, though that is a significant part of God's threefold revelation; God has revealed Himself in nature, in Scripture, and in the person of His Son.

Taken in its technical theological sense, "revelation" in this context must be primarily applied to giving the Scriptures originally. But Paul also seems to imply that God has communicated through revelation and now illuminates the heart and mind of a Christian teacher so he may communicate God's truth to others.

So spiritual growth depends on the double transmission of truth—God's Word to us and our explanation of it to others.

Note also that this passage emphasizes the depth level of such spiritual instruction. Teaching for spiritual growth is not a bare communication of the data of the Gospel or the constant repetition of the elementary facts of salvation (cf. Heb. 5:11—6:1).

Perhaps the biggest problem in evangelical churches today is spiritual immaturity. The cause of the problem is really simple, but its correction is complex. Spiritual immaturity results from lack of spiritual nourishment and exercise.

Of course, there could also be the complicating factor of disease in the physical domain, which is comparable to sin in the spiritual domain; but even here they are closely linked together. A person who does not eat the right food and get sufficient exercise is much more prone to illness.

So a Christian teacher has before him people who by virtue of spiritual age or spiritual infirmity are desperately in need of the truth he has to communicate on the basis of God's revelation. It is his goal through the teaching process to bring them to spiritual maturity as a result of consistent growth in the things of the Lord.

SPIRITUAL GROWTH REQUIRES CONFIRMATION

To be a Christian is to live in the best of two worlds. Paul frequently referred to it as a dual citizenship. He was quick to affirm his citizenship in the Roman Empire but even more concerned that people recognize the priority of his heavenly citizenship. First Corinthians 2:11-12 indicates how God confirms the communication of a Christian teacher.

There are three spirits spoken of; and because of *the spirit of man,* that is, because of his humanity, a person is able to understand natural truth. A secular scientist does not have to acknowledge God nor does he have the Holy Spirit resident within his life to uncover truths of nature. That is part of God's common grace and His natural revelation. To be sure, he will be able to interpret his findings much more accurately if he is a believer because then he can apply the lens of Scripture to his study of God's Creation. Nevertheless, he is able to understand natural truth because he has "the spirit of man."

By the same token, *the Spirit of God* alone understands the things of God. No man because of his humanity, because he is a member of the human race and therefore possesses a human spirit, can by that identification understand spiritual truth. The Holy Spirit understands spiritual truth because He is a Member of the Triune Godhead. He witnesses internally of God's gifts to us and confirms the relationship of both Christian student and teacher to the God who communicates of Himself.

The third spirit of the passage is *the spirit of the world.* There is a contrasting distinction that Paul makes plain in these verses. A natural man has the spirit of man because he is human. The tendency of that spirit is to draw him to the spirit of the world, which is in contrast with the Spirit of God.

A Christian also has the spirit of man because he is human. But because of the indwelling Holy Spirit, who manifests the life of Christ in his regenerated nature, he is able to resist the spirit of the world. He can seek the control of the Spirit of God, who confirms truth in his life.

The New Testament word "verily" (KJV) or "I tell you the truth" (NIV) is a word of confirmation. It is used in the Gospels only by Jesus and appears with great frequency (27 times in Matthew, 15 times in Mark, 8 times in Luke, 48 times in John). It is actually a translation, not of a Greek word, but of a Hebrew word, *amen,* now commonly used at the end of prayer. In his record of Jesus' teachings, the Apostle John uses the word always in the double form (verily, verily). Perhaps this is because John emphasizes more of the *words* of the Master than His *works*.

The word ought to be most meaningful to those of us who are teachers. It literally means "may it be confirmed." When used at the beginning of a phrase as Jesus used it, it could well be interpreted "Now hear this; now hear this." Surely our constant prayer is that God will confirm our communication so that spiritual growth can be demonstrated in the lives of our students.

SPIRITUAL GROWTH REQUIRES COMPREHENSION

The noted educator Benjamin Bloom, in his helpful and popular book *Taxonomy of Educational Objectives, the Classification of Educational Goals, Cognitive and Affective Domains* (McKay), talks a great deal about comprehension as a learning level. He indicates that though it may not be the highest level of learning, it is a good deal higher than knowledge and it represents a kind of learning which teachers ought to strive for more than they do.

A good common synonym would be our English word "understanding." May God deliver Christian teachers from always insisting that students *agree* with what we say. What is really crucial is whether they *comprehend* what we are trying to teach them. Persuasion is a much more important factor in the ministry of an evangelist than in the ministry of a Christian teacher. Our task is to communicate with the expectation that the Holy Spirit will confirm God's truth and that comprehension will result.

Notice again the text of our passage: "This is what we speak, not in words taught us by human wisdom but in words taught by the Spirit, expressing spiritual truths in spiritual words. The man without the Spirit does not accept the things that come from the Spirit of God, for they are foolishness to him, and he cannot understand them, because they are spiritually discerned. The spiritual man makes judgments about all things, but he himself is not subject to any man's judgment" (1 Cor. 2:13-15).

So comprehension results when a Christian teacher uses words given him by the Holy Spirit, who controls his mind and mouth. He expresses spiritual truths in spiritual words so that what educators call "differentiation" can set it.

Yet he teaches against the barrier of natural imperceptibility. To be sure, if all the students are believers, the Holy Spirit also confirms God's truth in their lives, and that is the ideal situation for Christian education.

But in dealing with a natural person—that is, an unsaved student—the teacher must recognize that he does not *receive* spiritual truth and does not *interact* with spiritual truth (the two important verbs of 1 Cor. 2:14 are different). The latter part of the verse says that it is impossible for an unsaved person to interact with spiritual truth because such interaction requires the confirmation ministry of the Holy Spirit.

First Corinthians 2:15 emphasizes that all-important educational task of *evaluation*. A Christian teacher tests the comprehension level of the students by evaluating spiritually both the process and results of his teaching. In short, he doesn't leave results to chance. And in the final analysis his own examination or evaluation is not of men but of God, for he serves the Lord Christ.

In the final verse of 1 Corinthians 2, Paul reverts to the classic device he uses in almost all of his epistles, the rhetorical question. "Who has known the mind of the Lord?" he asks. Answer: obviously nobody except the Holy Spirit. The middle phrase of the verse requires a careful delineation of the words "he" and "him." Exactly who is instructing whom? The grammar allows two possible interpretations. Paul may be emphasizing that all learning must come from above, since no one can instruct God, who knows all things and is the Originator of all truth.

But he might also be saying that a person who does not operate with spiritual communication, having his teaching confirmed by God's Spirit, is not able to instruct a natural person, who cannot discern or perceive or comprehend or understand spiritual truth.

But, praise God, the potential is there because "we have the mind of Christ." What a beautiful and comforting way for the passage to end! The task of Christian teaching does not rest on hidden ability but on divine power.

The process of bringing about spiritual growth in the lives of our students is something we do cooperatively with God, or rather something we do as His instruments because the Holy Spirit communicates, confirms, and produces comprehension in this wonderful experience which we call Christian teaching.

How to Understand and Teach about Worldiness

Humorist Robert Benchley once divided the world into two groups—those who divide the world into two groups and those who do not. Obviously the "two-group" classification is nonsense which could be dispelled with a laugh were it not carried over into so much Christian work.

Whether we admit it or not, we constantly divide people into those who do it the way we think it ought to be done and those who do not. We approve of those who dress the way we think people ought to dress and disapprove of those who do not. We admire those who run the kind of church we prefer and criticize those who run churches in different ways.

Of course, sometimes dual categorization is essential because it is biblical. Jesus spoke of those who believe and those who do not believe. Those who believe will not stand in judgment for sin, and those who do not believe have been judged already because of their unbelief (John 3:18). There are some obvious dual categories with which we must deal—saved and unsaved, men and women—but most categorization is unrealistic at best and deliberately misleading at worst.

For example, we talk about "children and adults." When does a person stop being a child and begin his life as an adult? We talk about black people and white people, but in various countries of the world, such as the island of Jamaica, there are all shades of brown. We talk about the educated and the uneducated, but who is educated? Does graduation from elementary school make a person educated? How about high school? College? The point is that our categories are so often false and so relative to variables which cloud the issue.

Such is the case with "worldliness"—a theological football which has been kicked up and down the ecclesiastical field for most of the history of the church. The Bible has a great deal to say about the world, and it is foolish to argue the point without beginning with a look at the passages which deal with the subject of worldliness.

INFORMATION ABOUT WORLDLINESS

"Do not conform any longer to the pattern of this world, but be transformed by the renewing of your mind. Then you will be able to test and approve what God's will is—His good, pleasing, and perfect will" (Rom. 12:2).

"You adulterous people, don't you know that friendship with the world is hatred toward God? Anyone who chooses to be a friend of the world becomes an enemy of God" (James 4:4).

"Do not love the world or anything in the world. If anyone loves the world, the love of the Father is not in him. For everything in the world—the cravings of sinful man, the lust of his eyes, and the boasting of what he has and does—comes not from the Father but from the world. The world and its desires pass away, but the man who does the will of God lives forever" (1 John 2:15-17).

"For, as I have often told you before and now say again even with tears, many live as enemies of the cross of Christ. Their destiny is destruction, their god is their stomach, and their glory is in their shame. Their mind is on earthly things" (Phil. 3:18-19).

These few texts do not exhaust the amount of Scripture relevant to the subject. But they are certainly representative, and the

1 John 2 passage may well be the high-water mark on the subject of worldliness in the pages of the New Testament.

INTERPRETATION OF WORLDLINESS

Now we get to the nitty-gritty. It is one thing to list passages and recognize that the Bible says a great deal about worldliness, but as Warren Wiersbe reminds his young readers in a helpful article, "What in the World Is Worldliness?":

> Your pastor will tell you that the *technical* definition of the Bible word *"world"* is "the present system of things actively opposed to Jesus Christ." Actually, the Bible uses the word in three different ways: the created world (John 21:25), the world of people (John 3:16), and the world as a system (John 14:30) (*The Alliance Witness*, May 7, 1975).

The concept of worldliness in Scripture almost always appears in contrast with the concept of righteousness or godliness. James 4:4 is a classic demonstration of this principle: "Don't you know that friendship with the world is hatred toward God?" So the biblical emphasis on *worldliness* deals with "the world" in relation to its ideas, its philosophies, and its system. These are the products of man's sinful condition which are opposed to the holiness that is found in God alone.

Primarily, worldliness is an *attitude* rather than an *act*. To be sure, such attitudes result in acts all too often, but one can be worldly without "doing" any of the so-called worldly things so often connected with carnality. Just as idolatry in its most general sense represents anything which comes between a person and God, so worldliness represents anything that keeps a person from thoroughly loving God. John sets forth a stark contrast: either you love the world or you love the Father; it is impossible to love both.

Quite obviously such an attitude results in an act or series of acts which we call "behavior." A person *behaves* in a certain way because of what he *values* and he values a certain thing because of what he *believes*; so we are right back to the cultivation of godly attitudes as the way to avoid worldliness and walk in the love of God. Wiersbe comes to the following definition of worldliness: "Anything that you love and do that keeps you from enjoying God's love and doing God's will is worldly and must be avoided."

On the positive side, it might be said that worship as a Christian virtue is not unlike worldliness as a vice. As worldly attitudes lead to worldly acts, so godly attitudes lead to worship. In both cases, worldliness and worship are better described by the attitude that produces the act rather than by the act itself.

INVOLVEMENT IN WORLDLINESS

If our goal as Christians is holy living—and that certainly is our biblical command—we will want to demonstrate attitudes and actions of worship instead of worldliness. Especially as Christian leaders and teachers it is important for us to offer our lives as models of holiness rather than as excuses for others to lapse into worldly behavior.

Perhaps that is why John makes his words so practical when he talks about worldliness assailing our lives through the lusts of our bodies, the lusts, or desires, of our eyes, and pride.

To be sure, there are certain aspects of Christian living which are absolute and others which are rather relative. Drunkenness as a behavior or lustful thinking as an attitude are both clearly condemned in Scripture and can never be right for any Christian at any time. They are absolutely negative aspects of worldliness and must be utterly avoided if godly living is to be maintained.

In other cases, individual circumstances become significant factors. To some Christians, purchasing a luxury automobile may be offensive. Others might regard owning a television set or theater attendance as evidence of spiritual decay. Condemnations in these instances are often based on individual economic standards.

Can a Sunday School teacher go to a party and stay up late on Saturday night without having his spiritual sensitivity dulled? Perhaps he can on occasion; and if he can, then doing so is a matter strictly between himself and God. However, he must come to grips with this issue on a personal basis. Sensitivity to the Holy

Spirit and awareness of what the Word says regarding the best use of time are imperative.

Notice how many individual factors can be involved in deciding a single issue. The relationship of Saturday night to a teacher's preparedness to teach on Sunday morning is an important question. So is the type of party he attends. Certainly he cannot dishonor Christ through immoral or unwholesome activities on Saturday night and expect to conscientiously honor Him on Sunday morning.

When it comes to worldliness, determinations cannot be made on the basis of surface generalities. There are individual questions that must be considered in order to distinguish between godliness and worldliness. That is why Paul calls us to consider the best, not just the permissible. He emphasizes that all things may be "lawful" for a Christian, but not all things build him up spiritually.

The secret to avoiding involvement in worldliness is found in one of the passages quoted earlier, Romans 12:2. J.B. Philips translates that first phrase, "Don't let the world around you squeeze you into its own mold." The Greek word translated by the English word "conform" (NIV) is the one from which we get our word "scheme," and it has to do with putting on a mask. At the same time, the word "transformed" is the word from which we get our English word "metamorphosis." It means more than a superficial change.

When a person who is truly born again engages in worldliness, he is putting on the mask of sin so that people cannot see the Spirit of the living God dwelling in his body. God wants him to take off that mask and adopt an attitude that reflects the nature of the living God who dwells within him because of regeneration.

Our task as teachers and leaders is to live this truth and then to teach it to others, not in laws of behavior admissible in church, not in a list of "no-nos" acceptable to the saints, but rather in an understanding of how the Scriptures and the Holy Spirit come together to produce an attitude of worldliness.

In my opinion the best approach is an appeal to Christian *principles*. That is, rather than legislating Christian conduct or attitude, we must take seriously the challenge to both church and home to teach principles of Christian living.

The New Testament abounds in such rich guidelines which apply to any people in any age. Romans 12:2 is one example: *the principle of mind-transformation.* Paul is led by God's Spirit to issue several guidelines to a church which was practicing "worldly legalism." *The principle of habit-freedom* (1 Cor. 6:12), *the principle of body-ownership* (1 Cor.6:13-20), *the principle of life-example* (chap. 8), and *the principle of self-edification* (1 Cor. 10:23) are just a few of the valuable passages in this great Corinthian letter (see the author's book, *The Family First*).

In order to implement this teaching, the church—in its Sunday School, youth groups, Children's Church programs, Bible study groups, and at all other opportunities—must bring individual Christians face to face with God's truth for Christian living. Avoiding mere don'ts, we want people to personally apply biblical principles as the way out of the woods of worldliness.

How to Choose Teaching Methods

When John Wesley began to promote an organized approach to the communication of the Gospel, he was sarcastically dubbed a "Methodist" by his Oxford classmates. There is a disorganized way to go about the process of communication of truth and there is also an organized way. Wesley's success, demonstrated by his place in history, is a strong argument for the latter.

CONSIDERATIONS IN SELECTING A METHOD

The word "method" simply describes the processes and techniques used by a teacher in communicating information from himself to his students. Because classes differ in such various factors as interests, mental abilities, and attention spans, a teacher should use teaching methods that are *appropriate for his group*. Children have *learning characteristics* that differ considerably from those of adults, so teaching methods that may be effective with adults will not necessarily achieve communication with children.

Another major factor is the *objective of the lesson*. What goals should be accomplished in the classroom period? Can the goals chosen be achieved best through a large amount of pupil participation, or do they require transmission of a generous portion of content? The teacher's clear understanding of his lesson goals will help determine how he goes about accomplishing them. Apart from the crucial concern for biblical theology, there is no more central importance in preparing to teach than a clarification of objectives.

In many years of working with college and seminary students preparing to be teachers, I have found their major collective hang-up to be a clumsy construction of teaching objectives. As Findley B. Edge has well reminded us in his book *Teaching for Results* (Broadman), good teaching objectives should be brief enough to be remembered, clear enough to be written down, and specific enough to be achieved.

More recent emphases focus on the necessity of writing objectives in terms of student behavior. For example, rather than saying, "To help the class realize the importance of daily prayer," one could rewrite that objective to look like this: "The student will understand the importance of daily prayer and begin a program of daily personal devotions." Such an objective is brief, clear, specific, and describes something that a teacher wants to see happen in the life of each student. When this kind of objective is developed, the road to selection of method can be walked more easily.

Still a third factor is the *content of the lesson* itself. A historical lesson from the Book of Acts for high schoolers could lend itself well to an illustrated presentation with the use of Bible maps. On the other hand, the principles of Christian separation expounded by the Apostle Paul in the sixth chapter of 1 Corinthians would be handled better in that same class through open discussion. One of the dangers in applying this factor is the constant temptation to offer excuses for one's lack of variety in teaching methodology. Many teachers excuse their excessive use of the lecture method by suggesting that the *amount* of content, or perhaps the *nature* of the content, requires that approach. Actually, they are probably guilty of not thinking creatively with regard to methodology.

The three factors just enumerated are perhaps the most important criteria for choosing teaching methods. Additional items include *available resources, educational backgrounds* of the students, and the important *time allotment* for the teaching period. A thinking teacher is aware of all these variable issues and applies them in his preparation.

TYPES OF METHODS

The variety of teaching methods is almost limitless. Perhaps it may be helpful to think in terms of categories of method. We can group them according to the type of communication they afford.

For example, one type of communication emphasizes the teacher as the performer in the educational process. One might call it *teacher-to-student communication*. Within this category such methods as lecture, storytelling, and demonstration are included. Obviously, these methods are primarily monological. They lend themselves to large groups, and learners who do minimal preparation for the classtime.

Usually teachers with less training and experience tend to gravitate toward this category since it is easier to use than most of the others. Unfortunately, they form habit patterns that persist years later after they have gained experience worthy of a greater variety of teaching methods. As someone has said, the only bad method is the one that is used all the time.

A second general category of method might be called *student-to-teacher communication*. This is a monologue in the other direction. The student performs and the teacher plays somewhat of a listening role. In this category we would expect to find such methods as recitation, reports, and testing. Obviously, such student performance must be planned and motivated by the teacher, but communication is still basically on a one-way track. Here the preparation time for the student is increased. He must know before the class period what is expected of him and how he should utilize his preparation time.

Two-way communication between teacher and student is another approach to teaching methodology. In the opinion of many professional educators this category exceeds the first two in effectiveness. It emphasizes an involvement of both teacher and student in the mutual quest for truth. The method called "Question and Answer" is distinguished from the method called "Discussion" by the kind of questions asked. When teaching by question and answer, the teacher either asks or answers objective questions usually based on some item of a factual nature. In discussion, thought questions are used. These generally lead the class to penetrate the subject with a much higher degree of perception and perspective. The discussion teacher spends a considerable amount of his teaching time preparing the kind and sequence of questions he will use. Successful implementation of two-way teaching depends on mutually effective preparation by both teacher and student.

Group activities represent yet a different kind of teaching method. There is a wide range of group activity that can be utilized as teaching methods, and its use is finding increasing attention and development in education. The emphasis here is on multiple involvement. Methods such as panels, debates, buzz groups, and all forms of drama could be categorized here. The collective planning, preparation, and participation contribute much to the learning experience of the class as a whole.

Teachers who work with smaller children would certainly want to include *instructive play* as a category of method. Methods in this list are generally used with children from the earliest years of instruction up through junior age: various kinds of games and toys, use of a sand table, puppets, finger plays, puzzles and contests, action songs, and simple role playing. At one time in the history of education it was thought that fun and learning were not compatible. Now we know, however, that interest is one of the important keys to learning, and good elementary teaching incorporates as much instructive play as possible.

A final category that might be designated could be called *"nonclassroom activity."* In all serious education the teacher is concerned that students prepare themselves for class by studying in advance. Guided preparation, carefully related to class sessions, can contribute much to mental and spiritual growth. Nonclassroom activity, however, refers to anything that happens outside of class, provided that it is a part of a planned instructional effort. Sometimes it happens before a given class session, and sometimes it takes the form of follow-up or carry-through. Such methods as field trips, guided research, and various kinds of projects fall into this general category.

A teacher who wishes to be really effective in methodology will be sure that his teaching is characterized by variety. In developing variety it is important for a teacher to become acquainted with various methods and use lesson plans for analysis of his methodology over a period of time. Variety of methodology implies an understanding of what happened in the past and insists that records be available to compare teaching strategy over a period of time.

A teacher's own attitude toward his ministry is important. If he recognizes teaching as genuine service for Christ, which must meet high standards, he may see variety as one of those standards of excellence toward which he must constantly be striving. A conscientious teacher can learn new methods by reading helpful literature on instruction, watching effective teachers in action, and attending workshops and conferences. In the final analysis, however, he will have to experiment, because continual effort and experience are a necessary part of the teaching process.

How to Communicate with Children

The greatest responsibility of God's people is not to the child but to his parents. Contemporary Christian educators all emphasize the importance of a family-centered church. New Testament priorities call for a focus on dad and mom and a ministry to the family unit in accordance with scriptural patterns.

But the Bible also reveals a clear love for children and an awareness of their significance. Jesus called children to Him on two occasions recorded in the Gospels (Matt. 18:2-6; 19:13-15), and there may have been many other times that are not recorded.

But many parents and teachers of children have difficulty communicating on a child's level. They forget that communication is the process of one person speaking to another in a language common to both—it is a *meaning exchange* rather than just a *word exchange*. In this chapter we will assume the importance of a loving teacher, the dynamic of the Holy Spirit, a Bible-centered curriculum, and adequate facilities. We will center on the principles of communication which enable children to learn better at home and in a classroom

PROPERLY GRADED GROUPS

Peer influence is an important factor with children as well as with teenagers. Knowledge levels, socialization and developmental task procedures are all facilitated if we teach children in groups which are as homogeneous as possible.

To be sure, the currently popular classroom seems like a violation of this time-honored principle, but remember that an open classroom rarely works with effectiveness unless one has very adequate facilities and a highly skilled team of teachers. In most cases we do not have either of these in the Christian home or the Sunday School. So we try to teach children the way God made them, one step at a time, associating new information with that which is already known (apperception), and giving the serious teacher an opportunity to work as much as possible with students who are at the same learning level.

CHURCH-HOME COOPERATION

The historic emphasis of God's truth is always centralized in the home. In the early days of the Old Testament, particularly when the Children of Israel spent forty years crossing the Sinai Peninsula, "home" was virtually the only center for growth and learning. Later on it was supplemented by more formal worship and educational institutions, notably the rabbinical schools of the postexilic times. But even as the New Testament opened, the synagogue had hardly displaced the home in importance but rather served as a supplement to the God-ordained teaching family.

The church has made great progress in its thinking on this recently, but we still have a long way to go. The development of parent-teacher fellowships and open houses in church educational ministries is just now beginning to find favor among conservative groups.

DEVELOPMENTAL TASK READINESS

This is the stair-step process I mentioned earlier. One truth must be built on a previous truth, as if a student were walking up the steps of learning. In the teaching of reading it could be demonstrated by sight recognition of a letter, sound reproduction of that letter, psychomotor skill in writing that letter, seeing the combination of letters to form words, and so forth.

A teacher who really wants to communicate with children in the home or at school must find out where those children are in their learning levels and prepare a developmental task pedagogy based on each child's readiness. This is extremely difficult to do when one is trying to teach too many children or children of too varied ability levels.

SENSORY EXPERIENCE

Though probably true of adults as well, it is particularly significant that children learn best through hearing, seeing, touching, smelling, and tasting. That fact alone points out that a home is a better place for learning than a school. It presents such reality, whereas a creative school teacher is constantly trying to produce representations of reality which so often turn out to be plastic or contrived situations.

The application of the principle is really very simple. The more physical or sensory experiences we can build into the learning procedures of a child, the better he will learn.

RELATIONSHIP TERMINOLOGY

Have you noticed how often children use the possessive adjective "my"? They constantly talk about "my daddy, my house, my class," and relate everything to themselves. They are, in short, constantly self-referential.

At first, parents and teachers are tempted to think this represents some kind of selfishness which must be purged from a child's thinking. But it is really quite normal because he is simply seeing everything by the only common measure he knows— himself.

To be sure, relationship terminology could get out of hand and turn into blatant egotism. But a teacher who wants to communicate with children will sense where the line should be drawn and use the positive benefits of relationship orientation to the best advantage.

CONCRETE IDEAS

Here we have a real problem. Children tend to think only in terms of concrete ideas, and they avoid abstracts. Their minds simply have a low tolerance level for things which cannot be measured, weighed, or touched. So an abstract concept runs counter to their dependence on sensory experience. Yet so many Christian truths are abstract—love, grace, peace, eternal life, and so forth. We must be extremely careful in trying to communicate these truths to children, avoiding heavy abstract theology.

SYMBOLISM

This is part of the answer to the problem we have with abstract concepts. Children can think of abstract truths through symbols, though not everyone agrees that the use of symbolism is good for children. Frankly I don't see how we can avoid it. God's sovereignty might be understood by the symbol of a crown, His love by the symbol of a heart, and His eternality by the symbol of a circle.

Of course, all symbols are inadequate at best; but since we can't deal with these important truths in concrete fashion, we are almost forced to use symbols to carry out the communication we so desperately desire. Here again a warning must be issued against going overboard. Sometimes we can press so hard to drive home a certain truth through using symbols that we cause a child to confuse a symbol with a reality. A cross may represent Christ, but it is not to be worshiped. A church may be the house of God; but if it is sold and turned into a boys club, no sacrilege has been committed because, as God has told us, He does not dwell in temples made with human hands (Acts 17:24).

IMAGINATION

Children are naturally imaginative because their creativity has not been stifled by tradition. It is amazing how we force children into adult ways of doing things, rigidly structuring their behavior and lives as well as their learning patterns. Then when they get to college we offer them special electives in creative thinking so they can learn how to do what we taught them not to do during their earlier years!

Though we should certainly never lie to children, even by allowing them to believe that such mythical beings as Santa Claus and the Easter bunny are real, there is value in sharing fairy tales and the world of imagination with children.

Child psychologist Bruno Bettelheim, in *The Uses of Enchantment* (Knopf), suggests that the two experiences which most strengthen a child's ability to find meaning in life are the impact of parents and others who take care of the child and the cultural heritage as transmitted through folk fairy tales.

Without diminishing the importance of reality and truth, or in any way giving fairy tales a place equal to the Scriptures, we can certainly develop the imagination and utilize the creative faculties of a child, thereby enabling him to learn to solve problems in life—an ability somehow absorbed unconsciously when he reflects on the meanings of stories. This may be why storytelling is such an effective method for teaching children.

INTERACTION

We talk a great deal about interaction when we teach young people or adults, but not enough with children. To be sure, teaching a class of preschoolers or even primaries is not a first-line opportunity for serious discussion. But the question and answer technique *can* be used, and children can be led through a series of carefully constructed questions to make applications of truth to their own lives rather than being always told what they should do and what God expects of them. Answering questions not only applies the truth of the moment; it also gives an opportunity for the child to develop the processes of reasoning, which is certainly the goal of all serious teaching in both home and school.

Some of the most interesting conversations a child-loving adult can have are with little folk. Their mixture of fantasy and reality, their quaint way of bluntly expressing anything they think, and their unique views of the world are the material of which the most interesting television interviews are made.

LIVING MEANINGS

Too often we try to explain to children why what we are teaching them will be of value someday. With a little effort, we can demonstrate the significance and value of truth *now*. Scripture memorization, a part of every effective Sunday School curriculum, is important, but never at the expense of comprehension. A child must understand and internalize what he is memorizing if lasting value is to result.

So, if you are a parent or a teacher of children, take a fresh look at the task God has given you. Consider yourself privileged to deal with these little ones whom Jesus thought so precious and whose angels guard them every moment of every day.

But don't be content just to spray them with words. Make sure that an understanding and loving communication, an interchange of meanings, results when you seek to carry out your ministry of communicating with children.

One more thought. These are skills which are learned. You may have the gift of teaching and a call from God to use it with children. But many hours of study and preparation are essential if you really want to be an outstanding teacher of children. In order to really improve your communication skills, learn children's characteristics, their needs, and their uniquenesses.

How to Teach Hyperactive Children in the Church

Occasionally one finds in Christian journals and magazines an article on special education with reference to either gifted children or slow learners. More rare are articles dealing with physically disabled or retarded children and how evangelical Christian education can meet their needs through local churches.

Virtually nonexistent, however, have been the treatments of a problem that is all too common in Christian homes and conservative churches—hyperactivity in preschool and elementary children. Much of the research on which this chapter is based is not my own but rather that of Mrs. Cathy Phillips, previously a graduate student under my supervision and now a missionary with her husband at the Portuguese Bible Institute in Lisbon. Her work should not be left sitting on a shelf; so I am taking this opportunity to share some of its implications with Christian parents and church leaders.

Hyperactivity is usually defined in terms of excessive movement. A hyperactive child is one who cannot sit still. She appears to be in perpetual motion. Such a definition, however, refers only to the amount of movement the child evidences.

An adult may exhibit excessive amounts of activity too; but in contrast with a hyperactive child, she is not considered a nuisance. The adult's behavior is labeled energetic, hard-working, enthusiastic, and ambitious. The same amount of activity exhibited by a hyperactive child would probably be called irritating, erratic, nervous, and uncontrolled. The difference is not primarily in the *quantity* of the behavior but rather in its quality. A "hyperactive" adult has channeled his actions into socially acceptable outlets, whereas a hyperactive child has not learned to do so.

Werry and Sprague define hyperactivity as "a disorder of movement which results in conflict with a social environment because of the amount of movement and/or its inappropriateness to the situation" ("Hyperactivity," in *Symptoms of Psychopathology,* edited by C.G. Costello, John Willey & Sons, Inc.).

CHARACTERISTICS OF HYPERACTIVITY

A hyperactive child may be identified by certain characteristic behaviors, learning difficulties, or "soft" neurological findings. No one child evidences all these signs, but if a teacher suspects that a child in her class may be hyperactive, she should observe the student carefully. The presence of many of the following characteristics in one individual *may* indicate what medical personnel call "the hyperactive syndrome."

What are these characteristics? Most authorities agree that many or all of the following terms can be used to describe hyperactive children: restless, fidgety, inattentive, easily distracted, highly excitable, hard to manage, unable to sit still, unable to take frustration (explosive), impulsive, irritable, and immature.

A study by Steward, reported in *The Scientific American* (April 1970), compares symptoms of hyperactivity that were observed in children already identified as hyperactive and another group of children that were identified as well-adjusted. Hyperactive children generally have a much higher incidence of inappropriate behavior in the eyes of parents and other adults, the study concluded.

CAUSES OF HYPERACTIVITY

Why does a hyperactive child have learning problems? One hypothesis suggests that *neurological impairment* causes learning difficulties, a view that gains strength by the fact that certain stimulating drugs can produce remarkable changes in the behavior patterns of a hyperactive child.

Though this may well be true in the case of some hyperactivity, it is imperative to note that not all hyperactive children have brain damage and that not all children with brain damage are hyperactive. So there must be other explanations for hyperactivity in addition to neurological deficiencies.

Another theory suggests that *increased physical activity* disrupts the attention to a task and thus prevents accurate intake of information. Successful learners are able to modulate activity, especially during crucial points of problem-solving. Unsuccessful learners cannot do this, and their *uninhibited movement destroys the concentration* necessary for accurate intake of information.

A third explanation of hyperactivity suggests that hyperactive children have *disturbed and speeded-up decision-making processes*. Kagan's 1966 study of impulsive and reflective children revealed that impulsive children make rapid decisions with many errors. On the other hand, reflective chidren take longer and make decisions with fewer errors (cited by Barbara Keogh, "Hyperactivity and Learning Disorders: Review and Speculation," *Exceptional Children,* October 1971).

If hyperactive children lack an ability to slow down their decision-making processes, it could partially explain the poor showings that such children often make in school and church learning situations.

A nonprofessional teacher (one who is not medically trained) may *tentatively* identify a hyperactive child by carefully observing his actions and comparing them with the characteristics we have discussed. Knowledge of the causes of hyperactivity may also help you to be more patient with a child who "misbehaves" in class. It is possible that a misbehaving student may not be mischievous. She may suffer from a malady that can be handled only after careful examination by a specialist. Be patient with the child, alert the parents to the *possibility* of hyperactivity without labeling the child "hyperactive," and offer whatever information you can.

METHODS OF TREATMENT

There are several methods of treatment used for hyperactivity with a good deal of variety in their recommendations and successes. The use of *drugs* to help control the hyperactive child has been employed since 1917 when Charles Bradley, of the Emma Pendleton Bradley Home, discovered that stimulating drugs tend to calm hyperactive children.

Both stimulants and depressants are initially administered in small doses and gradually increased until a satisfactory reduction in hyperactivity is obtained or until negative side effects appear.

A second approach to handling hyperactivity is through a *controlled environment.* Pioneers in this approach include Straus and Lehtinen, who in 1947 designed a clinical classroom that paved the way for later developments in controlled environment studies.

Their classroom was guided by six principles: a nondistracting school environment; individualized instruction; an elemental rather than a global approach to teaching (for example, a child learns individual letters, and later those letters are assembled into words); attention being focused on relevant materials through the use of colors and dividers; physical activity being used to enhance learning; and emphasis placed on basic subjects (*Exceptional Children in the Schools,* edited by Dean K. McIntosh and Lloyd M. Dunn, Holt, Rinehart and Winston).

Some experts believe *behavior modification* to be the best approach because, unlike the two previous methods, it provides for learning specific and appropriate behavior. The aim of behavior modification (as is that of all conditioning) is to extinguish unacceptable behavior and promote acceptable alternatives.

The primary means for accomplishing behavioral modification is the engineered classroom, which is designed to minimize hyperactive behavior and maximize academic success. It utilizes behavioral modification to reward the child for any socially acceptable actions he may display. The engineered classroom is a practical outworking of this technique in an actual classroom setting.

Progressive relaxation is another approach to treating hyperactive children. When moving a muscle, most children can differentiate between the muscle they move and the rest of their bodies. Tension or *tonus* is built up in the muscle to be moved while the other muscles remain comparatively relaxed. The hyperactive child, however, cannot make this distinction.

Whenever a hyperactive child moves a part of his body, the *tonus* of the whole body increases so much that even though the movement is made with maximum energy, *tonus* of the moving part is little higher than that of the rest of the body. Consequently, a hyperactive child is always under tension. Progressive relaxation seeks to teach the hyperactive child to relax one part of his body at a time, starting with his extremities and moving inward toward the center of his body, part by part.

Any teacher in school or church education can use this approach simply by creatively utilizing rest periods. As the children are lying down on mats or rugs, the teacher can help the hyperactive child by leading the entire class in this kind of relaxation technique without any reference to its particular purpose.

Ministering to the Hyperactive Child

Picture a "normal" Sunday School class of approximately eight to ten children. The subject matter to be taught will be predetermined by the use of a commercially prepared curriculum series. Suggestions for specific reference to a hyperactive child, however, can be built into any existing curriculum.

One of the crucial aspects of such a program is a *careful approach to discipline.* That discipline should be both preventive and corrective since both types will doubtless be needed with the hyperactive child. Remember that each hyperactive child will need *more personal attention,* even to the point of individualized instruction. Such children especially benefit from this attention because they tend to suffer from feelings of defeat and inadequate self-esteem.

Obviously, *modeling a role* (displaying proper behavior) is extremely important. Additionally, the use of *reinforcement* or reward for appropriate behavior utilizes the previously identified behavioral modification patterns. A good dose of *reality therapy,* helping the child to become aware of the natural or normal consequences of behavior, is useful. Sometimes even *physical restraint* is needed, though these last two methods should be employed only in conjunction with parental guidance.

All children become restless when a teacher does too much talking, and this is especially true of the hyperactive child. His attention span is shorter than others in his age-group. Obviously, the more active the class is, the less out of step the hyperactive child will seem.

To sum up, a Christian teacher of children, especially a teacher of hyperactive children, must have a style of life that demonstrates her love for the Lord. Her study of Scripture must be visible in life. She must honestly share from her own experiences, spend time with students, and allow students to share in learning experiences. Above all she must expect her students to grow in their Christian lives.

Rather than being disappointed or discouraged by the presence of a hyperactive child in your class, you should see this as an opportunity for God to teach you the fruit of the Spirit through the child.

A Christian teacher of a hyperactive child will especially have to be patient, sensitive, gentle but firm, faithful, and joyous. There are times when a hyperactive child aggravates his teacher beyond the limits of human endurance, but we should depend on the indwelling Spirit of God to empower us for effective ministry—even to hyperactive children.

How to Teach Teens a Christian World View

We talk a great deal in evangelical Christianity about a "holistic" view of man and the world. Presumably by this we mean an analysis of the total universe (or at least that portion of it with which we are acquainted) from a "divine viewpoint," attempting to see things as God sees them.

Another word that is important when we begin to talk about a Christian world view is the term "integration." In my classes, I frequently refer to the "integration of faith and learning," attempting to show students how the truth of God's revelation, both natural and special, relates to every aspect of sudents' lives and has an important impact on the way they deal with everyday things and ideas.

Where should young people learn this view? At home? Obviously they should, but most parents are not equipped to explain the theological significance of social and cultural issues to their children and young people.

What about the Christian elementary school? Again, serious attempts should be made, and indeed are being made, in many schools to thoroughly integrate the curriculum so that every subject is taught from a biblical point of view. But many teachers are untrained in theology or philosophy and are unable to see the relationship of their particular subject matter's fields to God's greater revelation, which should dominate the thinking of every true believer.

Is a Christian college any help? It ought to be, or it has no right to be called "Christian." Every Christian institution of higher learning has a responsibility for developing a distinctively Christian world view in the minds and lives of its students.

But isn't there another alternative, something the church can do? Is there any way that Sunday School and the youth group can get involved in grappling with the issues of our society from the biblical point of view? I think so, and some churches have already begun this kind of serious educational program.

It is the purpose of this chapter to lay down certain principles or ingredients of such a teaching process. Obviously, a special kind of teacher is needed, one who is not only well trained in theology and general education, but who is also able to see the kind of confrontational relationship that the Scriptures must maintain with the volatile pagan society around us. Some of the issues to which we have spoken arbitrarily in the past must be dealt with from a Christian point of view. Students in Sunday School as well as in Christian colleges should at least begin to grapple with a biblical outlook on their world.

The Value of the Mind

One of the essential aspects of a serious view of this kind of teaching is an appreciation of the dedicated mind. The Scriptures often speak about a Christian's use of his mind. We are to possess renewed minds (Rom. 12:2; cf. Eph. 4:23).

Paul prayed that the church at Colosse might be filled "with the knowledge of His will through all spiritual wisdom and understanding. And we pray this in order that you may live a life worthy of the Lord and may please Him in every way: bearing fruit in every good work, growing in the knowledge of God" (Col. 1:9-10). Notice the emphasis on mental processes and thinking in those verses.

Perhaps the key passage, however, is Luke 10:27, where Jesus afffirmed the validity of a lawyer's statement when he said: "Love the Lord your God with all your heart and with all your soul and with all your strength and with all your mind; and love your neighbor as yourself."

Churches and Sunday Schools should be centers of serious thinking. How unfortunate that both of these important educational ministries have fallen into disrepute and are almost thought of as places where one's mind is not used, rather than as places where minds are used to the greatest possible extent for the glory of Christ.

THE COUNTERCULTURAL NATURE OF CHRISTIANITY

Because God's truth *is* absolute and because certain portions of it have clearly been understood as foundational to orthodox Christianity throughout almost 2,000 years of its history, indoctrination is not an entirely objectionable form of teaching. The problem with indoctrination as a teaching technique, however, is that it tends to give itself not only to the absolutism of God's Word, the Bible, but also to absolutism concerning many relative issues that have grown up as cultural patterns in our day.

In one respect we say that Christianity is "countercultural" because the prevailing norm in almost any culture at any time leans in the direction of Satan, the god of this world. Perhaps a better word, however, would be "transcultural," emphasizing the fact that God's truth is not locked into any time or space frames, but speaks to every age where it is and when it is.

The people of God have always been a minority, and in many cases they have been a persecuted minority. They ran counter to the Roman culture in the first century to such a degree that they were hunted down and killed for their faith. That should not have been surprising, because Jesus predicted precisely such a reaction from the barbarian society in which His message would be proclaimed: "Remember the words I spoke to you: No servant is greater than his master. If they persecuted Me, they will persecute you also. If they obeyed My teaching, they will obey yours also. They will treat you this way because of My name, for they do not know the One who sent Me" (John 15:20-21).

Many churches are changing their focus from buildings, budgets, and programs to Bible study, discipleship, and helping people. They have seen that even the church in its organizational framework has been caught in the web of a culture that equates "good" with "big" and creates a cursed bureaucracy out of everything it spawns.

THE CHRISTIAN VIEW OF MEANING IN LIFE

Existential novelists have been telling us for several decades that humanism gone sour in the form of nihilistic existentialism has no answers for people in this confused world. Jean Paul Sartre came to the existentialist's only ultimate conclusion in his play *No Exit*—death is the final absurdity in a life of irrationalism.

The Christian answer is that meaning in life is impossible without morality, and morality is impossible without spiritual values. The believer responds to confusion and pessimism by affirming that a meaningful life takes its cue from the person of Jesus Christ. In other words, meaning comes from *outside* the human dilemma rather than from being dredged up by some kind of humanistic solution in the melting pot of man's sinful mind. C.S. Lewis has stated it as well as anybody since the Apostle Paul when he wrote in *Mere Christianity*:

> I am trying here to prevent anyone saying the really foolish thing that people often say about Him: "I'm ready to accept Jesus as a great moral Teacher, but I don't accept His claim to be God." That is the one thing we must not say. A man who was merely a man and said the sort of things Jesus said would not be a great moral teacher. He would either be a lunatic—on the level with the man who says he is a poached egg—or else he would be the Devil of Hell. You must make your choice. Either this man was, and is, the Son of God: or else a madman or something worse. You can shut Him up for a fool, you can spit at Him and kill Him as a demon; or you can fall at His feet and call Him Lord and God. But let us not come with any patronizing nonsense about His being a great human teacher. He has not left that open to us. He did not intend to (The Macmillan Company).

THE BIBLICAL ANSWERS TO CRUCIAL QUESTIONS

It seems that three central words describe most of the truly important questions being asked in contemporary Western culture—truth, morality, and ethics. Almost every problem we face, from sexual deviation to income tax fraud, from murder to international terrorism, is linked to these concepts.

The overall problem stems from the fact that our society has abandoned God's absolutes and chosen a relativistic view of human issues. As far as morality goes, man is perverted and cruel; but he has not always been so. Adam was not created cruel, but changed himself by his decision to go against God's plan. God, in His matchless and undeserved grace, has given man the possibility in Christ to opt out of his immorality and confusion. Man's way is the way of sin and death. If cruelty is abnormality, normality in Christ offers hope and peace and love. That requires a God big enough for absolutes.

Of course, even before morality is the question of truth. If I were to sketch it in a frame of deteriorating order, I would say that relative truth gives birth to relative morality, which in turn gives birth to relative ethics. Clark Pinnock suggested "an answer from the outside" when he spoke about the Christian's response to relative truth:

> The first problem to be cleared up is that of relativism. How is man to arrive at ultimate truth from his finite perspective within the human situation? By himself he cannot. But Jesus Christ, in whom God acted in time/space history, tipped us off to the nature of ultimate reality. Had He not come, how could we possibly transcend our cultural limitations and discover the real meaning of life and history? The Christian message is terribly exciting because it presents a solution which does not just bubble up out of the human situation, but comes to us from outside the flux of historical reality (*Live Now, Brother,* Moody).

When a man's concepts of truth and morality have been set straight and put in conformity with biblical patterns, then ethics will follow. A Christian businessman who genuinely believes what the Bible has to say about honesty and respect for government cannot cheat on his corporate or personal income tax.

A high school student who claims to know Christ must understand that no situation can legitimatize his cheating on an examination.

THE IMPORTANCE OF ROLE MODELS

Of course, all of this is possible only when students are able to see a model Christian world view lived out before them. They can be taught the components and try to put together their own version, but ultimately they must be able to see a practical demonstration of how truth fits into life.

The call for this kind of leadership is not a new one, but its relevance continues to the present hour. Speaking at the opening of the 101st session of Princeton Theological Seminary on September 12, 1912, J. Gresham Machen issued this challenge:

> The church is waiting. The church is waiting for men of another type. Men to fight her battles and solve her problems....They need not all be men of conspicuous attainments, but they must all be men of thought. They must fight hard against spiritual and intellectual indolence. Their thinking may be confined to narrow limits. But it must be their own. To them theology must be something more than a task. It must be a matter of inquiry. It must lead not to successful memorizing, but to genuine convictions.

How to Minister to College Students

What percentage of American young people go to church? Do you know? Well, you can be sure that it is lower than it was thirty years ago, but you may be surprised to know that it has not dropped since 1971. According to the Gallup organization, in 1967 four out of ten young adults attended church in a typical week. The proportion declined to about three in ten by the beginning of the 1970s, where it has remained.

Overall, adult patterns show 49 pecent church attendance in 1955 with a fairly steady drop-off (with the exception of 1958, which was also 49 percent) to a low of 40 percent in 1971, which has remained stable from that year right on into the 1980s.

Obviously, statistics for *evangelical* churches would be considerably higher among both youth and adults, but I was fascinated that the national statistic for church attendance is reportedly as high as 40 percent.

In this chapter I want to talk about college students in three categories. I am relating those three categories to the ministry of a local church, rather than to a denominational ministry on campus or to parachurch organizations.

Your Own Young People
Away at College

This is the category with which you as a church leader are most concerned. First of all, there is the matter of guarding the spiritual investment you have in these young people. But not only that, it is conceivable that they will return from college, settle again in your town, and become responsible adult leaders in the church.

The result which we are seeking is to create an attitude on the part of the students which will never let them forget their church and which will also make them anxious to return home to share with the members they learned to love and appreciate during their precollege years. Let me suggest four ways in which that attitude can be cultivated by a home church:

1. *Financial support.* Students from your church, when genuine need is demonstrated, who go to Christian colleges and seminaries should receive some kind of financial support from the church. The amount of support would depend on a number of factors, such as need, academic status, and the prospect of ministry. My own bias suggests that a student attending Bible college or seminary should get more consideration because the church is thereby investing not only in the student but also in the production of a servant for the church.

2. *Faithful prayer.* The church should not only pray for its students away at college, but it should let them *know* it is praying. Some churches identify a "student of the week," listing his name in the bulletin, praying for him on Sunday morning as well as at prayer meeting, and in general reminding the congregation to keep that person's name before the Lord during that week.

3. *Regular two-way communication.* Letters to and from the student, church bulletins sent to him each week, personal notes from members of the congregation as well as official notes from the pastor—all of these are important in the life of a student. No, he might not tell you he appreciates them, and he might not take the time to answer. But every time he goes to his mailbox (and college students away from home spend a good deal of time going to mailboxes!) and finds a letter from the church or someone in the church, it is another reminder that he has not been forgotten at home.

4. *Recognition and ministry.* Most young people away at college come home at one time or another. When they are home, *put them to work.* They ought to be giving testimonies, sharing in public services through music or other kinds of ministry, working in Vacation Bible School, and in general demonstrating that their involvement at a Christian college has taught them to be church leaders. You are not only giving them experience and opportunities for service, but are also checking on the faithfulness that college maintains to the ministry of the local church!

STUDENTS ATTENDING CHRISTIAN COLLEGES IN YOUR TOWN

If you are fortunate enough to be involved in a local church that is in a city or town which is also the home of a Christian college, Bible college, or seminary, you have much to be thankful for—access to library facilities, concerts, and other events held on the campus, internationally known speakers coming to speak to the students, and the frequent ministry of faculty members in pulpit and classroom.

But ministering to students in a college town requires a distinct skill on the part of a local church. Invariably students will gravitate to certain churches in a city while ignoring the vast majority of other congregations unless forced to attend by virtue of a Christian service assignment. Why is this so? What attracts Christian college students to certain local churches?

1. *They want to be wanted for themselves.* Too often a local church looks at the Christian college or seminary student as "free help." The standard procedure of calling the Christian service director and procuring six Sunday School teachers to fill slots left vacant by unwilling local workers is a common occurrence on Christian college campuses. Not that the ministry of Christian college students through the Christian service department is not a valid one; by all means, put your request in early. But the students want to be wanted and loved as individual persons, not just as students, Sunday School teachers, and youth directors.

2. *Design programs for them.* Imagine the frustration of a college student who comes to your church to participate as a

leader in a Children's Church program, but who has nowhere to go during the Sunday School hour because there is no college-age class. Consider the personal needs of a student who really wants to get involved in your church and has ample opportunity to do so as far as *service* is concerned, but who never reads in the bulletin that there is going to be a college skating party or a college and career class progressive dinner or a similar social event.

3. *Tie the college students to your church in some official way.* One of the complaints that churches have is that college students from a Christian college come and go. They are not dependable; they do not attend all the services; they may even switch churches in the middle of the year, if not in the middle of the semester. All of these criticisms are justified. These things do happen.

To some extent, the particular college is to blame if it does not encourage its students to be faithful in a certain local church for at least one year at a time. And, of course, the students must shoulder some of the blame because college-age young people are not yet fully mature, and they do not always make good judgments on important things such as church attendance and involvement.

But one way to alleviate the deficiencies which may be created by the college and the student is to design some program at the church that will tie that young person to your church for at least a year. I recommend "associate" or "collegiate" membership which is nonvoting and does not force the student to give up his regular membership at his home church.

4. *Keep the quality of preaching and teaching high.* There is nothing that will turn college students away from your church more quickly than deficient preaching or inadequate teaching in the college-age class. Keep in mind that these young people are under the instruction of professionals five days a week.

If you want to attract Christian college students to your church and keep them, the college class must be relevant and open-ended. Select a teacher who really has a love for students and who wants to meet their needs, even though they are temporary visitors in the congregation.

STUDENTS ATTENDING A SECULAR UNIVERSITY IN YOUR TOWN

You say you are interested in missions? Well, look around you. If you happen to live in a university town, God may send some pagans to your doorstep. Of course, they are not all pagans, and you will want to be ministering to the Christian young people in that state university as well as evangelizing the unsaved.

1. *Don't forget to emphasize retention among your own young people.* Not all of your Christian young people go away to college. Many stay right in town to attend a local Christian college or perhaps the secular community college or university. Many others go to work instead of to college. It is extremely important that you draw close to them and draw them close to you during these important years. The key word is *retention*. Students and nonstudents can be retained by using techniques similar to those one would use with Christian college students.

2. *Provide brotherhood and fellowship.* I am thinking now of those students from other evangelical congregations, perhaps even from your own denomination, who come to your church because they are attending a secular university or college in your town. The key word here is *refuge*. Your congregation ought to be a haven of necessary escape from the haranguing of godless students and unbelieving professors throughout the week.

3. *Carry out an aggressive program of evangelism.* Of course, the overwhelming majority of students on a state university campus are unsaved. Can you get many to attend your church? That depends on a number of things. I go back again to the quality of the preaching and the relevance of the teaching. There is also the variable of how well your own college young people (or the Christian students who are guests in your congregation) are sharing their faith on campus and bringing their classmates to church.

The key word with unsaved students is *regeneration*. And don't think of that just in terms of students coming to church. Let your congregation develop an active program of on-campus evangelism insofar as that outreach is legal and proper. Such evangelism is best accomplished by using college students from your own congregation who love Christ and want to witness for Him.

4. *Emphasize apologetics.* For both Christian and non-Christian students in a secular university, there is no area of Christian teaching (other than the direct study of the Bible itself) more meaningful, helpful, and desired than the field of apologetics. Christian students need to know that their faith is grounded in the facts of history and can be defended intelligently. They also need to know how to carry out an intelligent defense in their educational settings.

How to Help Adults Learn

One of the most highly respected American educators of the past four decades is Dr. Robert K. Havighurst of the University of Chicago. His most recent work has been with the problems and programs of urban school districts, but to many he will be remembered for his significant book *Human Development and Education* released in 1953. His research on developmental task education was begun in 1948 and appeared first under the title *Developmental Tasks and Education*.

Simply stated, the developmental task approach to education views the learning process as a series of stair-steps, rather steep at times but "interspersed with plateaus where one can speed along almost without ,effort." Since the learning process continues from the cradle to the grave, this includes all adults; productive adulthood is greatly enhanced by an understanding of the developmental task approach to learning. Havighurst himself defines the developmental task as "a task which arises at or about a certain period in the life of the individual, successful achievement of which leads to his happiness and to success with later tasks, while failure leads to unhappiness in the individual, disapproval by the society, and difficulty with later tasks."

As an individual grows, both in size and age, he discovers new physical, emotional, and psychological resources to meet tasks of increased difficulties. The tasks themselves arise not only from physical sources (learning to walk, etc.) but also from cultural pressures (learning to read) and from the value system of the individual (learning to be a success in business, etc.).

DEVELOPMENTAL TASKS IN THE CHURCH

Recognizing the needs in terms of developmental tasks which confront the individual at various points in his life, we can then produce "teachable moments" which coincide with the needs and interests of learners. According to Havighurst, "Of all the periods of life, early adulthood is the fullest of teachable moments and the emptiest of effort to teach. It is a time of special sensitivity and unusual readiness of the person to learn." Havighurst is right not only with respect to society in general but particularly with respect to adult education in the evangelical church. The need for biblical instruction, family life education, and solid answers to the many questions raised by Christians living in a complex society is clearly evident, but the inability of many adult Sunday School classes to meet these needs is just as evident.

Havighurst identifies "early adulthood" as the years eighteen to thirty and lists eight developmental tasks to which I have added two that seem particularly relevant to Christian adults:

1. Selecting a mate.
2. Learning to live with a marriage partner and achieving a fusing of two lives into one.
3. Starting a family: having the first child successfully.
4. Raising children with accompanying adjustment to the expanding family, the whole new life of the family, and the psychological problems involved.
5. Managing a home: that is, facing the financial problems as well as the general problems of living together in the home.
6. Getting started in an occupation.

7. Taking on civic responsibility: that is, responsibility for the welfare of the group outside of the family such as a church, lodge, or political organization.
8. Finding a congenial social group.
9. Accepting one's place in the church with its accompanying decisions and responsibilities.
10. Learning to assume Christian leadership and discipline with respect to oneself, one's family, and others.

QUALITY CONTROL IN ADULT EDUCATION

If Havighurst is correct in delineating the tasks to be met and achieved during the twelve-year span involved (and there is no good educational reason to believe that he is not), then the church must recognize its responsibility to contribute to that achievement. It must abandon its blind faith that learning will somehow mystically take place if someone stands before a group of adults and talks long enough and loud enough. Christian education committees in local churches must provide satisfactory answers to the following crucial questions:

1. How can we convince adults of their ability to learn?
2. How can we provide a desire to study outside of the classroom?
3. How can we provide adequate educative situations?
4. How can we coordinate interests and needs for our adults?
5. How can we provide social and fellowship activities that will be meaningful?
6. How can we help our young adults to build Christian homes which will be integrated with the program of the church?

Adult education in many churches is plagued by some rather common problems. The problems are "common" in that the same ones seem to characterize many or perhaps even most local congregations within the evangelical camp. Adult classes are often too big; teachers of adults are often poorly trained and frighteningly uncreative; time is wasted with "opening exercises" which provide nothing more than weak singing and a few announcements which are already printed in the bulletin; and both the facilities and methodology result in monological teaching which fails to involve adults verbally or mentally in a genuine search for biblical answers to the questions of life.

The grouping of adults in Sunday School has often been determined purely on the basis of what has been done in the past without any concern for a grouping which will produce the best teaching-learning situations. We scan lots of variable factors to make a good decision on grouping: the size of the Sunday School and the adult department; the availability and quality of teachers; the currriculum; the space; and, of course, the basic traditions which have been followed down through the years. All of these are important but none alone nor all of them together can approximate the importance of the crucial question: *How can we help young adults learn?*

Some churches have experienced satisfactory results by dropping age-grouping patterns in favor of the "elective" approach which allows adults to study subjects in which they are interested or for which they feel certain needs. Of course, it is essential for the Christian Education Committee to design an elective curriculum which meets the needs and captures the interest of adults. Sometimes a combination of age-grouping with limited electives is desirable.

Perhaps there is no *best* way and certainly no simple answer to the various problems that stand between where we are now and effective adult education in the evangelical church. One thing is sure, however. A closing of that gap demands our best attention during the rest of the century.

It is also interesting how the various developmental tasks of adulthood are related to emotional maturity. One psychologist defines maturity as "the giving and receiving of affection while continuing to function creatively in life and society." Tensions in contemporary society cause people to react in withdrawal, angry panic, or irrational confrontations of their situations.

All adults have certain basic emotional needs including a sense of security, a sense of belonging, a sense of adequacy, a sense of discovery, and the necessity of expressing one's individuality. If we think of developmental tasks in relation to emotional maturity, the picture takes on a perspective of attitudes which makes desirable behavior more achievable.

MARKS OF MATURITY

Reuel Howe in *The Creative Years* argues that the creativity of modern adults has been stifled by preoccupation with security. People, he claims, are not adequately interested in present opportunities. Evidence of this preoccupation shows itself in the gross conformity to society and the chains of technocracy. According to Howe, there are certain characteristics of a mature adult:

1. The mature person is guided by long-term purposes rather than immediate desires.
2. The mature person accepts people and things the way they are rather than pretending that they are the way he wants them.
3. The mature person accepts the authority of others without rebellion or "folding up."
4. The mature person can accept himself as an authority without extreme pride or guilt.
5. The mature person can defend himself from outside offenses with his own unacceptable impulses.
6. The mature person can work without feeling he is a slave and play without feeling he ought to be working.
7. The mature person can love so satisfyingly he is not dependent on being loved.
8. The mature person is able to accept his role in the larger scheme of things.

Havighurst and Howe are by no means the only writers who have drawn our attention to the crucial learning experiences of adulthood. They do represent, however, writers who have spoken in terminology understandable by local church lay leaders. Adult education in the church is the process of bringing interests and needs into harmony with each other. The collective result is harmony with biblical patterns of mature Christian living that are succinctly developed in the Word of God.

The use of small groups to achieve this goal has catapulted into prominence within the last fifteen years. Some Christian educators see groups as a quick fix for our problems. There is no doubt that a discussion motif structured in small groups can provide the church with a new approach to meeting the needs of adults. They ought to be used and used well. The inherent danger is that small-group discussions can easily degenerate into just pooling personal opinions rather than a search for biblical insights into human problems. The leader is the key.

The 1960s represented a decade of infatuation with youth work in the local church. In the '70s we "discovered" adult education. Now we have both the resources and the research to do the job right and really help adults learn.

How to Plan Adult Education

As the sketch indicates on page 215, there is a new slide in the microscope. During the 1940s and 1950s, Christian education in the local church focused on the child. With a few exceptions, most of the books on childhood education still used in college and seminary classrooms were written in the postwar years.

Then about 1960, a new slide was placed in the microscope, and we stared down for almost two decades at teenagers. The way to have a "going church" in the early and middle sixties was to emphasize young people, program for young people, and minister to young people. At the end of that decade, we began to think about the family, and that led us during the 1970s to become aware that we can neither think of the family nor minister adequately to children and youth without a proper concern for adult education.

Now the third slide is in the microscope, and perhaps we have come for the first time in the modern Christian education movement to a focus that is both reasonable and biblical. One would like to think that we stumbled on this emphasis through our sincere efforts to conduct a well-rounded program of church education, and that may well be true.

Another influence in favor of adult education is the population shift, which is forcing us to recognize that for the rest of the century, the spotlight will be on adults. The church had better stare into its microscope and come up quickly with some plans for adult education.

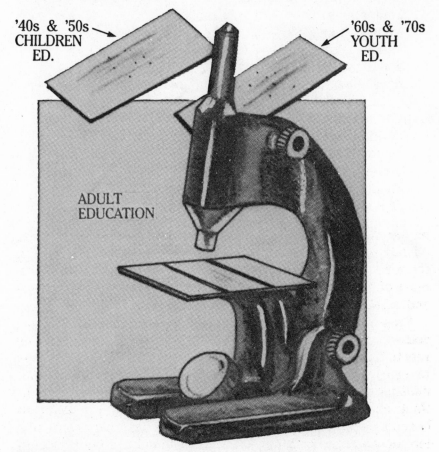

'40s & '50s
CHILDREN
ED.

'60s & '70s
YOUTH
ED.

ADULT
EDUCATION

DEMOGRAPHIC DATA

Demography is the statistical study of human populations, in an attempt to identify size, density, distribution, and other factors that tell us where people are going and what they are doing. The demographics of population shifts from 1950 to 2000 speak loudly and clearly: Adults are in.

The U.S. Department of Commerce, Bureau of the Census, has released charts entitled "Projections of the Population of the United States: 1977 to 2050." In round numbers, the charts show the population in 1950 as follows:

Children under 5—22 million
Children 5-13—17 million
Senior high teens 14-17—9 million
Young adults 18-34—40 million
Middle adults 35-64—53 million
Senior adults 65 and over—12 million

If we talk now about a future plan for church education, here is the same pattern projected for 1990:

Children under 5—19 million
Children 5-13—33 million
Senior high teens 14-17—13 million
Young adults 18-34—65 million
Middle adults 35-64—83 million
Senior adults 65 and over—29 million.

Except for the first group, children under 5, the number of people in each category will have risen between 1950 and 1990. Only the number of children under 5 is expected to be lower in 1990 than it was in 1950.

A quick look at 1970 and 1975 figures, however, shows that two other groups are also expected to be decreasing by 1990. The first group, children 5-13, is expected to go from 36 million in 1970 down to 33 million in 1990. The second group, teenagers 14-17, is expected to decrease from 17 million in 1975 to 13 million in 1990. According to these predictions, by 1990 the number of people under 18 will be decreasing.

Over the forty years between 1950 and 1990, the number of people under 18 will rise about 35 percent. And, as noted, by 1990 the number will have begun to decrease. Meanwhile, the number of people over 18 will rise by about 68 percent.

Though demographic data can be taken in various ways, in this case they seem most suggestive. They point to a pattern of ministry that the church must recognize and emphasize if it is to reach the maximum number of people during the next two decades.

DOCTRINAL DELINEATIONS

But a greater question remains than that raised by population statistics: Is adult education biblical? No aspect of Christian education could be easier to defend than the biblical and theological foundations for adult education in the church.

One can defend children's education and youth education quite nicely within the total framework of developing needs in contemporary culture. To do so through biblical exposition, however, is more difficult and may lead to distorted handling of texts, when viewed in their proper contexts. For example, Daniel, Timothy, and the three Hebrew "children" are actually references to young adults.

Perhaps no more definitive expression of adult education in the local church can be found than the words of Paul to a young pastor named Titus. He wrote: "You must teach what is in accord with sound doctrine. Teach the older men to be temperate, worthy of respect, self-controlled, and sound in faith, in love, and in endurance. Likewise, teach the older women. . . . Then they can train the younger women. . . . Similarly, encourage the young men to be self-controlled. . . . Teach slaves to be subject to their masters. . . . These, then, are the things you should teach. Encourage and rebuke with all authority. Do not let anyone despise you" (Titus 2:1-4, 6, 9, 15).

Paul's commands in Titus 2 are all aimed at adult education in the church. One catches on immediately that unless Titus carried out his role of adult educator, the ministry at Crete would be ineffective. It is a lesson we could well learn in the church today.

But ministering to adults can be difficult. To explain the problems involved, we tend unconsciously to believe that you can't teach an old dog new tricks, and we apply the saying to teaching adults. We may stress so strongly the importance of teaching children that we begin to sound as if we merely program blank children with Bible verses and precepts so that they automatically become good Christians.

In fact, no matter what a person's age, his decision to become a Christian or to live a more Christlike life is his own. By God's grace, no one is too old to change.

Spiritual change in anyone is not a matter of programming or conditioning. When we teach, we endeavor to nurture our students' growth in the Lord. We present truths to which each student responds as an individual. We must realize that we cannot make him be what he should be, regardless of his age.

Rather, the Lord Himself works in hearts to lovingly draw people to obey Him. With this in mind, we can cope with difficulties in teaching adults, knowing that change is possible for them.

DEVELOPMENTAL DISTINCTIVES

Adults are different. They are different not only from each other but also from other age-groups we are accustomed to teaching in the church. They are different in their *view of self,* much more aware of personal needs and the immediacy of learning. Educational settings for adults need to be psychologically, physically, and environmentally adult. That generally means informality, opportunities to participate, and dynamic relevance of content.

Adults are also different from children and youth in *life experience,* having stored up a wealth of background. This enables us to draw upon adults rather than just inform them. It means they should have opportunities to diagnose their own learning needs rather than have content imposed on them.

A third difference demonstrates itself in what we might call *readiness to learn.* Adults bring to the learning task much greater self-direction and willingness to "option" on issues. This ought to lead us to methods such as Scripture search and dialogue. The motivation for adult education is inseparably related to what we might call "ownership"—adult students must clearly understand that learning experiences are parts of their real lives and not contrived just to keep organizational machinery functioning.

Finally, adults are different in their *perspective of time,* possessed of a definite "now" orientation. Perhaps that is why Paul wrote that Titus ought to himself demonstrate and teach others to "live self-controlled, upright, and godly lives in this present age" (Titus 2:12). The words "in this present age" could well be translated "in the now age." Adult education focuses on immediate practicality and deals with specific problems.

So the task is before us. We can look at the real world where it is and gear up to minister effectively to adults, or we can ignore the demographic data, doctrinal delineations, and developmental distinctives and go about business as usual in the church.

Perhaps your church can begin to improve its ministry to adults by conducting a survey of adults already attending. Are they convinced that present Sunday School classes and other forms of adult education are meeting their needs? Do they come because the church provides relevant and practical help? Are they excited about inviting their friends? If not, what should be changed to make your adult education program more effective?

Adult education is a must in preparing adults for Christian leadership within home and community. It is vital for young, growing Christians to see adult models demonstrating a high level of maturity in the patterns of discipleship. Christian adults in the local church should be reflections of Christ.

In line with this modeling motif, here are six things to remember about adults:

1. They learn by their own initiative.
2. They want to know why it is important for them to learn a given subject.
3. They learn through knowledge of ideas and concepts.
4. They learn through creative participation and personalization of concepts.
5. They learn by assimilating behavior traits of a positive model.
6. They learn by practicing what they learn.

The challenge of the eighties and nineties is the challenge of adult education. Read about it; understand your present situation; then design a program to meet the challenge.

How to Evaluate Your Teaching

In church education we frequently talk about evaluating *learning* but rarely about evaluating *teaching*. Yet, we surely admit that the effectiveness of learning depends largely on the effectiveness of teaching. We need to get serious about analyzing what we are doing, how well we are doing it, and whether or not we are accomplishing stated goals.

This is not to minimize the evaluation of learning. But somehow in my own mind, I have never been able to separate the two. It seems that when we evaluate our students and what they have learned under our teaching, we are thereby evaluating ourselves and how well we have been communicating information, ideas, and attitudes.

EVALUATION BY STUDENT

Just as an effective teacher must frequently conduct an evaluation *of* students, he must also be willing to be evaluated *by* students. The teacher's evaluation of students is, in effect, an evaluation by students. Let me be specific.

Let's say that Jim Shelton gives a written test after one quarter of study in the Book of Acts with his junior high boys' class. Let's also imagine that out of a possible twenty questions, no one in the class scores higher than eight, and most of the boys answer fewer than five questions correctly. What do we conclude? Does Jim have a class of stupid boys? Is the Book of Acts too difficult? Did the boys fail to study?

Though all of these possible conclusions must be considered, I would suggest two other possibilities: Jim's failure to teach the content effectively so that the boys internalized and retained the information, and his ineffectiveness in testing.

Though I do not have space here to get into the essentials of testing as a teaching technique, let me list several guidelines which appeared in an article titled "Testing Is a Big Part of Teaching," written by Dennis Leuchtenburg (*NEA Journal,* October 1964):

Good tests give students a sense of accomplishment.

Good tests are challenging.

Good tests are fair.

Good tests teach.

Of course, a teacher's evaluation by his students is not limited to the tests which he prepares for them. He may also use some type of instrument to specifically secure information about his effectiveness. This is done frequently on college campuses and is mandatory in some colleges. Of course, such evaluation by students is most effective with junior high, senior high, and adult classes, but a more informal verbal exchange can be profitable for a teacher even in the children's division. In other words, let the people who eat the food you cook tell you how it tastes.

EVALUATION BY STAFF

Peer evaluation is important in effective teaching. Teachers in church education should not feel competitive among themselves but rather supportive. If I can learn something from you, some technique or idea you are using in your class which would work in my class, by all means share it. Or if I can give you some helpful hints to help you become a better teacher, I hope you will be willing to hear them. This kind of mutual exhortation is not only pedagogically sound; it is biblical.

But it will work only if teachers welcome the evaluation of their peers. I could hardly walk into your class, watch a class session or two, and then offer suggestions which you have not asked for and which, therefore, might be offensive. That might cause a split in our Sunday School and would do the Lord's work no good. But if you invite me to come in because you are particularly concerned about self-improvement, then we have a basis for cooperation, and perhaps I will invite you to visit my class on an exchange basis. Then our time of sharing and mutual prayer can help make both of us better teachers.

EVALUATION BY STANDARDS

Many evangelical denominations now prepare and provide standard evaluation forms for the total church education program and also for individual teachers. Publishers of Sunday School curriculum materials also have standardized guidelines which can be applied throughout an entire Sunday School and measure an individual teacher in comparison with his peers.

When this is done on a denominational basis, it gives us an even better understanding of how we compare with others who are doing the same thing we are attempting to do in our church ministries. Apart from materials produced by denominational and independent curriculum publishing houses, such forms are available in books on church education.

In one sense the following example is self-evaluation, as the title of the form suggests. In another sense, it is evaluation in accordance with previously designed standards prepared by professionals and utilized by others. It is the comparison with peers that is important in standardized evaluations. When we measure ourselves by ourselves, not much is achieved (2 Cor. 10:12).

EVALUATION BY SUPERVISORS

Every teacher is a man or woman under authority. That immediate authority may be the departmental superintendent, the general superintendent of the Sunday School, the director of some other church education program, or the Board of Christian Education. Whoever is directly responsible for the quality of teaching in a given class should also take the responsibility for evaluating that teaching.

Observation is the most effective method of evaluating teaching. A departmental superintendent should spend time in the classes of his teachers, checking on the effectiveness of their teaching.

Several things are implied here. First of all, it should be assumed that a superintendent or supervisor is an effective teacher himself and therefore has the qualifications to measure the work of other teachers. Second, the supervisor or observer must know what he is looking for when he makes the evaluation. Subjectivism can run rampant in supervisory evaluation if there is no clearly defined set of criteria. The observer must know the difference between those things which really pertain to the learning situation and those which are incidental. He must also be sufficiently flexible to allow for differences in teaching styles.

A third important guideline for supervisory evaluation is that those criteria for effectiveness mentioned above should be well known by the teachers who are being evaluated. If, for example, a certain teacher does not know that his supervisor is most concerned about the use of visual aids, he may make little effort to utilize visuals in his teaching and therefore be in for a negative report when the observer does his work.

What is of great importance is a mutual agreement of standards and objectives for the class. Some of these will be generalized throughout the Sunday School; others can be agreed on by the teacher and his observing supervisor.

Are the students attentive and interested in the lesson?

Is the classroom setting conducive to learning?

Does the teacher provide both time and initiative for interaction by the students?

Is the teacher effectively using visuals?

These sample questions are the type of thing which must be determined in advance of effective observation and evaluation by a supervisor. After the observation has taken place, several counseling sessions are in order to design a plan which will strengthen weaknesses and correct mistakes in the teaching.

EVALUATION BY SELF
In the final analysis only that teacher will improve who deliberately and designedly wants to improve. A teacher who really is concerned about quality in his teaching will seek out forms of evaluation, utilize the information he gathers, and constantly strive to be a better teacher.

A teacher who is already doing a good job is interested in evaluation so that he can do a better job, whereas a teacher who is suspect in quality probably will be offended by the thought that someone wants to check up on him.

Self-evaluation should be going on constantly. If a teacher is properly using his lesson plan, he probably will have evaluative remarks written down after each teaching session. If he is spiritually minded, he probably will be constantly praying that the Spirit of God will show him weaknesses in his teaching.

Finally, self-evaluation can be done by designing a simple form which no one need see but the teacher himself. In that way it is different from the evaluation by standards which I have described. The form on the next page is a simple self-evaluation form which I have used with teachers in various churches. It is by no means exhaustive and perhaps not even sufficiently complete. But it is a start, and any Sunday School teacher can develop or adapt a similar form for self-evaluation which will help him to constantly improve the teaching of the truth of Jesus Christ.

CHRISTIAN TEACHER
Self-Evaluation Form

1—Always; 2—Usually; 3—Rarely   Circle One

1. I spend time each day in Bible study and prayer.   1 2 3

2. I pray for each of my students by name several   1 2 3
   times a day.

3. I accept my teaching responsibilities as a direct   1 2 3
   call from God within His will.

4. I enter my classroom with clear-cut objectives   1 2 3
   for achievement.

5. I spend at least two hours per week preparing   1 2 3
   my presentation.

6. I use a variety of methods each quarter.   1 2 3

7. I use adequate visual aids to facilitate   1 2 3
   communication of the lesson.

8. I solicit and achieve student participation in the   1 2 3
   class sessions.

9. My students bring their Bibles to class and use   1 2 3
   them in class.

10. I have definite means of evaluating whether my   1 2 3
    students have learned during the week, quarter,
    or year.

11. I visit absentees.   1 2 3

12. I attend both Sunday services and prayer meet   1 2 3
    ing.

13. I take advantage of any opportunity for further   1 2 3
    training, such as conferences, workshops, read-
    ing, and so forth.

14. I make an effort to be with my students outside   1 2 3
    of class.

15. I maintain proper discipline and order in my   1 2 3
    class.

PART FOUR

STRENGTHENING TOTAL CHURCH RELATIONS

How to Develop a Family-Oriented Church

One healthy trend that the evangelical church experienced in the 1970s was a reawakening to the biblical emphasis on the importance of family life. Prior to 1968 almost no books on this significant subject had been written from an evangelical point of view. But now the shelves of Christian bookstores are giving increasing space to the growing library of volumes on this important subject. Churches that have never previously scheduled a family conference are now making it an annual affair. A renewed emphasis on adult education is being introduced in many church education programs.

Some churches are finding it difficult to make the transition. Decades of emphasis on children and youth have left their mark, and reorienting ourselves to a family ministry is difficult. We read articles about the importance of family life in the church, and occasionally we hear conference speakers emphasize this crucial aspect of ministry; yet to really put it into operation is a much more *complex* task. In this chapter it is my purpose to make eight suggestions for practical implementation of family-centeredness in a local church.

PREACH ABOUT THE CHRISTIAN HOME

One of the most educational ministries of the church is pulpit teaching. Paul reminded his readers that pastors ought to be "able to teach" (1 Tim. 3:2). Though there are numerous informal teaching situations, a pastor is cheating his congregation if he gives himself to so many tasks of the church that his schedule is too full for serious, regular study of God's Word and preparation for preaching. His primary ministry is of proclamation and teaching. If that is neglected, no substitute is satisfactory.

Preaching that will build Christian homes should include an expository treatment of the key family passages in Scripture, such as Genesis 2:7-8, 13-25; Deuteronomy 6:6-9; Psalms 127—128; 1 Corinthians 7; Ephesians 5:22-33; Colossians 3:18-21; and 1 Peter 3:1-7. Biblical principles of family living should be explained and applied to current social settings.

PROGRAM WITH FAMILIES IN MIND

Some churches develop schedules which occupy the family almost every night of the week. Apparently it is their assumption that church is the primary organization and it is the task of family members to fit themselves to the church. Biblical principles, however, indicate that the home is God's primary organization. A church should see itself in a supplementary, secondary role. It would follow, then, that a church's responsibility is to structure its programs so as to support rather than fragment family life (see chapter 38).

POPULARIZE FAMILY LIFE

The message of the importance of the family ought to be ever before the congregation. It should be standard procedure for the people to "think family" in all the things they do. This can be accomplished through the establishment of special days. Posters should decorate announcement boards, and notices should appear regularly in church bulletins and mailing pieces.

The mass media (and particularly television soaps and sitcoms) give us a negative view of family life. With the added influence of the women's liberation movement, some high school students are even concluding that they want no part of marriage and all that it brings. Part of our teaching task is to reestablish a positive outlook in the minds of our people.

PROSPECT FOR FAMILIES
One of the popular approaches to church growth in our day is the use of a busing program to reach out to various areas of a city and bring in children and young people for Sunday School. In some churches the busing program has been expanded to reach adults and even families. But as a general rule, a traditional Sunday School bus still says to parents, "We have come for your children. Go back to bed."

But prospecting for families includes more than just welcoming adults aboard the Sunday School bus. It means that the visitation program and the people who participate in it must "think family" every time they visit a home. Their task is to win families for Christ and incorporate them in the local body of Christ.

Another good approach to family outreach is what some churches have called "friendship evangelism." A Christian family from the congregation attempts to make friends with an unsaved family. This plan usually works well when the interests, geographical locations, and ages of the children of both families are similar. A Christian family takes the initiative to invite their friends on outings and into their homes and, in a generally low-key approach, shares Christ consistently with them as a family.

PLAN WITH FAMILIES IN MIND
A church considering the construction of a new educational facility can orient that facility toward any given segment of its congregation. It could be a building geared primarily for ministry to children. Or it could be a youth-centered plant. It is also possible to develop a building to minister primarily to adults. Still a different construction would emphasize family ministries.

Also, the planning of the church year and its various events will show our concern for families. Rather than camps for only youth and children, a family-oriented church develops family camps, even encouraging its parishioners to use their own trailers and tents for this kind of ministry. One church in the Midwest holds its annual Sunday School picnic as a family overnight camp-out and always selects a spot where campers and trailers can be used. Cabin facilities are available for anyone else.

A church with a family orientation will also put great emphasis on the quality of its nursery program. In addition to operating during every service, it will also be categorized into at least two compartments (cribbers and toddlers) and sometimes three (cribbers, creepers, and toddlers). The nursery should be properly staffed and, of course, kept spotlessly clean at all times.

PRAYER FOR FAMILIES

Prayer for families should be a vital part of the intercession of the pastor and also of every other member of the church staff. A church that emphasizes prayer for families may also develop a family prayer partner program. Each family is linked with another for a month, during which time they try to share ideas of family living, visit each other at least once as a family, and pray regularly for each other on a personal and specific basis. If this program is made to work effectively, not only does it increase the volume of prayer support from the congregation, but it also binds families together in a "body" relationship, which is so necessary to effective congregational unity.

PREPARE HELPFUL MATERIALS FOR FAMILIES

Commercial publishers are catching the vision for printing family-oriented helps and guides. Meanwhile local congregations can put together need-meeting packets of educational items offering information on family worship, recreation, ideas for vacations that are distinctly Christian, and many other significant activities. One church in Phoenix has developed a complete home study plan, correlated with preaching and Sunday School topics.

PURPOSE TO BE A SERVING CHURCH

Too many churches want to control rather than serve their families. They have adopted an authoritarian attitude which expects that the congregation must take priority over the lives and homes of each individual. But the biblical picture of church leadership is *service* (Acts 6:1-7; 1 Peter 5:1-5). A serving church will become a family church if it observes a few simple principles:

1. The church should concentrate on discipling people toward maturity in Christ.
2. The church should get serious about adult education.
3. The church should emphasize family units.
4. The church should not monopolize its families' time.

A church that has fragmented its ministries by emphasizing first one and then another of its age-groups can coordinate its program around a central theme of developing maturing Christian families. Such a church will soon become known in its community as a "family church."

How to Design Family Cluster Programming

As indicated in chapter 37, churches are beginning to catch on to the New Testament principle that their primary responsibilities are to *support* and *supplement* Christian homes, not to *substitute* for them. Such a welcome awareness is demonstrating itself in a number of ways: family life conferences, sermons which center more and more on the biblical emphasis of the home, and a greater concern for Sunday School classes and informal discussion groups which seek biblical answers to the questions many family members are asking.

But one of the clearest evidences is a church's willingness to restructure its program so that its centrality of emphasis is no longer on the church but rather on the homes which make up its constituency. The traditional approach to programming, particularly in a large and active church, is to grab up every night of the week for use by some Christian education agency, committee, or meeting of some kind. The "new look" in programming is almost bare by comparison. Rather than a *maximum* of evenings, now a *minimum* is the goal. Rather than tying up as much of the congregation's time as we can, now we attempt to free it. In such a program, it is apparent that the pastor and the board have been working hard to rethink and restructure a meeting-centered church.

THE PURPOSE OF FAMILY CLUSTER PROGRAMMING

Though individual churches would think about it in different ways, the kinds of objectives they are trying to achieve might well be grouped into three areas:

1. To alleviate tight schedules
2. To allow time for the family to be together at home
3. To force ourselves to avoid overloading

Before we look at each of these in greater detail, let me suggest a definition which may be helpful. Family cluster programming is an effort to capsule all activities of the church into as few nights as possible by scheduling as many concurrent activities as the building and personnel will allow.

Larry Richards stated the problem about two decades ago:

There's no doubt that the overprogrammed church, packed with activities each night of the week, breaking up the family by alternately attracting mom, then dad, then son, then daughter, is not an effective church. And overloaded laymen, tied down to too many jobs, so involved with church programs that they have no time to be involved with lost neighbors, are not effective Christians (*Moody Monthly,* January 1967).

The tight schedule we are trying to alleviate is not only the schedule of the church, if we are thinking about "church" as the organization. It is the collective pressure felt by all the people who *are* the church as they attempt to be faithful to the ministry and activity of their congregations while making a living in this busy and confusing society. It is becoming more and more difficult for churches to find workers and to attract those workers to various meetings. This is partly a result of the industrialization and urbanization which have made us citizens of a technocracy.

Allowing time for a family to be at home really has a varied pattern of concern. Family members should have time to themselves for general togetherness. They also need time to pray together and to learn how to worship as a family unit. In the article mentioned previously, Richards suggests that "the home is at least thirty-three times more significant in communicating religious faith than is the church!" Yet most of us would have to admit that many Christian families have turned over their children by default to the public school for general education and to the Sunday School and church for Christian education. *It is not the responsibility of the church to teach children and young people so much as it is our responsibility to teach parents to teach those children and young people at home.*

In a sense, the purpose of avoiding overloading is a positive factor that at first looks negative. One of the complaints against family cluster programming is that we simply cannot gather enough workers on one or two nights to have all those activities going at the same time. But the point is that we recruit workers so that each person serves at only one job (as a general rule), and something like family cluster programming may force us to stick more closely to that worthy ideal.

THE PROGRAM FOR FAMILY CLUSTER SCHEDULING

Most churches are fairly well committed to scheduling activities on at least two days of the week, Sunday and Wednesday. In some areas Thursday substitutes for Wednesday as the evening for the midweek services, but the principle is the same. We must free ourselves from the bondage and tyranny of special days. Obviously Christians will always consider Christmas, Easter, and Thanksgiving crucial to the total program of the church. But a local church will *not* collapse if its programs are moved to other nights or days of the week. Flexibility and adaptability are keys to a developing family orientation.

Having decided which weeknight we want to use, the next step in designing a family cluster is to make a list of all the ministries we now have and to specify when they meet. It will help if we know how many people attend and, of course, which leaders work with what groups. Now here is another point of flexibility. Programs should stem from objectives which are based on needs. If these needs should vanish or change, the programs may be obsolete and need either abolition or revision.

Next we try to see whether there is any way that all these meetings can be handled in our facilities on the same evening. Let's not limit ourselves in terms of thinking about where some of those activities might meet. A church in Illinois has a very small building. However, on Wednesday evenings from 6:45 to 9:30 P.M. it has found space and leaders for the following: two boys' club sessions totaling over fifty boys; three sections of Pioneer Girls with an almost equal number; twenty-five children from ages four through seven in a group called "Kids Klub"; a senior-high teenage Bible study; an adult Bible study; and choir practice. But the only way such a program could ever be possible is through the use of every bit of space in the church building, perhaps the rental of a gymnasium for the boys' club program, and the opening of a private home for one of the girls' club programs. They have not been able to schedule their visitation and committee meetings for Wednesday evenings, but these two activities and an occasional party or social event are their only transgressions of the "Sunday and Wednesday only rule."

The simple fact is that many churches unduly stretch out activities and meetings which could, with a little creative thinking, be compacted and concentrated. It is a question of emphasis. One pastor proudly told me once that he *deliberately* programs every evening of the week as fully as possible. He intends by such a schedule to keep his people away from television. It seems to me that such a view of pastoral ministry completely misses the key: to teach people how to relate biblically to their culture, considering both its banes and its blessings.

THE PROBLEMS OF FAMILY CLUSTER SCHEDULING

Surely most of the problems have become apparent already if you have read this far. Space is the tough one unless we can find rental facilities or utilize spacious family rooms and recreation rooms near the church. Availability of workers is a problem that immediately becomes obvious; but it is one that can be alleviated if we get away from the problem of overloading, which was discussed previously. Sometimes noise can be a difficult factor,

particularly when club programs are meeting in the same building as the prayer meeting. The use of carpeting and the acousti-
cal treatment of walls and ceilings have actually helped some
churches bypass the need of putting up another costly building.

Some pastors oppose family cluster scheduling because it cuts
down on prayer meeting attendance. True, it probably will cut
down on the attendance in your prayer session since many of the
people who work in the club programs would also attend prayer
meeting if it were held on a different night. On the other hand, if
we count all the people we have involved on our family night, it
can be an exciting figure when the program is working properly.
What we really face here is a value choice. Is it more important
for Bill Kline to spend three nights at church so that he can
attend Sunday services, prayer meeting, and work with clubs one
night? Or, is it more important for him to spend two nights at
church and one additional night with his family at home?
Churches switching to the family cluster are saying that the
family must come first!

One church in Kansas even includes its committee meetings as
a part of its Wednesday night cluster. Their Wednesday evening
schedule looks something like this:

	7:00-8:00	8:00-9:00	9:00-10:00
BRIGADE	X	X	
PIONEER GIRLS	X	X	
PRAYER MEETING	X		
CHOIR PRACTICE			X
COMMITTEES		X	X
NURSERY	X	X	

In their program each of four major committees in the church
has been assigned one week in the month for its meeting. The
chairman and all the committee members know what night that
is, and the committee meets at the church immediately after
prayer meeting. In order to facilitate the committee schedule,
however, they have had to move the choir practice to the hour
immediately before the evening service on Sunday.

Again, let me say that the keys are flexibility and adaptability. Your program does not have to look like either of these, or like any other that you might know about. What nights should you use? What groupings can be put together in what rooms to pull your program together into a cluster? What leaders need to be removed so that some of the groups which they now head can function with new leaders? Remember that the important thing is the people and the purpose, not the program. Family cluster scheduling is only the first step. Now we have to help our families understand what to do with the new time that they have and how to carry out successful family relations and togetherness at home.

How to Help the Church Help the Family (I)

We have come a long way in our emphasis on the family in evangelical churches since I wrote *The Family First* in 1970. No doubt many families are being helped by the vast production of resources made available since then. A list of titles on family life from the evangelical publishers now numbers into the hundreds of volumes; most of them are less than ten years old.

But there is still a tremendous implemental gap between what scholars, researchers, professors, and theorists are saying and writing about family life and what churches and families are really doing about it. Perhaps Emerson was right when he said, "What all of us need is someone to make us do what we are capable of doing." I might add that we also need someone to make us do what we know we *should* be doing.

The continuing pressure on the family in our society was emphasized in a *Harper's* magazine article penned by Michael Novak for the April 1976 issue:

> The role of a father, a mother, and of children with respect to them, is the absolutely critical center of social force. Even when poverty

and disorientation strike, as over the generations they so often do, it is family strength that most defends individuals against alienation, lassitude, or despair. The world around the family is fundamentally unjust. The state and its agents, and the economic system and its agencies, are never fully to be trusted. One could not trust them in Eastern Europe, in Sicily, or in Ireland—and one cannot trust them here. One unforgettable law has been learned painfully through all the oppressions, disasters, and injustices of the last thousand years: *If things go well with the family, life is worth living; when the family falters, life falls apart.*

There is no question, in my opinion, that the mediator between theory and practice in Christian family life is the local church, with particular emphasis on the pastor, the educational leaders, and the teaching staff. We have seen a new enthusiasm and optimism in the last quarter of the twentieth century, and there is no doubt that a significant upturn in interest exists in the attempt to structure church educational programs that are oriented to families.

But the same kind of monolithic overshadowing that a denomination can sometimes present to our local churches, a local church can present to an individual family. We are in constant danger of thinking of ourselves as substitutionary rather than supplemental in the nurturing process of children and young people. However, let's be specific. How can a local church really help a family?

THE CHURCH CAN HELP BY BEING THOROUGHLY BIBLICAL IN ITS APPROACH TO FAMILIES

There is no question that we can profit from the input of social science, particularly as it helps us develop inquiring minds that seek answers to problems that Christians as well as non-Christians face in our culture. But it is certainly axiomatic that secular psychology and sociology can never help a Christian family unless their findings are first poured through the grid of genuine biblical theology.

What frightens me is that even so-called Christian psychology at times suffers from an unwillingness to submit to biblical authority. As we think about the problems of our culture,

I believe we will have to honestly admit that each one has poignant theological implications. In fact, all social problems for the Christian are, in the first sense, theological problems.

Let's take just one example—abortion. The Christian's response is not primarily one of concern for population or even the health of the potential mother but rather a search for guidance from the God of the Bible on whether the practice is right or wrong.

On another issue, premarital sex, the Christian answer is not the use of contraceptive pills to avoid pregnancy and its social side effects but rather a prophetic claim that sex outside of marriage is sin because God has condemned it. Lovingly, patiently, with a concern for serving and nurturing its people, the church must teach God's truth while walking a balanced line between permissive contemporary values on the one hand and a judgmental Pharisaism on the other.

I might say something here about intergenerational learning, which is a relatively new idea on the educational scene. Intergenerational learning might be defined as intentional interaction among persons of two or more generations, acknowledging in style and kinds of activities the concerns and the characteristics of each generation involved. Quite obviously, the informal family clusters we have been talking about are intergenerational in nature. More and more churches are experimenting with this approach.

THE CHURCH CAN HELP BY TEACHING PARENTS HOW TO BE COUNSELORS AT HOME

Perhaps there is some value in mentioning again at the beginning of this section the important difference between family life education and premarital counseling.

In talking about family life education, I am thinking about parents and churches teaching the biblical principles of marriage and family living throughout the entire eighteen years that we have children and teenagers under the influence of the home and the church. That's a great deal different and infinitely more valuable than a few sessions or even six or seven weeks of premarital counseling during the extremely emotional state just preceding a wedding.

A thorough climate of famiy life education includes proper role patterns in the home; a family-oriented church program; biblical preaching on marriage and family passages which permeate the Scriptures from Genesis to Revelation; special family education events, such as conferences, family camps, and seminars; a good and well-used church library of family books, both for adults and teenagers; carefully planned classes for teenagers; and a serious program of adult education which teaches parents to teach their children at home.

Parents are even more important than pastors when it comes to providing information and attitudes regarding marriage. I am old-fashioned enough to believe that Christian teenagers who really want to do the will of God still listen to godly parents whose counsel they have learned to know and trust for years. They may outwardly make noises about independence and show a great anxiousness to get out on their own; but dad and mom still do know best. And if parents go about it in the right way, they can provide a most positive influence during the years of dating, courtship, and marriage.

Research studies reveal that marriages having the sanction and cooperation of parents are more likely to succeed than those which do not. Let's not make any mistake about it; there's no reason to let dad and mom run the life of a new couple after the marrige has taken place, but they can provide helpful information in the year or two before the day wedding bells ring.

According to Dr. Clyde Narramore, parents can contribute three very important things to a decision and plans for marriage: maturity, experience, and frankness. The Book of Proverbs says that there is wisdom in a multitude of counselors, but a committed Christian young person who can really communicate with a godly dad and mom can cut down on the need for that multitude by a little serious listening. Here are Narramore's own words:

> When you're in love, parents can often be more objective than you are; and they are usually interested enough to help dismantle your castle of dreams and get at the structure to see if its base is sound. Parents

can be especially helpful because they know their children. They have seen them grow from babyhood; they know the years of experience that have made them the young adults of today. For these reasons, parents have an important role in your romance (*Psychology for Living,* No. 3, Zondervan).

Of course, in order to make this kind of counseling system work, both sides have to work at it properly. The young people have to listen, trust, and commit themselves to a certain amount of follow-through if the advice is sound.

Parents, on the other hand, need to avoid an arrogant dictatorial attitude in their attempt to help young people in their proposed relationships, and demonstrate great flexibility and patience in the discussions.

Above all, the continuing openness and love of the family unit must be there. Certainly it is possible that our children may grow up and marry someone we would not have picked for them. Worse yet, they may marry someone we really don't approve of and may never ask our advice, much less our consent, about the marriage. With aching hearts and no small emotional distress, serious, mature Christian parents still let that young person and his or her new partner know in no uncertain terms that they are always welcome and loved "at home." In such difficult circumstances, Christian parents have to be like Mary who "treasured up all these things and pondered them in her heart" (Luke 2:19).

Of course, a willingness to listen has to be cultivated long before the last few weeks preceding the wedding. That's where family life education comes in. While our children are young, we should help them understand verses such as: Proverbs 12:15: "A wise man listens to advice"; Proverbs 11:14: "For lack of guidance a nation falls, but many advisers make victory sure"; Psalm 1:1-2: "Blessed is the man who does not walk in the counsel of the wicked. . . . But his delight is in the Law of the Lord"; Psalm 33:11: "The plans of the Lord stand firm forever."

Basic to Christian marriage, and certainly basic to proper counseling for Christian marriage, is the recognition of the role of God in the marriage. Well-known leaders with divergent theological viewpoints have emphasized the trinity of Christian marriage.

Too often it has been assumed that only two are needed for love—you and I—when really it takes three—you, I, and God. As evangelist Vance Havner said: "There is with us a third Person, nonetheless real because to sight unseen, making the only three that isn't a crowd."

How to Help the Church Help the Family (II)

In chapter 39 I emphasized that the church can help the family by being thoroughly biblical in its approach to family life and by teaching parents how to be counselors at home with particular emphasis on their role in preparing teenagers for marriage and family roles.

Now let's be quite specific and candid regarding what the church has *failed* to do, assuming that by correcting past deficiencies we will thereby be taking positive steps toward the establishing and equipping of stronger Christian families.

THE CHURCH CAN HELP BY CORRECTING SOME OF THE FAILURES IT HAS SHOWN IN FORMER YEARS OR WITH RESPECT TO FAMILY MINISTRIES

I think one of our problems has been the *failure of inflexibility*. We have not been able to adapt to changing lifestyles. By that I don't mean we should be changing morals and values. A commitment to absolute truth links us at least in some measure to a commitment to absolute morals and values. But we need to understand the contemporary issues and help parents grapple with modern-day problems, instead of the problems that confronted the North American society in the more agrarian culture of 150 years ago.

The church has also been guilty of the *failure to adequately teach adults.* Somehow we have to find a way to emphasize the parents' responsibility to nurture their children, as the Bible describes it. I think I can be specific here in terms of practical suggestions. Pastors need to preach regularly on family life. Maybe one Sunday out of every month or perhaps one month out of every year the sermons and the whole church life should revolve around a biblical focus on the family. Texts such as Genesis 2, Deuteronomy 6, 1 Corinthians 7, Ephesians 5, Colossians 3, 1 Peter 3, and many others could be used as foundations for expository sermons on the family, always with the application that parents should practice in the home what the pastor is teaching them in the pulpit.

The adult Sunday School class is another area of concern. It is fine to focus on the vision of the great image in the Book of Daniel and the eschatological niceties of the Book of Revelation. But along with other kinds of Bible exposition in those adult classes, let's squarely treat the family passages of the Bible in a practical way.

Home Bible classes can focus on family subjects, particularly when those classes are made up of young parents and potential parents.

A third way the church can correct past deficiencies is to treat its *failure to adjust its programming* to favor family participation and togetherness. Family cluster programming is not particularly new, but it is catching on in churches that formerly tried to program every night in the week. Family cluster programming isn't just scheduling the church's activities on only one or two nights of the week instead of six or seven, but doing specific and intelligent family things when the people get there.

A family cluster is defined as a family unit that meets together regularly for a shared learning experience. These family units provide a faith sharing and caring testimonial time where purposeful interaction encourages personal growth. There are a lot of different ways that we can make up a "family" for the purpose of family cluster groups.

We can use the nuclear family, made up of dad, mom, and the children, and relate it to similar nuclear families. We can use a simulated nuclear family, involving substitute adults or children, where none exists in the formal nuclear pattern. We can use a nuclear family plus single adults in the church who would be built into the system. We can use adults and children who are not necessarily related in nuclear families but only in the total family of God, the body of Christ.

There are several guidelines we need to watch when using family cluster programming:

1. Don't let any family cluster become a clique. This may suggest that clusters should be changed with some regularity.

2. Try to keep families (however you interpret that term for your cluster purpose) related to each other outside of formal church groups. For example, a family could "contract" with another family for a limited period of time for purposes of prayer, sharing, fellowship, and general support.

3. Make sure that each person has a corresponding peer in the group. A completely adult group with the exception of one teenager would create identity problems for that isolated young person.

We can do this kind of family cluster programming in a number of different ways. One good way is the family camp, which provides separated activities for each age-group as well as cluster activities during the week. Another is a weekend outing or the informal long- or short-term contract recently mentioned. Remember, we don't want to overstructure, because the setting should be as informal and life-related as possible, leaving room for spiritual spontaneity.

THE CHURCH CAN HELP THE FAMILY BY BEING SENSITIVE AND COURAGEOUS IN PROBLEM AREAS

Families have multitudinous problems in our day. Among the more frequently appearing are the following six:

The senior citizens or the elderly. Already the average child born in America can expect to live to over seventy years of age, about 50 percent longer than he would have at the turn of the century. The number of persons over age sixty-five in the United States has grown at three times the rate of the total population. Today, at over 27.4 million, the elderly constitute 11.6 percent of all Americans.

Take another look at Paul's words to a young Christian leader in Titus 2:1-5: "You must teach what is in accord with sound doctrine. Teach the older men to be temperate, worthy of respect, self-controlled, and sound in faith, in love, and in endurance. Likewise, teach the older women to be reverent in the way they live, not to be slanderers or addicted to much wine, but to teach what is good. Then they can train the younger women to love their husbands and children, to be self-controlled and pure, to be busy at home, to be kind, and to be subject to their husbands, so that no one will malign the Word of God."

The young. Here we want to avoid our previous error of *over*emphasizing youth in the church. In the 1960s evangelicalism indulged itself in a distorted emphasis on teenagers. Now we need to focus attention on solving youth problems by catching them before they really begin by adequately instructing parents how to be biblical nurturers in their own homes.

The formerly married. There are a number of ways that a church can meet the challenge of the formerly married. Here are suggested guidelines used by some pastors which have proved helpful:

1. Provide a Christ-like attitude toward divorced persons (John 4:6-26).
2. Create friendships with these who are especially needful of companionship.
3. Commend those who participate in church-related activities.
4. Help involve them in acceptable areas of service.
5. Recognize the need for security and purposeful living among the formerly married. Attempt to provide answers in these areas.
6. Help the formerly married feel accepted within the church family.

7. Encourage the presently married to learn from the formerly married.
8. Encourage single adults to recognize the importance of biblical standards in choosing a mate through the testimony of the formerly married.

The unmarried. There is disillusionment with marriage in our society, and the church must clearly recognize that it is not necessarily God's will for every person to be married.

Remaining single is gaining increasing respectability in North American culture, and that means we need to develop significant programs for single persons and recognize the importance of this growing special group. Dr. Mark Lee suggests that the church needs to do several things if it is to effectively minister to singles:

1. It must accept the state of being single as an appropriate option to marriage for single persons who envision this as the will of God for their lives.
2. It must recognize that the interests of singles are considerably different from those of the married. For example, singles are more attracted to extended education, culture, the arts, and travel.
3. It needs to recognize the role that singles can play in extended family and surrogate family situations.
4. It needs to help singles grapple with sexual problems that come from following God's absolute standards of morality.
5. It needs to help singles see that they have in many ways much more to give to Christ by way of service than do married people. This was precisely Paul's point in 1 Corinthians 7.

The remarried. Of course, the remarried are also the formerly married, but they are not singles, so their situation is different. Here the church is grappling with what to do with the issue of divorce and remarriage. There may well be some specific guidelines in your church, either in its doctrinal statement or constitution, or both, regarding limitations on divorced and remarried persons as far as certain ministries are concerned. But there surely can be no biblical reason for rejecting the genuinely repentant remarriedperson from the love and shelter of a church family.

Single parents. Here again, of course are people who could be grouped with the formerly married. But I am particularly thinking of young parents who for one reason or another find themselves attempting to raise a family alone. The problem is twofold—the absence of a mate and the presence and responsibility of one or more children. Demographers expect that by 1990 one half of all American children will be living in single-parent families. Here is an enormous challenge for the Church to provide nurture, encouragement, and support to a very special kind of family.

Whatever the problem, whatever the need, we can help the church help families by first of all being godly family members who apply biblical principles at home and then teaching those principles throughout the church educational program.

How to Handle Trouble at Home

Psychologists tell us that the most important influence in the life of a young married lady is the relationship she had with her father when she was young. During those early years she develops both a conscious and a subconscious ideal of what a husband and a father ought to be—an ideal which she then carries through both in her search for a husband, and in her relationship to him. Of course, this is not a matter of fixed finality. A girl who has had negative experiences with her father may well compensate for those problems, but the influence is, nevertheless, real.

Complicating this basic axiom is the unfortunate cultural division of moms and daughters on one "team," with dads and sons on the other. During the early years of childhood there is not much evidence of this sexual division, but when children enter their teenage years, a natural division seems to emerge. It is during those years that Christian moms have to work extra hard to relate effectively with their sons and likewise dads with their daughters.

There is not a great deal of biblical evidence in either narrative or biographical form concerning the relationship between fathers and daughters. The single clear-cut story we have is one of crisis in which a religious leader discovered Jesus to be the only solution to the problems in the home. It is the record of Jairus and his twelve-year-old daughter, recorded in each of the synoptic Gospels (Matt. 9:18-19, 23-25; Mark 5:22-24, 35-43; Luke 8:41-42, 59-56).

A Dad's Dignity

It is incorrect to call Jairus a "Christian" leader, though he was certainly a religious leader and, in reality, a religious educator. He was ruler of the synagogue at Capernaum and, therefore, the religious and civic leader of that town. To be sure, the Romans held ultimate political control. But synagogue rulers even in Jerusalem, and more so in the outlying areas of the nation, held a strong religious and civic hold on the allegiance of the people.

Perhaps Jairus' parents knew that he would be a professional religious teacher one day because his name means "he will enlighten." It is possible that his family may have served in the synagogue for a number of years and he was next in line to be its likely leader.

Like many church leaders today, Jairus was a busy man with a demanding schedule away from home. He had responsibility for the religious instruction of many people—children, youth, and adults—but as we encounter him in Scripture, we see that he has but one concern. It is not for the growth of the synagogue or the welfare of the people of Capernaum, but for his little girl who was desperately ill.

Perhaps the first lesson we learn in the story of Jairus and his daughter is that *a godly father is important.* He has awesome responsibilities, both at home and on the job, which no church leader should take lightly.

A Dad's Despair

Mark 5:42 tells us that Jairus' daughter was twelve years of age. How long had she been ill? I have no idea, but rather presume that Jairus had tried every means at his disposal for medical aid before he came to Jesus. There is no record that he was a disciple or that he had ever before confronted Jesus in a personal way. As a resident of Galilee, he no doubt knew about the miracles the Lord had done. Perhaps this confrontation at the shoreline of the Sea of Galilee was a last desperate effort to get help for his dying girl.

Imagine the conversation which might have gone on between father and daughter by that bedside:

"Daddy, do you have to go to the synagogue again tonight?"

"Yes, dear. People need me, and I have a class to teach."

"But Daddy, couldn't you please stay with me this evening? I feel so sick, and I see you so rarely."

"Of course, dear. I'll send word to the synagogue that someone else should take the class tonight so I can be with you here at home."

Why do many families draw close only in crises? Perhaps the word "only" is too strong. It certainly is true that Christian families can take their love, unity, and relationships too much for granted by going about daily business in the rigorous schedules which mark the homes of most Christian leaders.

But then despair hits. Here we can learn a second lesson from Jairus: *a godly father is human*—he hurts, he cries, he needs. Few things can tear at his heart like the potential death of one of his children. Jairus was a broken man as he made his way down the incline of the hill from the city of Capernaum to where Jesus' boat was being beached, as He returned from the east side of the lake.

A Dad's Dependence

How openly Jairus comes to Jesus about his child! Look at the words of Mark 5:23: He "pleaded earnestly with Him, My little daughter is dying. Please come and put Your hands on her so that she will be healed and live."

I imagine that Jairus was a self-sufficient man. He had a standard of leadership to uphold, a dignity to defend, and a reputation to stand by. But all of that was nothing compared with the impending death of his daughter. He threw aside all restraints which probably would have led him, under normal circumstances, to wait in the synagogue or at least in the city until this itinerant Prophet came to him. Instead, Jairus elbowed his way through the gathering crowd. He probably heard people whisper suggestions as to why their synagogue leader would lower himself to come and beg in this fashion.

But of course we must always approach God from a position of weakness, a position of complete dependence on His resources. The problem is that we tend to wait until a crisis comes, or until we have exhausted all possible human resources and have no other alternative.

Imagine the consternation of Jairus when Jesus was delayed by a woman who had suffered from prolonged hemorrhaging. What might Jairus have been thinking as the conversation played back and forth regarding who touched Jesus and as the crowd slowed to a stop while He talked with the woman?

Didn't Jesus understand the seriousness of his need? Didn't He realize that Jairus' plea was of the utmost urgency? Why did Jesus spend time with this woman when Jairus' daughter could have died at any moment? Certainly the only logical thing for Jesus to do was to rush to Jairus' home, heal his little girl, and then return to take care of anyone else who needed help or healing!

On the page in my Bible containing this account I wrote, "God's delays are not denials, but they are discipline." Jesus was in command of the situation at every moment. He was in no more of a rush to get to Jairus' house than He was to get to Bethany during the sickness and death of Lazarus (John 11). It made no difference to Him whether He was dealing with a sick person or a person already dead, because the miracles of the Son of God could overcome sickness or death with equal ease and power.

I am impressed with the fact that Jairus did not complain. He certainly had the authority to argue the issue, to "pull rank" as ruler of the synagogue. But he shows that when a man truly puts his dependence on Jesus, even for those problems at home which are so heartbreaking, he must follow the timing of the Master as well as trust in His power.

This leads us to a third lesson from the story of Jairus: *a godly father is courageous and patient* because his strength is in Jesus. I doubt that Jairus was thinking about Jesus' power to raise the dead any more than the disciples considered the resurrection of Lazarus. But he had crossed the point of no return. His complete faith was now in the Lord, and he became a beautiful picture of those three frequently lauded New Testament virtues, faith, hope, and love, all wrapped up in one father.

A DAD'S DISAPPOINTMENT

The crowd had not even begun to move again up toward the city when news of the little girl's death reached the ears of her hopeful father. Note the blunt and discouraging words of his friends. Death is such a great enemy that somehow, even people in biblical times, those who saw the power of Christ, believed that He had power only on this side of the grave.

Mary and Martha had no doubt that Jesus could have healed Lazarus if He had arrived in time. But it never occurred to them that the One who has the power over life and death could also bring their brother back to life. Their discussion about resurrection power gives us one of the most dynamic statements from the lips of our Lord: "I am the resurrection and the life. He who believes in Me will live, even though he dies; and whoever lives and believes in Me will never die" (John 11:25-26).

Before Jairus even had an opportunity to react to the news of his daughter's death, Jesus spoke these words of comfort: "Don't be afraid; just believe" (Mark 5:36). This could well be translated, "Stop fearing, only be believing." The grammar of the text leads us to believe that Jairus was experiencing the mixed emotions of fear and faith. Jesus wanted to stifle his fear.

The mockery of Jesus' words by the friends of Jairus indicates that they were not honestly concerned about his family. Notice how they went from mourning and wailing to laughing in just a moment of time. They were most likely professional mourners hired for the occasion, perhaps even on standby, pending what everyone expected to be the imminent death of the little girl.

Here we find a fourth lesson abut crisis at home for a Christian: *a godly father is a man of faith, not fear.*

A DAD'S DELIGHT

Jesus entered the bedroom of the little girl in a moment of tense crisis. Seven people were in the room—dad, mom, the little girl, Peter, James, John, and Jesus. He worked a miracle in the daughter's body, and she returned to life. The record shows that Jesus attended three funerals during His earthly ministry, and He closed them all down.

Both parents were amazed at what God could do in their home. Their little daughter ate (a sure sign of life) and was well and strong again. The family was reunited because a father put aside the external restrictions of his position, cast himself completely on the mercy of God, and brought Jesus to his home.

The concern Jairus showed for his daughter and family provides a fifth lesson for us: *a godly father is a man of love who works at famiy unity.*

The lessons of this story are clear not only physically, but spiritually: Dad, your daughter needs you. Your son needs you. Your wife needs you. Your family needs you.

Christian leadership begins at home. Recognize the centrality of Christ there when things are going well; but when crisis hits and you find yourself in despair, remember Jairus and cast yourself in complete dependence on the Son of God.

As a matter of fact, don't wait for a crisis. Make sure that Jesus is recognized as a constant Visitor at your house now, so that your children get to know Him and treat Him as a Friend.

How to Practice Biblical Discipline

One of the greatest problems our nation faces today in its homes as well as its schools is the breakdown of order and discipline on the part of children and young people. The problem has been frequently attacked in the secular press as well as by various Christian writers. The problem not only continues but actually worsens week by week.

The tragedy is that so many Christian parents and teachers in Sunday Schools as well as Christian school classrooms find themselves defeated on this crucial ingredient of the nurturing process. There is in the New Testament a passage of Scripture which speaks pointedly to the whole matter of discipline, urging earthly parents to consider the way the Heavenly Father handles discipline.

That passage is Hebrews 12:5-13. After describing those heroes in the honor roll of faith in chapter 11, and then focusing our eyes on Jesus, "the Author and Perfecter of our faith" (12:2), the author of the Book of Hebrews reminds us that God deals with us as children and thereby sets an example of the way we should deal with our children.

The purpose of discipline is to create maturity. Nurturing is bringing up a child along the process of growth from dependence to independence, at which point he assumes responsibility for starting the process all over again with others. This process is precisely the same in both the physical and spiritual realms. In the physical realm we call it "parenting" and in the spiritual realm, "discipling."

DISCIPLINE IS A NECESSARY COMPONENT OF LOVE

If discipline is an ingredient of love, it follows that discipline should be *loving*. Note Hebrews 12:6: "The Lord disciplines those He loves, and He punishes everyone He accepts as a son."

The whole climate for bringing up children in Christian homes and teaching them in Christian classrooms should be one of love and acceptance. Once such a climate has been established, discipline can be structured within the framework of love rather than as a departure from the loving pattern. The previous verse reminds Christians not to make light of the discipline of the Lord or to be discouraged when rebuke comes. Perhaps this would be a good reminder for us to share with those we teach.

Paul reminds parents not to make their children bitter, or they will become discouraged (Col. 3:21). Of course, children can also discourage their parents. I recently talked with a Christian mother who told me how much effort she and her husband put into raising their children for the Lord. I empathized as she appealed, "All we want from them is a little cooperation!"

DISCIPLINE IDENTIFIES A CHILD AS A MEMBER OF THE FAMILY

That is the central thrust of Hebrews 12:7-8: "Endure hardship as discipline; God is treating you as sons. For what son is not disciplined by his father? If you are not disciplined (and everyone undergoes discipline), then you are illegitimate children and not true sons."

Of course, some parents do not discipline their children, but God is telling us that they are not real parents in the biblical sense. It is impossible, says the Scripture, to be a member of a family and not undergo discipline, because discipline is a part of a total family structure. Legitimacy in a family is marked or perhaps even guaranteed by discipline.

By the same token, a Sunday School teacher who fails to discipline members of his class, or to carry out a structured atmosphere of discipline for the class, is showing that he really doesn't identify those students as his own.

DISCIPLINE AND PUNISHMENT ARE DIFFERENT

Perhaps this is the most important concept we must recognize, and it comes through quite clearly in the use of two different words in Hebrews 12:6. We are told that the Lord *disciplines* those whom He loves and *punishes* everyone who is accepted as a son. This is reminiscent of Proverbs 3:12: "The Lord disciplines those He loves, as a father the son he delights in."

What, then, is the difference between discipline and punishment? I think of discipline as that order or design which characterizes a properly functioning home or classroom. It is erecting the fences and notifying children and young people where the fences are and what will happen if they cross over them. Punishment is the retribution which comes when discipline breaks down. So a home or classroom which is effectively disciplined will have less need for punishment.

The word "discipline" comes from the word "disciple" and therefore has a unique meaning for Christians. *Webster's New Collegiate Dictionary* defines *discipline* as "training that corrects, molds, or perfects the mental faculties or moral character" and "control gained by enforcing obedience or order" and "orderly or prescribed conduct or pattern of behavior."

In my opinion, these definitions are much to be preferred over identifying discipline synonymously with punishment, though punishment definitely enters into the definition.

DISCIPLINE BY HUMAN PARENTS IS NEVER PERFECT

Hebrews 12:9-10 tells us that earthly parents disciplined children "as they thought best." That is not intended to mean that family discipline is generally capricious, but rather that even the best parents are imperfect and can do only what they think best at the time. One problem in discipline is psychological role playing, when an adult behaves like a child, responding to a child's behavior or actions in emotional rather than rational ways.

To immediately strike a child for an act of disobedience without explanation or an opportunity to carefully think through the punishment is not an act of responsible adulthood but rather the way one child would respond to another.

DISCIPLINE ALWAYS SEEMS PAINFUL AT THE TIME BUT EVENTUALLY PRODUCES VALUE

The Scriptures are plain on this point: "No discipline seems pleasant at the time, but painful. Later on, however, it produces a harvest of righteousness and peace for those who have been trained by it" (Heb. 12:11). How many times we have heard and used that worn expression, "This hurts me more than it hurts you"! No child believes that, of course, but when he becomes a parent, he understands that statement's truth.

This principle is true of both discipline and punishment. Having to live structured, ordered lives (such as one might experience in the military or even on some college campuses) produces in us a spirit of rebellion. When we break those rules and violate the discipline, thereby incurring punishment, the momentary pain is increased. But if we can become detached from the emotions of the moment and look back on the value of the experience, then we see that the Scripture is right—discipline leads us to righteous living and peace.

DISCIPLINE TAKES COURAGE ON THE PARTS OF PARENTS AND TEACHERS

Hebrews 12:12-13 almost seems out of place: "Make level paths for your feet, so that the lame may not be disabled, but rather healed." Like water, we find it much easier to take the road of least resistance in dealing with children and young people, both at home and at church.

But the Scripture admonishes us to "strengthen" our own "feeble arms and weak knees" when it comes to the matter of discipline. God's discipline in our lives as adults is gauged to produce righteousness and strength. And we owe it to our children to reproduce those qualities in them through effective use of both discipline and punishment.

But it takes courage and endurance to be a good parent or an effective teacher. Because of sin, disobedience and rebellion run rampant in our society today. A Christian adult who would advance the cause of biblical discipline must indeed strengthen his spirit to do God's will.

DISCIPLINE REQUIRES COOPERATION

In the home this cooperation is between both parents. They should agree on the rules and structure of the family and on the kinds of punishment that follow if that structure is broken down. One parent should never argue with another in the presence of the child regarding matters of discipline and behavior. Strategy meetings are held in private, not in front of the troops.

It follows, of course, that parents and teachers who want to be effective in their discipline of children must be disciplined persons themselves. Part of the problem that we have as adults is our own sloppiness and careless behavior toward the habits of our own lives. A mother who maintains a careless house can hardly expect her young daughter to keep her own room clean. A classroom teacher who consistently hands tests and papers back late cannot ethically demand that students turn in their assignments on time.

DISCIPLINE DEMANDS CONSISTENCY

Proverbs 29:15 reminds us, "The rod of correction imparts wisdom, but a child left to itself disgraces his mother." And in verse 17 we read: "Discipline your son, and he will give you peace; he will bring delight to your soul."

Too often parents and classroom teachers discipline and punish according to their own whims. As the Scripture says in our

Hebrews 12 passage, they are imperfect and fallible in their handling of those over whom they have responsibility. Such inconsistency in discipline breeds lack of discipline.

The psychological principle of reinforcement indicates that there must be repetitive positive results in order to encourage a person toward the behavior we desire. By the same token, a consistent negative punishment is required to drive out behaviors which are unacceptable.

Perhaps we could ask why discipline always seems to be a problem for parents and teachers. The subject invariably shows up on workshop titles at conventions and in chapters of family books.

Surely one of the reasons is the link between rebellion and sin. An attitude or act of rebellion on the part of children or teenagers is representative of the old nature, which they possess as part of the human race. Sin doesn't want to recognize authority, to submit to those who have responsibility over us, or to obey quickly and humbly. Discipline then becomes the process of breaking the selfish will (not the spirit) of children in the process of bringing them to maturity.

Discipline is also a problem because of the negative climate which both discipline and punishment so often create. Since no chastening seems pleasant at the time, the easy route for teachers and parents is to avoid confrontation. But the price of such avoidance is high.

So the task is before us, and the model is Jesus Himself. It is no accident that Hebrews 12 reminds us to "consider Him who endured such opposition from sinful men, so that you will not grow weary and lose heart" (v. 3).

How to Make Sure our Children Get Their Three Strikes

In the spring of 1976, baseball fans in the United States were submitted to a nationwide baseball strike. Quaint stories of six-figure-salaried stars practicing on Little League ball parks or trying to break into college stadiums for warm-ups highlighted the salary war between baseball owners and players. It wasn't settled until the season was half over.

So the season began and the alleged "national pastime" once again unfolded with scores of umpires in hundreds of games giving the previously "striking" players a different kind of opportunity to "strike" as they stood at home plate facing opposing pitchers.

Ever since the rules of baseball were solidified, the phrase "three strikes and you're out" has become common in American vocabulary. Keeping in mind that though a player who swings three times and misses is "out," the strikes actually represent *opportunities* rather than *penalties* until that third one has been missed. It is expected that, given the opportunity to do so in three attempts, a player should sometimes make a hit or at least get on base in some fashion if his team is going to win.

The game of life is not greatly different. There are a limited number of "strikes" allowed all of us. In the measure of God's grace, we may frequently get even fourth, fifth, and sixth chances to redeem what may have been an inferior performance on previous attempts. But even so, there is clearly a limit to opportunity.

One of the ways to think of the opportunity a child has in a Christian home is to focus on the major influences in his life and to think of them as opportunities or "strikes." As he stands at the plate, facing life before him, we want to maximize his opportunities to get that hit, physically, spiritually, emotionally, and in every other domain of human existence. So let's consider three strikes, and more specifically, how some parents deny their children that third opportunity at the plate.

FAMILY IS THE FIRST STRIKE

There is no question that the primary influence in the life of a child is his family. It is clearly written in the Scriptures from the earliest chapters of the Old Testament through God's record of the New Covenant. The primary responsibility for spiritual instruction of children rests not with pastors and Sunday School teachers, but rather with parents. It is a responsibility which cannot be abdicated, a privilege which dare not be minimized.

This is the first strike a Christian child gets at the plate of life. And it is one most Chrisian parents are quite willing to let him have. In fact, though we might not always do it in exactly the right way, most of us believers who have brought children into the world want God's best for them and attempt to raise them according to biblical principles.

To be sure, life's curves, fastballs, and sliders come by just as fast on the first strike as on the others; but as in baseball, they are less of a threat because other opportunities are still ahead.

CHURCH IS THE SECOND STRIKE

God has also created the family of families to provide opportunity for His people. The church is not only an opportunity for communicating the Gospel of salvation to those who put their trust in Christ, but also an opportunity for Christian children and young people to get a second strike in their quest for growth and maturity.

Because that second strike is so important, we must ask ourselves some hard questions about programs in our churches. Are they really providing the opportunities essential for Christian growth? Is there really a clear teaching of the Word of God as well as the presentation of the message of salvation so that people have an opportunity to move on to maturity in the things of Christ? Is the church really serving the whole family, or is it geared just to young people or children? Does it really supplement the ministry of the home?

CHRISTIAN SCHOOL IS THE THIRD STRIKE

The decade of the 1970s saw a veritable explosion in the development of Christian schools. Paul A. Kienel, executive director of the Association of Christian Schools, Intl., writes in that organization's publication:

> Everywhere I go there is abundant evidence that the Christian school movement is keeping pace with its reputation as the fastest-growing educational movement in America. The rapid growth of Christian schools which I have observed in California (from 68 to 408 member schools in 9 years—an increase of 600%) is happening in almost every other area of the United States. *U.S. News and World Report* and other national magazines have referred to this phenomenon as "the Christian school explosion" (*Christian School Comment*, Volume 5, Number 9).

Christian school growth, though particularly noticeable of late, was not at all unknown during the '50s and '60s. It was more common then, however, for Christian schools to spring up as the effort of parent groups generally independent of church control and operated by a self-perpetuated or society-perpetuated boards.

The trend today is clearly toward the parochial school; that is, the school operated by a local church—or, less frequently, by a denomination. Given the size and cost of today's church buildings, it makes sense. Churches invest large amounts of money in physical plants which are used minimally in the functions which are distinctly oriented to the church's own program. With more careful planning, a Christian day school can be built into the system, utilizing the same facilities and providing a service not only to the congregation but to the entire community as well.

But many evangelical parents have been suspicious of Christian schools and have deliberately denied their children the third strike. Some of their reasons appear to be valid, at least on the surface, and require some explanation.

One of the issues frequently raised is the *cost* problem. Christian parents, already paying taxes for state-supported schools, are doubly burdened when required to pay tuition (which can run over $2,000 per child per year) for a Christian education. Some families are able to fit the cost into the budget; others believe the value of the third strike is sufficiently important to make the necessary sacrifices. Others simply cannot afford the added financial burden on already taxed family resources.

In an attempt to deal with the cost factor, some local churches have started schools on "shoestring budgets," trying to keep tuition costs at the bare minimum, thus making Christian education available to almost anyone who wants it.

But problems emerge here as well. There *is* a positive correlation between quality and expenditure in education, and though it does not follow that a maximum expenditure will always lead to a higher quality education, it certainly must be recognized that the equipping of adequate facilities and the hiring of qualified faculty members do require a respectable budgetary commitment on the part of a church that wants to have a quality Christian school.

In some ways, poor quality Christian education serves as a negative testimony to Jesus Christ and may be doing more harm than good.

Another objection many parents raise with respect to the third strike is the matter of *facilities*. Of course, a state-supported institution with its mandatory tax funds can afford laboratories and gymnasiums far surpassing what a Christian school can provide. But once the issue of adequate facilities to care for the instructional program has been dealt with, a fascination with facilities can become a fallacious argument. Unfortunately, this is frequently used as nothing more than a convenient excuse to deny our children that third strike.

Still another argument Christian parents raise is the old *"hot-house" issue*. It is argued that children in a Christian school are isolated from the real world and are therefore unprepared to cope with its problems upon graduation from eighth grade or high school. Thinking Christian educators in recent years, however, have finally come to realize that the hothouse argument with which we have struggled so long is really an indictment on the public education system rather than on Christian schools.

It is the student in the public school who is isolated from the real world because *the real world is God's world*. To hear only evolutionism rather than creationism; to view history only as chance rather than God's handiwork in His universe; to attempt to understand the nature of man in purely mechanical terms rather than as the image of God—*this* is being isolated from the real world and from the real truth!

Perhaps that brings us to some positive arguments for allowing our children that third strike we have been talking about. Certainly, one argument must be the *current availability* of Christian education. There was a day when it was extremely difficult for a Christian parent to find a Christian school, even if he had the inclination to enroll his children and had the funds to pay the tuition. Now with the boom of the past decade, an evangelical education at the elementary and secondary levels is possible for millions more children than ever before.

Atmosphere is another important factor. The influence on children during their school years is not only brought about by teachers and administrators, but also by the children with whom they study and play day by day. Since values are more "caught" than taught, this peer exposure is an important factor in the spiritual development of our children.

But perhaps the most important factor is the *philosophy of the classroom* itself. Far greater than the influence of other children is the influence of trained, professional teachers who in the public school system are committed to the systematic inculcation of secular humanism as a philosophy of life. To quote Kienel again,

> Not only are Christian youngsters by the multiplied thousands being "secularized" by a secular system of education, but non-Christian educators are driving a devastating wedge between children and their parents and between children and the church.

So if you have children at the plate or if you serve as the coach of a family, church, or Christian school team, don't restrict the batting average of the youngsters under your leadership. Give them all three strikes in the game of life.

How to Strengthen the Base of the Teaching Triangle

At the risk of overemphasis, I want to call up again the issue of home, church, and school but change the metaphor from strikes to a triangle. As indicated in the last chapter, one of the most significant recent trends in the field of Christian education has been the explosive growth of the Christian school movement. It provides the third side of what I am calling "the teaching triangle," with the home serving as the base and the church as the other supporting side.

A proper relationship among all three agencies is essential to a satisfactory program of triangular Christian nurture for children and young people. In another article, I talked about the relationship between church and home; so here I want to emphasize the partnership that must prevail between Christian families and the administrators and teachers of a Christian school.

PARTNERS IN A DISTINCTLY BIBLICAL PATTERN OF EDUCATION
A proper understanding of the unity of church, home, and school is at the heart of the Christian school movement. This familiar

triangle emphasizes a three-sided approach to total Christian nurture. Its three sides represent the home, the church, and the Christian school. At times leaders of Christian schools have not recognized the importance of the family.

To have a proper understanding of Christian nurture, we must grasp the philosophy behind Christian schools. At the heart of the philosophy is the belief that parents must be actively involved in the educational process. In partnership with the administration and faculty, they assist in the task of educating their children.

PARTNERS IN ACHIEVING INSTRUCTIONAL GOALS

One of the reasons Christian parents choose to send their children to a Christian school is because they feel that they no longer have a significant voice in the educational process of a public school. In contrast, most Christian schools make a conscious effort to involve parents in the various aspects of the instructional process.

A Christian school must actively solicit parental assistance, not only for classroom activities but also for home study. Such a concept is in direct contradiction to such popular advice-to-parents books as Haim Ginott's *Between Parent and Child* (Avon Books). In his book Ginott offered this advice to parents, advice which I reject:

> From the first grade on, parents' attitudes should convey that homework is *strictly* the responsibility of the child and his teacher. Parents should not nag children about homework. They should not supervise or check the homework, except at the invitation of the children....Much misery could be avoided, and much joy added to homelife, if parents would show less interest in the minute details of the child's assignments and instead convey in no uncertain terms: "Homework is your responsibility. Homework is for you what work is for us."

PARTNERS IN BUILDING FAMILIES, NOT TEST SCORES

The greatest priority of both home and school is the nurture of children and young people. Consequently, a Christian school that is concerned about building families will engage in prayer for the families making up its constituency. Obviously, in order to pray intelligently for families, the teachers need to know the parents. If parents won't come to the school for various parent-teacher functions, teachers may have to visit the parents in their homes. A teacher cannot pray adequately for his students and their families until he understands their home situations.

It is easier to achieve this degree of intimacy at the elementary than at the secondary level. Nevertheless, creative secondary school teachers can develop relationships with their students and their families that will enable them to pray for the needs of specific families.

One goal of prayer in the broader program of Christian nurture is to foster parent-child unity and to strengthen husband-wife relationships. It should be clear too that the familial relationships of the faculty and administration of the school serve as models for the students. This is especially important when good parental relationships do not exist in certain homes.

Schools that support parents should place a strong emphasis on family life education as a part of the curriculum. This takes us into the area of the affective domain as opposed to the straight cognitive realm, where we tend to spend too much of our time. Though Christian schools must strive to convey knowledge, they must also remember that their primary concern is to teach moral and spiritual values, a task that cannot be accomplished as effectively without the aid of parents. Family life educator Paul Popenoe wrote:

> Not much can be expected of the schools until education for family living has found a firm place in teacher training. It should not be too difficult to establish such a place....Family life education can easily be worked into the curricula of schools, be they progressive or old-fashioned or revolutionary ("The School Must Help," *Family Life*, May-June 1973).

PARTNERS IN DEALING WITH TOUGH ISSUES

I wish we had more space to deal with this extremely important aspect of the Christian school's ministry because I feel that it is one area in which we have been grossly deficient. What responsibility does a Christian school have in helping parents assist their children in combating the worldly influences of our pagan society? What is your school doing, for example, to point out the negative influence of rock music in the lives of Christian young people? I agree with Paul Kienel's observation:

> It is profoundly inconsistent to send young people to a Christian school to learn biblical values and the virtues of our great country and then smile at them while they listen to the beat and subtle message of a band of rock revolutionaries that are busting their vocal chords and the eardrums of their listeners to tell our kids that biblical values and the greatness of America are hopelessly old hat and high-button shoe (*Newsletter.* Educational Research Associates, April-May 1976).

What about other troublesome issues? Where are the lines to be drawn? What should be the attitude of a Christian? What is the role of the Christian school in helping parents and young people grapple with these issues? Where can we draw the line without being judgmental on the one hand or too lenient on the other?

These are primary concerns to Christian parents who are seeking to raise their children in accordance with biblical standards of conduct. Since these parents often look to a Christian school to provide guidance, the school provides a valuable service to both parents and students when it promotes biblical standards. The Christian school that does not take a biblical stance on such issues as rock music, drinking, drugs, and premarital sexual experiences is simply not living up to its responsibility.

PARTNERS IN RELATIONSHIP TO THE LOCAL CHURCH

Here we stand as one side of the triangle, assisting the base to also properly support the other side. Christian schools assist parents in their relationship with the local church in a number of practical ways:

1. The churchmanship example of administration and faculty at the school.

2. The frequent visitation of pastors from various local churches, in chapel services and other special events.

3. The willingness to make homework assignments flexible enough to allow students to take part in prayer meetings and other midweek service activities.

The church needs help today, and Christian schools are in a position to offer some of that help. Through its doors pass numerous potential professional and lay Christian leaders. As they find their roles in local churches, the body of believers is strengthened and encouraged.

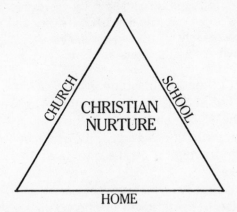

To cultivate an attitude of partnership with the families involved with our schools is both our responsibility and our privilege. It is a responsibility because of God's priorities wherein He puts the family first. We have no choice about this if we are to be faithful to a truly biblical philosophy of education. It is also a privilege because it meets the needs of our students' families and, in a general sense, of society as well.

A recent Gallup poll clearly indicated that the nation's schools must forge new bonds between the home and the classroom in order to prevent continuing strife and turmoil in public education. George Gallup commented on the results of the poll by saying, "For every dollar spent in making parents an integral part of the teaching team, the returns in savings to society will come back one hundredfold."

There is a lesson here for the church as well. Just as Christian schools need to forge strong bonds between parents and teachers, so the workers in the church's educational program must think of the family. I believe that Gallup's remarks fit church life as well. We need to spend less money on frills, gimmicks, and gadgets and more on solid, ongoing family life programs that strengthen the teaching triangle.

How to Keep Your Child Out of Christian Service

The opportunities for vocational Christian service in the 1980s are as great as, or perhaps even greater than, they have ever been in the history of the church. Bible college enrollments are up and evangelical seminaries are crowded. The church is popular again, and some of the statistics we talked about in the late sixties (35,000 pastorless churches in the United States, for example) have been swept aside by a new commitment to Christ within the evangelical community during the past fifteen years.

But the world population explosion continues, and there are still 2,000 languages without a translation of the Scriptures. New ministries have developed on university campuses that could help meet this need—media ministries and specialized technical skills necessary to almost every mission field of the world.

The challenge to Christian service is still offered by pastors, missionaries, and other Christian leaders, but the response is somewhat hampered by the materialism of our society. Thousands of young people made a commitment for missionary service at Explo '72 in Dallas, but the mortality rate of those original decisions was tragically high.

Besides the negative influence of society, young people often face an enemy at home in the person of Christian parents. Warm, friendly, committed believers often stand in the way of their own children, for reasons which seem to them to be valid.

A father explains: "I always anticipated that John would take over the family business, which my father taught me. It was started by my great-great grandfather, and it has been traditional in our family for each son to take on the responsibility."

A Christian mother argues: "Of course we believe in missions, but Susan is our only daughter. We couldn't think of her being halfway around the world; we'd never see our grandchildren!"

Still another couple emphasizes the need for good Christian leadership in secular vocations such as law and science, urging their son to attend a university rather than a Bible college or seminary.

Yes, it is possible to keep your child out of Christian service; and if that is your intention, this tongue-in-cheek chapter offers some helpful suggestions.

CRITICIZE YOUR CHURCH AND PASTOR REGULARLY

This maneuver will assist your children in developing negative ideas about a Christian ministry. If they can see that a pastor is underpaid, overworked, and rarely appreciated, they may think twice about responding to God's call to a pulpit ministry.

But if you have no objection to your son becoming a pastor, then let him see constant prayer and concern for the local church at home. Teach him from passages such as Matthew 16:18 the centrality of the church in God's total plan for the world. Demonstrate your own faithfulness to the church's ministry by attendance and also by involvement. Encourage him to get involved early in ministries open to young people in your church.

IMPRESS ON YOUR CHILD THE NECESSITY OF PERSONAL SECURITY

This feeling for security is quite easily taught in a society that is already committed to materialism. Constant talk of income levels, bank accounts, larger homes, job status, and good investments will develop a value system that is well in line with the standards of contemporary society. Obviously, the child must attend the best college and select a job that has the best market potential during the next several years, or even decades, insofar as that can be determined.

But if that does not appeal to you and you are interested in creating a Christian value system, show him an example of what Jesus meant when He said: "Do not store up for yourselves treasures on earth, where moth and rust destroy, and where thieves break in and steal. But store up for yourselves treasures in heaven, where moth and rust do not destroy, and where thieves do not break in and steal. For where your treasure is, there your heart will be also" (Matt. 6:19-21).

Do your children see in you a systematic dependence upon God to provide the needs of the family, or is your family marked by an independence which teaches your children to do for themselves rather than looking to God to supply their needs?

Teenagers are already caught up in an annual spending level of over 20 billion dollars. Madison Avenue created "the teenager" in 1941 and now successfully sells him everything from transistor radios to expensive automobiles.

In an affluent society, this kind of behavior by middle-class Christian parents is commonplace. Do not misunderstand; affluence is not a sin in itself. But the philosophy of life which we call materialism—a love for and a coveting of things—is sinful. It is quite possible—yet quite difficult—for a family to be extremely affluent and yet demonstrate in their home a sacrificial spirit of giving and serving.

I remember a woman who spoke with me after a service in which I had been ministering on the theme of commitment to Christ for Christian service. She wanted me to pray with her that her daughter would become a missionary because she herself had rejected God's call in her earlier years and the guilt had haunted her all of her life. Now she was hoping that somehow her daughter could take her place as a second-generation substitute for her mother's failure to respond affirmatively to God's leading in her life.

IN EDUCATION, EMPHASIZE ONLY
ACCREDITATION, DEGREES AND CAMPUS

Quite obviously, what is important in Western culture is the attaining of satisfactory credentials which will lead to the obtaining of a satisfactory job. This is the corollary to the second suggestion of seeking personal security. The way to achieve that satisfactory job, many feel, is to attend the right kind of institution, where one can earn maximum qualifications to achieve and get ahead in the competitive society which surrounds us.

The thinking may sound worldly, but I assure you it represents the conclusions of many Christian parents, particularly those in the more affluent segment of our society. By "affluent" I do not mean wealthy, but the middle and upper-middle classes, which certainly characterize many families in evangelical churches today in the massive sprawling suburbs of our land.

As a former college president, I would be among the first to affirm the importance of accreditation, degrees, and an adequate campus. But for a Christian student, knowledge of the truth is the really essential component of education. A Christocentric philosophy of education stands opposed to the secular humanism characteristic of public education from kindergarten through graduate work at a secular institution.

A Christian college, and more specifically, a Bible college, stands in contrast, emphasizing the foundation of truth which comes solely through a knowledge of Holy Scripture: "The fear of the Lord is the beginning of knowledge, but fools despise wisdom and discipline" (Prov. 1:7).

How tragic it is that many Christian colleges cannot compare favorably with the equipment and scholarship of secular institutions. That in itself is an indictment on the failure of the evangelical community to recognize the importance of learning for the propagation of truth in the best possible settings.

A church that talks about missions but gives nothing to Christian colleges should understand that without these institutions there would be few missionaries or missions to concern us.

Are you interested in missions? Be interested in Christian higher education. Do you want to support missions? Support Christian higher education. Without the Christian college there is no local church, no sending home base, and no sustained work on the field. When we strengthen the Christian college, we strengthen the work on the field, we strengthen the home base, and we strengthen the local church (Kenneth O. Gangel, "The Neglected Word of the Great Commission," *Communicare*, Spring 1977).

LEAD HIM TO MAKE HIS OWN DECISIONS ON THE BASIS OF NATURALISTIC CONSIDERATIONS

There are certain issues that every person must consider in this world. Among them is looking out for number one. Obviously, if we fail to pay attention to our own needs and concerns, no one else will do so. Consequently, we must teach our children to be independent. They must understand that they can expect nothing from anyone else in this kind of society; and they must, with determined effort, take advantage of every opportunity that comes, because opportunities will be few and far between.

To be sure, Christians should never cheat or do anything unethical; but why miss an opportunity to do something for self-advantage which is legal and can be justified or at least rationalized by socially acceptable people?

Such an independent mentality recognizes no restrictions. It lives within a system of relative morality and creates its own rules, which differ according to each situation.

The New Testament talks about Christian living as a privilege. It emphasizes the responsibility of believers to understand the will of God and to live committed to that will: "From everyone who has been given much, much will be demanded; and from the one who has been entrusted with much, much more will be asked" (Luke 12:48).

Obviously, it is the task of Christian parenthood to bring our young people to the place where they can make intelligent decisions. But these decisions should be guided by the significant support of almost twenty years of parental, pastoral, and pedagogical training.

In the early twelfth century B.C., a humble family lived in Mount Ephraim during a time when Israel was passing through a great spiritual crisis. The problem of the nation was not materialism or affluence but rather a genuine dearth of godliness, which reflected itself in superstition, a quasi-religious atmosphere, and a rampant desecration of religious behavior in the tabernacle at Shiloh. One commentator wrote that during these years the nation reached its lowest ebb of degradation.

But a godly couple, Elkanah and Hannah, understood clearly the responsibilities they had as parents. After praying for and receiving a son, they committed him to God for service at the temple.

I am sure it was extremely difficult to see little Samuel only once a year. But what a marvelous encouragement and blessing it must have been for them to know that their son was being trained for the Lord's service and would someday be used mightily by God in significant leadership of His work in the world. But it all began when Hannah was able to say to Eli, "So now I give him to the Lord. For his whole life he will be given over to the Lord" (1 Sam. 1:28).

Yes, you can keep your child out of Christian service, unless God in His sovereignty decides to overrule your efforts. But do not underestimate the influence you have as a parent, and do not minimize the enormous responsibility of stewardship which is yours in raising these, God's children, in His behalf.

How to Build Leadership in Teens

Michigan psychologist Joseph Atelson once wrote that "an over-whelming majority of the young—as many as eighty percent—tend to be traditionalists in values." Atelson claims the evidence suggests youth's politics and passions still largely reflect those of their parents. One teenager quoted in his article thinks that there may even be a return to a larger parental role in helping teens establish beliefs and attitudes. He says:

> Kids will go to their parents not just for pragmatic advice and information but also for guidance and understanding in the art of becoming a person. They will learn not only how to make a living but also how to live.

Of course, all of this relates to the continuing problem of the church with respect to its youth. The sixties saw us cavorting from one idea to another in order to somehow develop a program that would reach, teach, and retain teenagers in the local church. Most often our quest led us to the flamboyant "fun" type of program with a focus primarily on entertainment with consequent shallow results. The 1980s seem to be offering a return to a more biblical orientation, namely that God has created a definite order for instruction and nurture and *that* order places primary focus on the Christian home with mom and dad playing the leading roles in the relationship drama.

The Bible is an adult Book written *by* adults *for* adults. Most of the passages which youth evangelists are able to come up with in preaching to teens tend to be wishful hermeneutics at best or contextual perversions at worst. It's not that God doesn't love young people or that the Bible doesn't relate to them. It rather emphasizes again that parents and other adult figures in church and school are ordained of God to be strategic influences in bringing a teenager from dependence to independence, and from immaturity through the process of maturing.

So what? How about some constructive suggestions? OK, let's center on a few ideas that have worked in some churches which seek to develop a commitment to Christ and a bent toward leadership on the part of the teens. Of course, there are some principles which must precede any kind of practice of an educational nature.

God's order of priority places the Christian home in the primary spotlight and the local church as a collective community of God's people doing the work of Christ on earth. In this context parents, pastors, and other God-ordained leaders possess an authority which cannot be given up by default if the position of Scripture is to be honored. Another principle is that participation or involvement in actual Bible study and Christian service is the most biblical and practical way to teach and train teenagers in the Christian life. Consequently the following sugestions emphasize training for involvement and involvement in training.

One of the problems, however, that precedes even the training period is the problem of motivation. How do we get teens really fired up about the possibility of serving Christ through the church? How can they be inspired to *want* the kind of training which we can make available to them through various kinds of programs? How can we make them aware of their strategic place in the ministry of the church, rather than letting them wander out the back door or become passive adults who listlessly float from year to year performing perfunctory tasks of custodial management?

One of the best answers is not a new one, but it has been tried experientially by too few churches. Those churches which have tried it have repeatedly expressed the success with which their efforts have been crowned as they put into operation an *annual youth conference.* No church is too small or too large to involve its young people in this kind of spiritual enrichment and leadership training at least once a year.

A youth conference can take many forms. For example, it could be held over a long weekend in the early part of the fall. Labor Day is an excellent choice since it comes early in September and adds another full day to be utilized in conference. Sometimes such a conference is referred to as a "Fall Retreat." Planning for such a weekend should be done well in advance and with very careful consideration. Planning can be handled by the young people themselves with adult leadership and guidance. The planning committee will decide such matters as dates, time, transportation, cost, and food service.

The place is extremely important, perhaps a campsite or resort area at least 50 or 100 miles away from the church and in an area sufficiently remote to give the idea of "being away from it all for a while." There should be some recreational area as well as satisfactory sleeping and eating facilities. The rental cost of a facility may be a significant factor in its selection.

Many of these decisions will also relate to another kind of youth conference, one that would be held over a full week during the summer, Christmas vacation, or perhaps even in the spring. This latter, of course, is less practical than the weekend idea since the cost and the time involved are inhibiting factors.

Sometimes the leaders and the young people decide to conduct a conference in the form of special meetings for the young people at the church. Again, this can assume the form of a weekend or a full week of activities. The emphasis might be evangelistic or a challenge for Christian living, but the activities ought to be youth-centered and not entirely dependent on a series of formal services.

Whatever kind of youth conference you decide to have, programming is an extremely important factor. Bring in an outside speaker who can really challenge young people from the Word of God. If your conference is being held over a weekend, three major services with this speaker would probably be sufficient. These would be supplemented by lively discussion groups centered around relevant topics. Trained youth leaders may be in charge of these groups or you may use the teens themselves and again you would utilize your special speaker. Certainly you would want to include a good athletic program, consisting of contests and games played just for fun.

Plan some time for personal devotions and quiet worship before the Lord. Some churches include planning sessions during which the youth sponsors and the teens map out in general the youth programs for the year ahead.

Of course, any such endeavor at a site away from the church needs careful supervision and requires a sufficient amount of mature leadership. Music should play a big factor also, so there is a need for someone who can really get kids to sing. Maybe a contemporary guitar and folk session could replace some of the light choruses which we so often use, but also have the young people sing some of the great meaningful hymns which have been collected in various songbooks, such as those published by InterVarsity Press.

Whichever form your youth conference takes, one of the most significant ingredients must be the participation of the young people themselves. They must have a large share in planning the program and in carrying it out. It must be *their* conference, not something handed down to them by youth sponsors or pastors. Remember that the basic objective is training for service. Sessions should place a strong emphasis on personal Bible study. Regardless of the accent, however, your youth conference should be a program for the young people, of the young people, and by the young people.

While the conference is in session, keep the activities moving but let everything be permeated with an informal air. Structure opportunities in which the young people can get to know the special speaker personally. Some churches have found it profitable to bring in a Gospel team from a nearby Christian college so that the music, testimony, and life-influence of college-age young people who are dedicated to the Lord can have a real impact on junior high and senior high teens during the conference.

One more thing. Remember that building leadership in teens is a process, not an event. Any conference must be consistently supported by daily feeding and leading of your young people in all of their activities, over a long period of time.

How to Train Parents to Be Biblical

Born September 23, 1800 in western Pennsylvania, and raised on the Ohio frontier, William Holmes McGuffey was a clergyman, a professor of ancient languages and philosophy, a college president, and an advocate of public education. But he is most noted as a textbook compiler. It is fascinating that in the late twentieth century some people are again discovering McGuffey's readers, which stand with *The New England Primer* as perhaps the best-known schoolbooks in the history of American education.

McGuffey, though a distinctively evangelical Christian, did not leave us much in print on his ministry in the local church. He was a servant of public education, not Christian education (which was virtually unknown on the frontier in McGuffey's day). Nevertheless, he had a grasp of the distinctive role of the home in Christian nurture, particularly as it related to the role of the school. The schoolmaster made a fascinating distinction between methodology and content when he wrote:

> Teachers ought to know best *how* to do that which is required of them—
> the parents are, or ought to be, the better judges as to *what*

is to be done. We fellow teachers are the servants of the public. We have a deep interest, as has been shown, in the results of our labors and their effects upon public prosperity and national character. But, as we love and ought to love those committed to our care, they are but our pupils, not our children. This last relation is one which can be constituted only by the Author of our being. All attempts artificially to form it must end in comparative defeat. None but the *natural* parent can feel that natural affection which is adequate to the duties of *properly educating* an immortal mind (John H. Westerhoff III, *McGuffey and His Readers*, Abingdon).

What McGuffey said about public school teachers is certainly applicable to teachers in a local church. Our responsibility is to build the Christian home in its various biblical functions, not to offer a substitute for parents who have failed to realize their responsibilities.

As I pondered this unique relationship between teachers and parents, I began to think of it in terms of two ideas used frequently and with great impact by a contemporary management expert, Peter Drucker—*efficiency* and *effectiveness*. Drucker suggests that *efficiency* describes the leader who does things right, whereas *effectiveness* describes the leader who does the right things. When we apply these to parenting, we can draw a picture of the Christian home that ought to result from proper Christian education functions at the church. It takes form as a three-dimensional model, describing parenting that is efficient, effective, and effluent.

EFFICIENT PARENTING: DOING THINGS RIGHT

Parents who do things right have grasped the fundamental understandings of Christian responsibility in the home. For example, an efficient parent accepts the responsibility for *providing,* in accordance with 1 Timothy 5:8. Providing for one's family has been God's plan from Creation to the present and cannot be minimized or compromised without great negative results. God does not bless a home in which the parents deliberately fail to exercise this function adequately.

A second aspect of efficient parenting is *discipline*. Efficient discipline must be in accordance with the principles of Hebrews

12. That most practical Bible passage patterns parental discipline after the disciplinary behavior of the Heavenly Father.

A fascinating book by Peter Marshall and David Manuel titled *The Light and the Glory* (Revell) pinpoints behavior of the early American family with respect to discipline:

> And here's the greatest difference between the Puritans and most present-day American parents. For we are not willing to risk losing the "love" in our relationship with our children by persevering with them in matters of discipline. The biggest single cause of the breakdown of the American family is that so much of what we could call *love* the Puritans would have another name for: *idolatry.*

Still a third aspect of the dimension we are calling efficiency is the act of *propelling* growing children into their own lives, replacing dependence with independence as adolescence gives way to adulthood. It is necessary for an efficient parent to let his "eaglets" go when the launching time arrives. If providing has been carried out adequately and discipline has had its proper role, propelling should follow at the appropriate time and in the appropriate way.

EFFECTIVE PARENTING: DOING THE RIGHT THINGS

An efficient parent should also want to be an effective parent, and proper adult education in the local church will help him achieve both ends. As we selected three elements in the first dimension, let's focus on three here, the first of which is *modeling*.

Perhaps *modeling* is the greatest responsibility of a Christian parent, and he can never do the right things as a parent without concentrating on the necessity of demonstrating Christian values and behavior in the home. The classic Old Testament passage, Deuteronomy 6, emphasizes the responsibility of parents' modeling the practical effects of God's Word so that their children may respond in ways God wants them to.

From the earliest days of simple mimicking, in which a preschool child may walk, talk, or in some other way behave like a dad and mom, to the subtle absorption of value systems which occurs in early adolescent years, modeling is a strategic aspect of effective parenting.

A second idea we might choose to describe parental effectiveness is *ministering*. Here the priestly function of the home emerges, and one is reminded of the importance of godly example and education by parents.

Still another aspect of the second dimension is *multiplying*. Those who work professionally in Christian education often speak of teaching as a ministry of multiplication. Since every parent is a teacher, parenting is also, indeed more so, a ministry of multiplication.

Obviously parenting includes physical reproduction. But it also ought to include spiritual reproduction. Christian parents ought to be rearing children who possess Christian values and general commitment to Jesus Christ.

It should be immediately obvious that it is possible to be *efficient* (that is, to provide, to discipline, and to propel) without being *effective* through modeling, ministering, and multiplying. But both are essential in a three-dimensional family.

EFFLUENT PARENTING: DOING THINGS FOR THE RIGHT REASONS

The word "effluent" describes something that flows out; therefore it is quite in line with what we are trying to suggest for the three-dimensional family. Parenting is not a static or a passive activity. There should be a constant outflow of love, nurture, and self. What, then, are some of the right reasons parents ought to take into consideration when they choose behavior patterns in their homes?

One basis for choosing to instill a particular behavior in a home is *determining whether that behavior is biblical*. A Christian home requires a commitment to truth in a world of error. The implication here is that parents should know and be committed to what is biblical.

Effluent parenting also results when Christian fathers and mothers carry out their responsibilities *because the results are eternal*. There is an enormous need in the 1980s for the inculcation of timeless values in an ethical, moral, and spiritual vacuum.

Our culture is besmirched by secularism, sensuality, and selfishness; and it becomes more and more difficult for a Christian home to offset these social "diseases" by creating a focus on eternality which directs the attention of dads, moms, and children to a divine viewpoint in the crucial decisions of life.

Finally, effluent parenting is advanced when parents make a choice or select a plan *because it is consistent.* How can we raise children who are responsible in the midst of an irresponsible society? The answer to that question is by providing an entire lifestyle in which values and patterns are cultivated over the long haul.

We could talk about the role of the Christian school in helping to develop the three-dimensional family, but let's not confuse the issue by adding an additional resource for the task. An effective local church program of adult education, a serious commitment to personal Bible study, the application of Scripture to life, and a sensitivity to the Holy Spirit's leading in the lives of parents are sufficient resources to get the job done.

What is your church doing to assist in the production of three-dimensional families—families that are carrying out the parenting task with efficiency, effectiveness, and effluence?

How to Promote Family Renewal

In the last chapter I attempted to lay some groundwork for the whole matter of renewal by emphasizing that Christian renewal begins when we accept parental responsibility. The principle of renewal centers in Colossians 3:15—4:1. There the Apostle Paul identifies the qualities which are demonstrated by Christians in community relationships.

RENEWAL EXHIBITS GODLY QUALITIES

There are three godly qualities mentioned in Colossians 3:15-17 which catch the eye of a careful reader: peace (v. 15), wisdom (v. 16), and thankfulness (v. 17).

The quality of "peace" is the peace of God which takes over as a controller in the life of a Christian who yields himself to God's way (Col. 3:15). The word "rule" in the English text is actually an athletic word which is best represented in our day by the word "umpire."

A.T. Robertson spoke eloquently of the role of Christ's *peace* in the life of a believer:

Christ is the Lord of peace, and He will give peace to each of us in the midst of and in spite of all the clanging passions of our complicated natures. He can break the complex that holds us fast and give calmness. So then, pleaded Paul, let the peace that Christ gives cast the deciding vote in our struggles. We shall never go wrong in that case (*Paul and the Intellectuals*, Broadman).

Notice four sets of triplets in Colossians 3:16 which can help produce renewal in a church:

Word	Teaching	In you	Psalms
Dwell	Admonishing	With wisdom	Hymns
Richly	Singing	With gratitude	Spiritual songs

Interestingly there are several present tense verbs in Colossians 3:16. Paul said we should "Let the word of Christ" be continually dwelling in us, and we should be continually teaching, admonishing, and singing to the Lord.

The third godly quality demonstrative of renewal is *thankfulness.* Colossians 3:17 indicates the comprehensive nature of that attitude in the life of a Christian: "And whatever you do, whether in word or deed, do it all in the name of the Lord Jesus, giving thanks to God the Father through Him."

We should be thankful in everything we do because everything we do should be done "in the name of the Lord Jesus" (3:17). There is no compartmentalization of the sacred and secular in the life of a Christian, for all things belong to Christ. The idea of comprehensive thankfulness of life is also emphasized by the Apostle Paul in his letter to the church at Thessalonica (1 Thes. 5:18).

RENEWAL BEGINS AT HOME

Again the order of thinking and writing in Colossians 3:18-21 is characteristic of the Apostle Paul. In these four verses he capsuled much of the information which we find in Ephesians 5:22—6:4. The first English word of each verse indicates the group of people to whom it is written: wives, husbands, children, and fathers.

Renewal for Christian wives is linked to the central New Testament command for them, namely, submission to their own husbands. Colossians 3:18 might be translated, "Be constantly subjecting yourselves with implicit obedience." But we must remember that we are talking about order and rank—the way the family functions—not about equality or essence. The Bible in no way denies the equality of women. In fact, wherever the Gospel has gone, it has been a source of the genuine liberation and elevation of women.

Husbands engage in family renewal by following their central New Testament command: "Love your wives" (3:19). Here we have an interesting line which does not appear in Ephesians 5:25, namely, "Do not be harsh with them." Are husbands generally more impatient than wives? I think so, and apparently God thinks so. That is why He included verses like this in the Bible: "And you husbands, show the same kind of love to your wives as Christ showed to the church when He died for her. . . . That is how husbands should treat their wives, loving them as parts of themselves. For since a man and his wife are now one, a man is really doing himself a favor and loving himself when he loves his wife!"

Children engage in famiy renewal by obeying their parents (Col. 3:20). It is not up to the children as to which of their parents' commands they should obey. They should obey them *all*. The Greek word for "children" shows that Paul was stressing a filial relationship—those born into the family. Thus the focus is on offspring relationships, and the matter of obedience is binding on teenagers as well as on younger children. First-century society made no distinction such as that made in our society over the past four decades.

Finally, the word translated "fathers" in Colossians 3:21 is used of both parents in Hebrews 11:23. It can be translated "parents" here because the command which follows the word certainly applies to both mothers and fathers.

The emphasis is on avoiding behavior of continual irritation to the children. As Phillips puts it, "Don't over-correct." The purpose of restraining oneself in stern, austere discipline is to present a sufficiently positive atmosphere in the home so that children will not become discourged or pessimistic.

Think of the impact of Christian homes in pagan Colosse! Think of the impact of really biblical Christian homes in your community! Be a teacher who focuses on homes, centers his own primary interest and concern on his own family, and then teaches his students, at whatever age-level, to be properly functioning biblical family members.

Leadership begins at home and extends to the church. The Old Testament implies and the New Testament clearly states that a man ought to have a positive record of leadership and control in his own home before the congregation gives him authority to lead in the church (1 Tim. 3:12).

Those of us who are Christian teachers are a part of the team responsible for building families through the ministry of our congregation. In an article written over ten years ago, I noted:

> What it boils down to is that the church's responsibility in building the Christian family is by no means completed when a system of premarital counseling has been developed by the pastor, even if that system is totally effective. Churches must be concerned with a total instructional program in Christian family living which reaches into all facets of biblical injunction and practical problems. And programs should be spread over all age-groups in the church with special concentration on young parents (*United Evangelical Action,* Winter 1973).

RENEWAL EXTENDS TO THE JOB

"Slaves, obey your earthly masters in everything; and do it, not only when their eye is on you and to win their favor, but with sincerity of heart and reverence for the Lord. Whatever you do, work at it with all your heart, as working for the Lord, not for men, since you know that you will receive an inheritance from the Lord as a reward. It is the Lord Christ you are serving. Anyone who does wrong will be repaid for his wrong, and there is no favoritism. Masters, provide your slaves with what is right and fair, because you know that you also have a Master in heaven" (Col. 3:22—4:1).

Three of the four lessons we find in Colossians 3:22—4:1 are given to employees and the other one to employers.

Colossians 3:22 says that employees should be obedient. It has been estimated that there were about sixty million slaves in the Roman Empire at the time these words were written. Certainly, the Gospel does not teach one man to enslave another; Paul's Gospel was that in Christ all men are spiritual brothers (v. 11). On the other hand, no social revolution is indicated in the New Testament. Instead of encouraging Christian slaves to revolt, Paul taught them to be better slaves because they were Christians. They were not to picket or join protest marches in order to cause social renewal.

The second lesson is that employees must recognize that they are working for Christ (Col. 3:23-24). Certainly it is easy to consider ourselves to be working only for the one who pays our salaries week by week or month by month.

But the Bible teaches that ultimately every Christian is working for Christ. This does not apply only to Christian vocations such as the ministry of pastoring or missionary service. Working as a bricklayer, accountant, engineer, or chimney sweep is also sanctified and sacred employment when carried out by a Christian because all work is ultimately work under the lordship of Jesus Christ.

Colossians 3:25 teaches that employees will be judged by God. Wrong behavior brings retribution, and that retribution will be impartial because God engages in "no respect of persons." This links very closely with Romans 13:1, which tells us that all powers in civil government are ordained by God. Apparently a Christian employee also should recognize that the authority over him in his employment is an authority backed by God.

Finally, our passage shows that bosses or employers must be fair in all their dealings. Colossians 4:1 continues the content of chapter 3 and warns Christian employers to offer the just thing and the equal thing.

Toward the earlier part of this century, the great Baptist scholar A.T. Robertson wrote of the social implications of a passage like this:

> Class revolution and class hostility would have no place and no chance to terrorize capitalists if they always had been careful to do what is right and just, what is human and fair, to their employees. A better day is coming,

but there is room yet for common justice to those employed in our homes, in our stores, in our factories. We talk more today about social theories but Paul touches the real thrust in all of them—treating each other as brothers in Christ (*Paul and the Intellectuals,* Broadman).

There is a Christian philosophy of labor, and these verses from Colossians 3:22—4:1 are a significant part of that philosophy.

As churches around the world revitalize their educational ministries, their leaders search for approaches that are both grounded in Scripture and applicable to life as it is. These forty-eight chapters offer principles and procedures drawn from experience and tested in the crucible of congregational service. They are published here in the hope that servants of Christ everywhere will be encouraged and better equipped to continue their labors under the Son.